FLOODS

Floods

A Geographical Perspective

Roy Ward

Reader in Geography, University of Hull

A HALSTED PRESS BOOK

JOHN WILEY & SONS
New York

First published in Great Britain 1978 by
The Macmillan Press Ltd

Published in the U.S.A. by
Halsted Press, a Division of
John Wiley & Sons, Inc.
New York

Printed in Hong Kong

Library of Congress Cataloging in Publication Data

Ward, Roy
  Floods.

    "A Halsted Press book."
    Bibliography: p.
    Includes index.
    1.   Floods.   2.   Floods—Psychological aspects.
3.   Title.
GB1399.W37   1978   363.3   77–18543
ISBN 0 470–99383–9

Contents

List of Figures

List of Plates

Acknowledgements

The author and publisher wish to thank the following for permission to use copyright material: Princeton University Press for extracts from William G. Hoyt and Walter B. Langbein, *Floods* (© 1955 Princeton University Press); Methuen and Co. Ltd for extracts from T. O'Riordan and R. J. More Choice in water use in *Water, Earth and Man* (ed R. J. Chorley) (© 1969 Methuen & Co. Ltd).

For permission to reproduce or adapt figures: the American Geophysical Union for material from H. A. Einstein, A. G. Anderson and J. W. Johnson (1940) A distinction between bed load and suspended load in natural streams *Trans. Am. Geophys. Un.*, **21**, 628–32 for figure 5.1c; from S. G. Heidel (1956) in *Trans. Am. Geophys. Un.*, **37**, 56–66 for figure 5.2a; from D. M. Hershfield and M. A. Kohler (1960) in *J. Geophys. Res.*, **65**, 1737–46 for figure 6.1; from C. H. Hardison (1974) in *Wat. Resour. Res.*, **10**, 745–52 for figure 6.4; from H. J. Day, G. Bugliarello, P. H. P. Ho and V. T. Houghton (1969) Evaluation of benefits of a flood warning system in *Wat. Resour. Res.*, **5**, 937–46 for figures 7.4c and 11.4c; and H. Kunreuther and J. R. Sheaffer (1970) in *Wat. Resour. Res.*, **6**, 659–67 for figure 11.1b; the Oxford University Press from M. D. Newson (1955) in *Flooding and Flood Hazard in the United Kingdom* for figure 10.6a and b; the Controller of Her Majesty's Stationery Office from *Met. Mag.*, **81**, (1952) 354 for figure 2.3; from Meteorological Office *Daily Weather Report* for figure 4.4b; and from the Ordnance Survey map (Crown copyright reserved) for figure 10.2; the International Glaciological Society from Thorarinsson (1953) in *J. Glaciol.* for figure 3.3b; the Geographical Association from A. H. W. Robinson (1953) in *Geography*, **38**, 134–41 for figure 4.4a and d; from K. C. Edwards (1953) in *Geography*, **38**, 182–7 for figure 4.4f; from A. H. W. Robinson (1961) in *Geography*, **46**, 18–24 for figure 4.5c and d; and from A. T. Grove (1953) in *Geography*, **38**, 164–70 for figure 5.3c; W. H. Freeman and Company (copyright © 1964) from Luna B. Leopold, M. Gordon Wolman and John P. Miller in *Fluvial Processes in Geomorphology* for figure 5.3a and b; © National Environment Research Council by permission of the Institute of Hydrology from NERC (1975) for figure 6.5c; the National Water Council from N. Medrington (1969) Twenty years of land drainage progress in the area of the Lee Conservancy Catchment Board in *Association of River Authorities' Yearbook* (eds N. Whincup *et al.*) pp. 303–20 for figures 10.5a and b; the Institute of British Geographers from G. M. Howe *et al.* in *Trans. Inst. Br. Geog.*, **41**, 33–58 for figure 9.1; the United Nations from *Methods and Problems of Flood Control in Asia and the Far East* for figure 10.1; NOAA from

U.S. Weather Bureau map for figure 4.3b and publications for figure 6.2; from W. C. Conner, R. H. Kraft and D. L. Harris (1957) Empirical methods for forecasting the maximum storm tide due to hurricanes and other tropical storms in *Mon. Weath. Rev.*, **85,** 113–16 for figure 4.3c; from U.S. Weather Bureau (1959) in *National Hurricane Research Project, Rept,* **32,** figure 4, p. 8 for figure 4.5a; from M. A. Kohler and R. K. Linsley (1951) Predicting the runoff from storm rainfall in *U.S. Weather Bureau Res. Pap.* 34 for figure 7.1a; from NOAA (1973) in *The National Weather Service and Water Management,* U.S. Dept. of Commerce NOAA/PA 71004 for figure 7.4a and b; and from C. E. Jensen (1974) in *The Federal Plan for Meteorological Services and Supporting Research,* U.S. Department of Commerce for figure 7.5; the Princeton University Press from W. G. Hoyt and W. B. Langbein (1955) in *Floods,* Figure 10, page 42 (© Princeton University Press) for figure 1.3; the Severn – Trent Water Authority for figure 8.2a; the *Sunday Times* from S. Fay and P. Knightley (1975) Will inflation sink Venice rescue Party? in *Sunday Times,* 13 April 1975, p. 5 for figure 10.9d; the U.S. Army Corps of Engineers for figures 8.3 and 12.1; the U.S. Department of Agriculture from W. E. Reifsnyder and H. W. Lull (1965) in *U.S.D.A. Tech. Bull.*, 1344 for figure 3.1b; the U.S. Department of Commerce from U.S. Corps of Engineers (1956) for figure 3.1a and from *Climatological Data, National Summary 1972* for figure 11.2 a,b and c; and the Yorkshire Water Authority from their maps for figure 10.9c.

For permission to reproduce tabular material: NOAA for table 8.1; Sheaffer (1960) for table 8.2; and Task Force (1966) for table 12.1.

For permission to use photographic material: © Aerofilms Ltd. for plates 3 and 10; Associated Newspapers Ltd. for plate 4; R. E. Laudick, Jr in *U.S.G.S. Circ.* 418 for plate 2; the Lea Division of the Thames Water Authority for plate 9; *The Louisville Courier-Journal and Times* for the photograph by Billy Davis for plate 6; the Severn – Trent Water Authority for plate 8; the Tennessee Valley Authority for plate 11; the USDA Agricultural Research Service for plate 1; the U.S. Forest Service for plate 7; and the U.S. Geological Survey from *U.S.G.S. Prof. Pap.*, 422-M, Figure 10 for plate 5.

Preface

Nature is blamed for failings that are Man's,
And well-run rivers have to change their plans
                    (from the poem 'Water' by Sir Alan P. Herbert)

Water is of universal concern and interest, and the study of its movement and distribution through the hydrological cycle forms the basis of Hydrology. Some of the most challenging aspects of this subject involve the interactions between Man and his Environment which have always concerned geographers and have recently assumed even greater general interest with the growth of Environmental Studies and Environmental Sciences and the development of a wider public concern in the problems of environmental pollution and control.

Floods are one of the most dramatic interactions between man and his environment, emphasising both the sheer force of natural events and man's inadequate efforts to control them. Floods are always news, from the road washed out by a small freshet, reported in the local weekly paper, to the major disaster of August 1974, when floods inundated almost half of Bangladesh, killing thousands of people and occupying international press and television headlines for weeks. But although man has been responding to floods since long before the days of Noah, they are still not fully understood by the hydrologists, engineers, agriculturalists, planners and politicians. Still more is this true of the general public, for whom floods are an unexpected, often inexplicable and always traumatic experience.

In recent years there have been major attempts in many countries to improve knowledge of the flood hazard and of the possible responses to it. For example, in the United States a Federal Task Force reporting in 1966 called for a more imaginative response than merely building flood embankments and reservoirs; in Leningrad in 1967 an international symposium on 'Floods and their Computation', jointly convened by the International Association of Hydrological Sciences, UNESCO and the World Meteorological Organization, attracted almost 100 papers from 23 countries; while in Britain the NERC Institute of Hydrology's major study was published in 1975, marking this country's biggest advance in the understanding of flooding for nearly half a century.

This seems an appropriate time, therefore, to review the state of knowledge in this field in terms of past achievements, present understanding and future prospects. Floods are treated here both as physical and socio-economic phenomena which affect, and are in turn affected by, man's activities. After introducing and defining the problem in chapter 1 the main types of flood are discussed in some detail in chapters 2 to 4 and then the role of floods in shaping the landscape is briefly considered in the next chapter. There follows a detailed review of the procedures for predicting and forecasting floods in chapters 6 and 7 which leads on, in chapters 8 to 10, to a consideration of the ways in which man may respond to the flood hazard. Some economic aspects of this response are discussed in chapter 11 and in the final chapter the book concludes with a brief consideration of likely future developments.

Throughout, I have attempted to present the material in a form which will be useful not only to the specialists concerned with the flood problem but also to university students in a wide range of subjects, such as hydrology, geography, civil engineering, agriculture, environmental sciences, planning, administration and public health, and finally to the informed layman who may be exposed to the risk of flooding. Inevitably this has meant some compromise. Clearly, a treatment aimed at one specialist group may not be useful to another and would almost certainly be too technical for the layman. Therefore, each topic is treated on its merits; some chapters are more technical than others, although even in the 'difficult' ones, such as chapter 6, fairly simple summaries are provided which will guide the skimmer safely through to the next chapter. The detailed bibliography for each chapter should provide a sound basis for further study.

I am sincerely grateful to all who have helped in the preparation of this book. I particularly wish to thank the University of Hull and Professor J. Allan Patmore and my other colleagues in the Department of Geography for making it possible for me to take a period of study leave to complete this manuscript; Keith R. Scurr, Wendy Wilkinson and Anthony I. Key for the preparation of all the diagrams; Margaret Micklethwaite, Pixie Gwilliam, Diana Cooper and Jean Rowland for typing the manuscript; and finally, my wife, Kay, for her encouragement and help.

Roy Ward

1 Introduction

FLOODS ARE NEWS!

Floods are repeatedly in the headlines of local, national and the international media. Most of the stories concern comparatively minor events which cause little damage and are soon forgotten except by those most directly affected. Some, however, concern major disasters involving loss of life and the destruction of property, bringing in their wake hardship, suffering, disease and famine. In the early 1970s alone there were at least ten major flood disasters around the world. A tropical cyclone struck the shores of the Bay of Bengal in November 1970 and devastated the emerging nation of Bangladesh as the effects of flooding rivers were intensified by winds and tidal surges – 6000 people died on just one small island when the protecting levees broke. In the following year flooding in India caused damage exceeding £300 million. June 1972 saw Hurricane Agnes cause the single largest natural disaster, in terms of damage, in the history of the United States with estimated losses approaching $3000 million. In August 1973 the worst floods for a century hit Mexico when the tail of Hurricane Brenda lashed the south of the country and left 200 000 people homeless. In the same month 1500 people died and damage worth £400 million occurred as floods devastated huge areas of Punjab and Sind provinces in Pakistan. Eastern Australia was subjected to widespread flooding in January 1974 when freak tides caused by tropical cyclone Wanda held back river floodwaters – in Queensland alone 650 000 km² were inundated and estimated damage exceeded A$100 million. A few months later more than 2000 people died in the worst floods ever recorded in Brazil. A similar death toll was recorded in August 1974 when disastrous flooding inundated almost half of Bangladesh leaving over 5 million people homeless. Finally, in the following month Hurricane Fifi struck Honduras and, with the death toll approaching 10 000, this may with justification be regarded as one of the worst natural disasters in recent history.

Earlier decades witnessed similar catalogues of disaster with, occasionally, individual catastrophes of outstanding proportions – such as the 1887 flooding on the Hwang Ho and the 1911 flooding on the Yangtze Kiang which claimed 900 000 and 100 000 lives, respectively. Such disasters rarely occur in the British Isles, but when they do (for example, the Lynmouth floods of August 1952 or the North Sea coastal flooding of January 1953), they have deeply impressed the public conscience. Normally, however, major disasters tend to recur in the same unfortunate areas. India, for instance, expects an annual flood disaster, and over the past twenty years has suffered average annual losses of more than 700

1

people, 40 000 cattle and £60 million.

The prevalent impression is that the flood situation is worsening. To some extent this is a function of the shortness of human memory; how often is each new flood described in the press as 'the worst in living memory'? However, there is evidence that the flood situation may indeed be deteriorating. Climatic change is undeniable. Small changes in the atmospheric circulation and subtle changes in the delicate interrelationships between ocean temperatures and the overlying atmosphere may well cause *local* alterations in the frequency of intense or prolonged precipitation, and thus in flood magnitude and frequency. The available evidence is, however, largely circumstantial and often difficult to interpret. It is equally undeniable that land-use is continually changing. The spread of urbanisation, of forest clearance and of agricultural under-drainage and the ploughing-up of natural grasslands have increased flood potential. There is, moreover, some evidence of the changed character of flooding itself, particularly in an intensively developed country like Britain. In early historical times rivers probably flooded much more frequently than today, responding to what would now be regarded as comparatively minor precipitation. Because of the primitive, poorly drained character of catchments and floodplains the floodwaters once rose comparatively gradually to the peak and drained equally gradually back into the channel. Land-use changes and drainage improvement quickened the movement of water into stream channels which thus, over the centuries, have been slowly dredged, straightened and embanked. Now minor floods are contained and only major floods overtop the banks, although when they do inundation takes place rapidly and the floodwaters are unable to drain back into the channels.

Finally, there is clear evidence that the flood situation is getting worse in terms of the damage caused by flooding. Despite massive expenditure on flood control, flood losses continue to rise in many countries around the world. Protective measures are, in fact, often counter-productive since, by engendering a false sense of security, they may result in even higher damages than would otherwise have occurred.

This relationship between flood protection and flood damage brings into focus a characteristic of the flood problem which has been implied but now must be stated explicitly as a major theme of this book – floods are not *natural disasters*. Although this term is commonly used it should be made clear that floods are *natural phenomena* and form part of the normally occurring range of stream-flow conditions (just as does drought, at the other end of the scale). Since stream channels can carry only a fraction of peak floodflows, part of the excess must flow through and over, or be stored on, the floodplain. In flood conditions, therefore, channels and their adjacent floodplains are complementary and inseparable and together form the proper conveyance for the transmission of floodwaters. However, flood *disasters* are *man-made* in that man has put himself at risk by developing floodplains for settlement, agriculture and industry and by building roads, bridges and railway lines in floodable positions. Such intrusions into the floodway may result from ignorance or for economic reasons (that is, the risk is worth taking or worth safeguarding against). Either way, man's affinity for floodplains has a long history and now affects a substantial proportion of the world's population. For example, it is estimated that in the United States 10 million Americans live in significantly defined floodplains and another 25 million where they could be affected by floods (AWRA, 1972) while nearly half the population of the Far East continually faces the danger of floods.

In many cases, of course, even major floods simply spill their waters on to unoccupied floodplains or 'washlands' where they do little damage and may even be beneficial, as in arid zones where irrigation and soil fertilisation still depends on the natural flooding of rivers. However, for the millions at risk where *floods* are equated with *disaster*, there is no easy solution. It is neither possible to prohibit all development in areas prone to floods nor to abandon those which are already at risk. This raises a number of important problems which will be discussed at length in ensuing chapters, namely: the need to understand the natural and man-induced reasons for flooding; the need for adequate prediction and forecasting of flood occurrence and magnitude; the need to evaluate and then educate man's awareness of the flood hazard; and finally, the need to develop sound economic responses to flood situations through properly costed programmes of adjustment, abatement and protection.

HISTORICAL PERSPECTIVE

Since early times floods have been a major aspect of man's interaction with his environment, and epic stories of flood disasters are found in the traditions and literature of many ancient peoples. Some of these legends have been verified by subsequent archaeological findings and today people still climb Mount Ararat in eastern Turkey to search for the wreckage of Noah's Ark.

Sometimes man has successfully harnessed and adapted the natural flood regime. In Egypt the Nile flood has been the basis of successful agricultural irrigation for more than 5000 years. The most important date in the Egyptian calendar was the one on which the annual inundation took place, and records of flood levels can be traced back to 3000 to 3500 BC, while remains of what is possibly the world's oldest dam, built between 2950 and 2750 BC, are still in existence near Cairo (Biswas, 1970). Field systems, dating from before the discovery of the New World, have been found on Columbian floodplains, where construction must have required large-scale operational effort and a high degree of social organisation to take advantage of the seasonal floods (Parsons and Bowen, 1966).

In other cases, however, successful utilisation of the floodplain is frequently interrupted by major tragedies. Chinese history is full of tales of the struggles against the notorious Hwang Ho, often called 'China's Sorrow', which not only floods frequently but also tends to change its course bringing unexpected disaster to new areas. The first recorded flood on the Hwang Ho was in 2297 BC, although shortly afterwards the rivers of China were supposedly controlled and tamed by the massive waterworks of the legendary Yu the Great (Biswas, 1970). Over the next 4000 years, however, the successful waterworks of 'good' dynasties fell into disrepair during 'bad' dynasties and times of war, causing inundations which in one surge drowned the millions who farmed the fertile riverine land.

Probably the best-known flood epic is the biblical story of Noah, saved from the floodwaters with his family and birds and animals by building and entering the Ark. Ten months after the flood's onset the gradually subsiding waters encouraged Noah to send out the raven and the dove to see if the first traces of land had appeared, and eventually the dove returned with an olive leaf. Other similar stories exist. There are clear parallels, for example, between the Hebrew and Babylonian traditions of man's early history and they both may have chronicled the struggles with the wayward rivers of the Tigris and Euphrates valleys, the legends spreading to Syria and Palestine in about the middle of the second millennium BC (Lambert and Millard, 1969). Certainly, archaeological evidence of flood deposits separating the strata of different Sumerian and Babylonian civilisations indicates that floods did destroy existing cultures, although it is not clear whether the tradition of the flood as an historical time-reference reflects one severe flood or the memory of several disasters. In the Babylonian flood saga (Lambert and Millard, 1969) King Atra-ḥasīs was given seven days by the god Enki to pull down his reed house and build a boat with the materials. The boat was loaded with his possessions, animals and birds. As soon as they were aboard the flood came and, apart from Atra-ḥasīs, his passengers and family, the entire human race was destroyed. In Babylonian tradition the flood lasted seven days and seven nights.

By comparison, our scientific interest in floods, based on programmes of intensive and organised data collection, is very recent. In the United States, for example, it dates back only to the mid-nineteenth century when the Federal Government first actively participated in flood protection and organised surveys of the Mississippi system. In fact it was not until 1928 that a modern approach to flood studies began when Congress authorised the expansion of the Mississippi flood control project – an action which was broadened by subsequent legislation, including the significant Flood Control Act of 1936 (Chow, 1956). In Britain, the Institution of Civil Engineers' *Interim Report of the Committee on Floods in Relation to Reservoir Practice*, published in 1933, has been the basic guide to engineering practice in this field. Although clearly in need of revision, the report in effect survived until the publication in 1975 of the findings of the NERC Flood Studies Team which will, hopefully, provide the basis for future flood practice in this country.

DEFINITIONS

Before proceeding further, we must attempt a more precise definition of our subject. Defining a flood is difficult, partly because floods are complex phenomena and partly because they are viewed differently by different people. Floods can occur in many ways, usually in valley bottoms and coastal areas, and be produced by a number of influencing conditions. Their locations and magnitudes vary considerably and as a result they have markedly different effects upon the environment. For most practical purposes and certainly in popular usage a meaningful flood definition will incorporate the notions of *damage* and *inundation*.

As might be expected, most flood definitions relate to river floods and the one by Ven Te Chow (1956) is not untypical:

A flood is a relatively high flow which overtaxes the natural channel provided for the runoff.

In fact, so many stream channels have been artificially improved that the definition by Rostvedt and others (1968) is probably more appropriate:

A flood is any high streamflow which overtops natural or artificial banks of a stream.

However, because the banks of a stream vary in height throughout its course there is no single bankfull level above which the river is in flood and below which it is not in flood. In a strictly hydrological sense, therefore, a flood may be any relatively high water level or discharge above an arbitrarily selected flood level or flood discharge.

In order to incorporate the rarer coastal as well as the more common valley-bottom inundations, a more general definition is needed:

A flood is a body of water which rises to overflow land which is not normally submerged.

In this example inundation is explicit and damage is implied in the final three words of the definition.

CAUSES AND CONDITIONS OF FLOODING

Floods result from a number of basic *causes* (see figure 1.1), of which the most frequent are climatological in nature. Excessively heavy and/or excessively prolonged rainfall is the most common universal cause of floods, although in cold-winter areas, where snowfall accumulates on the surface, substantial flooding frequently occurs during the period of melt in spring and early summer, particularly when melt rates are high. Similarly, floods may be caused by melting ice, intensified by the formation of ice-jams and by other pondage and surge effects. In many snow-covered areas floods result from the effects of rain falling on to an already decaying and melting snowpack.

In other types of flooding climatological factors are only partly or indirectly responsible. Thus, in many estuarine situations, the immediate cause is the ponding back of streamflow by the rising tide, particularly during spring-tide conditions, or by various tidal surge effects. Again, along low-lying coasts flooding may result from excessively high tides associated with storm-surge effects caused by a combination of very low barometric pressure and high windspeeds.

Finally, there are other, rather infrequent, causes of flooding which are associated only indirectly, if at all, with climatological events. Of these, tsunamis produced by earthquakes, landslides into enclosed or semi-enclosed water bodies and the failure of dams and other water control structures are the most important.

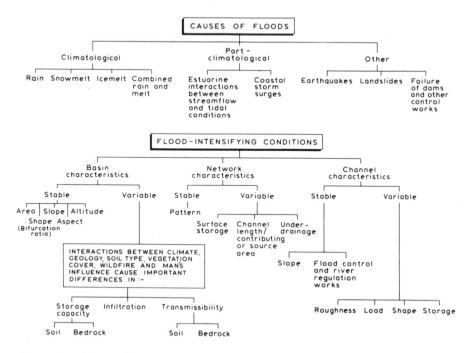

Figure 1.1   Causes of floods and flood intensifying conditions

Floods resulting from these various causes will be discussed in more detail in chapters 2, 3 and 4. At this stage it is pertinent to note that identical flood generating mechanisms, particularly those associated with climatological factors, may result in very different floods from one catchment to another or, indeed, within a given catchment from time to time. These differences are due to the effects of a number of flood intensifying *conditions* (see figure 1.1,), most of which operate to speed up the movement of water within the catchment, that is to reduce the time of concentration when this is defined as the time required for water falling on the most remote part of the catchment to contribute to streamflow at its outlet. The time of concentration is thus the shortest time in which the whole of the drainage basin contributes to streamflow either directly, as water moves over and through the surface layers, or indirectly through the translatory flow or push-through mechanism whereby water infiltrating on the higher parts of the basin will cause a related amount of water to be pushed out lower down the slope.

The main flood intensifying conditions (which are, of course, flood-ameliorating conditions when operating in the reverse direction) may be conveniently grouped into basin, network and channel characteristics, each group having some characteristics which are comparatively stable and unchanging and others which are relatively more variable. These are tabulated in figure 1.1.

Of the *stable basin characteristics*, area is probably the most important since this affects not only the time of concentration but also the total volume of streamflow generated by a given catchment-wide precipitation event. Shape is also important, particularly in association with the disposition of the channel network within the basin. For example, as figure 1.2a illustrates, where a high bifurcation ratio is associated with a long narrow basin, flood peaks may be low and attenuated, whereas in the more normal case of a low bifurcation ratio associated with a comparatively rounded basin, flood peaks are both higher and sharper. Water movement both over and through slope materials tends to increase as slope increases, while aspect and altitude affect both the amount and type of precipitation intercepted by the basin as well as the extent to which the effectiveness of precipitation is modified by evapotranspiration. The integration of stable basin characteristics effectively defines drainage basin geomorphology which has been shown by numerous workers to relate significantly to flood response.

Variable basin characteristics are numerous and their effects on flood hydrology are often complex. However, three important secondary characteristics result from the complex interactions between, for example, climate, geology, soil type, vegetation cover and the effects of wildfire and particularly of man in burning, clearing, cultivation and urbanisation. First, the capacity for water storage of both the soil and deeper subsurface layers may affect both the timing and magnitude of flood response to precipitation, with low storage potential often resulting in rapid and intensified flooding. Secondly, high infiltration values allow the bulk of precipitation to be absorbed by the soil surface and thereby reduce catchment flood response, while low infiltration capacities encourage the normally swifter over-the-surface movement of water associated with rapid increases in channel flow. Thirdly, even in a basin where most precipitation infiltrates the soil surface, flood response will be greatly modified by subsurface transmissibility, which is the ease with which water can move through the subsurface materials.

Channel and channel-network characteristics within a drainage basin are essentially dynamic and variable, often changing markedly within a few hours. Drainage pattern is, perhaps, the most *stable network characteristic*, its effect closely related to that of bifurcation ratio and basin shape. Generally speaking, drainage patterns which result in the coalescence in the lower drainage basin of the floodflows from a number of major tributaries, (dendritic drainage), are associated with sharp high-magnitude flood peaks at the basin outlet; while those patterns which permit the evacuation from the basin of floodflows from the downstream tributaries before the floodflows from the upstream tributaries have arrived (trellised drainage) result in a more muted flood response.

The relatively more *variable network characteristics* are often very important in modifying the flood response of a catchment to precipitation. Initially, large volumes of unconnected surface or depression storage act as a storm reservoir

Floods

which can contribute to direct streamflow only when the necessary interconnec-
tions have been made by continued precipitation. One of the most important of

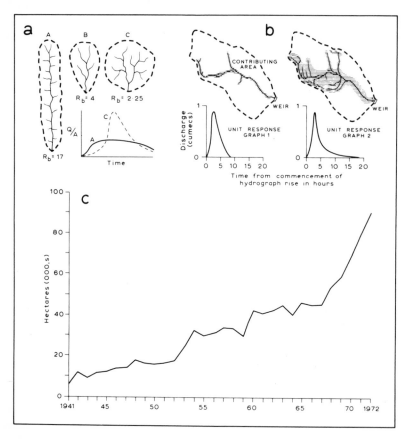

Figure 1.2 Some flood intensifying conditions: *a*, Relations between basin shape, bifurcation ratio and shape of flood hydrograph; *b*, Quickflow contributing areas in a small
catchment at the end of a dry and a wet period; *c*, Graph of increased area of under-
drained land in England and Wales, 1941–1972
Source: *a*, Strahler (1964) section 4 – III; *b*, Walling (1971) p. 77; *c*, Green (1973) pp.
377–91.

all flood-producing conditions is the total area of interconnected water and
waterlogged surface within the catchment where the effective infiltration capacity is zero and on which, therefore, all falling precipitation contributes
directly to streamflow. During the early stages of precipitation, or at the end of a
prolonged dry period, these contributing or source areas may be restricted to the
water surfaces of the channel network, but as precipitation continues so the
contributing area expands (see figure 1.2b) with consequent major increases in

the volume of rapid runoff entering stream channels. Artificial drainage, such as the furrowing often associated with afforestation or the underdrainage of arable farmland, helps to speed up the movement of water towards the stream channels. In some areas artificial drainage has been steadily increasing for a number of years (see figure 1.2c).

Turning now to the relatively more *stable channel characteristics*, it is clear that the passage of a floodwave down a channel will be faster in unregulated steep channels and slower in well-regulated, relatively flat channels. The downstream velocity and magnitude of a floodwave will also be greatly affected by *variable channel characteristics*, particularly roughness, which depends largely on constituent bed and bank materials and vegetation growth, as well as channel shape and storage properties, which may vary rapidly with changing streamflow and streamload conditions. The load being carried in solution and suspension or as bedload within the channel is also important for the augmenting effect it has on total water depth and discharge, and may range from virtually zero in some clearwater streams to 100 per cent or more in a mudflow.

THE FLOOD HYDROGRAPH

A continuous trace of discharge or water depth against time during a flood event defines the flood hydrograph. In the comparatively rare coastal flood event, water depth rather than discharge is the crucial variable and the flood hydrograph is defined by the tidal curve or, more accurately, by the departure of the 'observed' from the 'expected' tidal curve. Although such events will be discussed later, particularly in chapter 4, the main emphasis will be on the more usual floods generated by climatological events in river basins. In such cases the flood hydrographs have certain common features.

Let us examine the hydrograph of a river flood, figure 1.3. During dry periods streamflow decreases exponentially (section AX). At such times discharge consists solely of baseflow which is largely sustained by unsaturated interflow in small, steep, impervious catchments, by groundwater flow in flat, permeable catchments or by a combination of both of these in intermediate catchments. Rainfall begins at time X and the rapid increase of discharge between X and Y results from the generation of quickflow from the expanding channel-network contributing areas which are fed from above by infiltrating precipitation and from below by interflow (see chapter 2). The hydrograph peak occurs at time Y, shortly after the cessation of rainfall, and thereafter discharge is largely determined by the amount of water held in storage both on and under the surface of the catchment. The rate of exhaustion of storage is reflected in the shape of the recession limb of the hydrograph (section YB). The early part of the recession will be sustained largely by saturated interflow while the later stages (sections ZB and AX) will be sustained by the combination of unsaturated interflow and groundwater flow, depending on catchment conditions.

It will be clear from this that during a flood event the discharge hydrograph is dominated by the quickflow component, with a time base XZ and a peak *Y*. Equally clear is that in most circumstances, flood conditions do not begin immediately discharge increases at time *X*, since the initial discharge in-

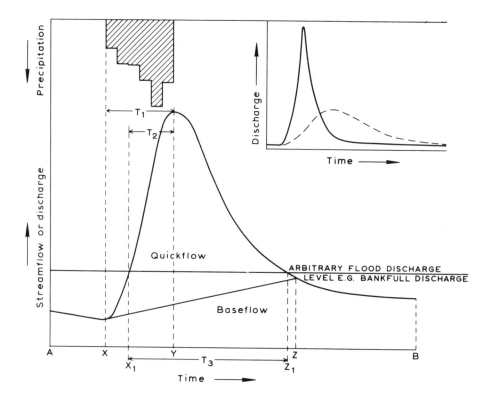

Figure 1.3   River flood hydrograph: *Inset* Hydrographs on flashy and sluggish streams
Source: Hoyt and Langbein (1955) p. 42.

crease is either contained within the stream banks or results in elevated water levels, but with the raised stream surface still below the arbitrary flood level. Consequently, the flood hydrograph proper, consisting entirely of quickflow, may be considered to begin and end when the preselected flood level or discharge is equalled on both the rising and falling limbs. Thus, although still peaking at *Y* it will have a shorter defined time base X_1Z_1.

As indicated in the preceding section, the general form of the flood hydrograph will be greatly modified not only by variations in the nature and intensity of the climatological input (rainfall intensity, rate of snowmelt, etc.) but also by variations in the many potential intensifying conditions. Thus, at one extreme the hydrograph may have the low peak and long time base of a sluggish stream, while at the other it may have the high peak and short-time base of a flashy stream (see figure 1.3, inset).

MEASURABLE FEATURES OF RIVER FLOODS

Since floods are both physical and socio-economic phenomena which impinge upon, and are of direct interest over, a wide range of activities, it is perhaps not surprising that they may be categorised by a wide range of measurable variables.

Undoubtedly the oldest and still probably the most common index of flood magnitude is *water depth* or *stage* which has the advantage that it may be measured directly and is of immediate relevance if flood-retaining structures are likely to be overtopped. This index is popular in Britain because most flood protection schemes involve embanking lowland rivers rather than providing reservoir storage in upland reaches (Smith, 1972). Another common measure, particularly in the United States, is the *discharge rate*, which provides the basis for most methods of predicting flood magnitude (see chapter 6). Discharge is normally derived indirectly from measurement of stage by means of a stage–discharge rating curve. Understandably, interest normally focuses on peak stage or discharge (time Y in figure 1.3) since this is the moment of greatest danger and maximum inundation. Also of interest are the changing relationship between *magnitude* and *time*, which defines the *shape of the flood hydrograph*, and the *discharge volume*, which is the total quantity of water measured on the flood hydrograph in the time period X_1Z_1 and which is a significant factor in the optimum design and operation of flood control and multi-purpose reservoirs (Chow, 1956).

Flood magnitude, defined by any of the above indices, determines the *depth* and *area* of inundation and to a large extent the *duration* of flood (time T_3 in figure 1.3). In turn, water depth and discharge are directly related to the *velocity* of floodwaters, about which comparatively little is known due to the difficulties of measurement. One promising approach is the use of aerial photography to record the movement of special floats dropped at intervals into floodwaters (Popov and Gavrin, 1970). These three characteristics of floods – depth and area of inundation, duration of flood and velocity of floodwaters – largely determine the potential flood damage of a given event. Thus, in postulating two meaningful flood stages, Sheaffer (1961) suggested that a depth of inundation of about one metre, with a velocity of one metre per second, could cause widespread structural damage and even loss of life, while an inundation depth of 3 m will result in damage to the contents of buildings above ground floor level. The damage intensifying effects of velocity and duration need no further emphasis at this stage.

Seasonality of flooding is another important measurable characteristic. Although floods may occur at any time of the year, they tend to be most numerous in the wet season (either the rainy season or, in areas of uniform precipitation, the season of lowest evapotranspiration) and in the melt season (in high altitude and high latitude areas). Large rivers, which normally show very marked seasonal characteristics, invariably attain their peak flows during these seasons. On smaller streams, however, the most severe flooding may be associated with intense convectional storms in summer. Clearly, where flooding has a marked and reliable seasonal character, adaptation to the flood hazard is easier, for example by the provision of adequate flood storage at multi-purpose reservoirs.

Flood frequency is a statistical measure of the probable occurrence of a flood of a given magnitude. Large floods occur relatively infrequently – they have large return periods or recurrence intervals of perhaps several hundreds of years – while small floods occur frequently, perhaps two or three times a year, and therefore have a very small return period or recurrence interval. The one year flood and the 1000-year flood can occur at any time, but naturally the former is more likely. This has important repercussions in terms of encroachment on to floodplains since the only floods likely to have been experienced are the more frequent minor ones whose impact is comparatively small.

The statistical likelihood of a given flood occurrence provides important evidence for the hydrologist and engineer. The average floodplain occupant, warned of an incipient flood event, will be more concerned with the time left to remove his furniture and drive his car or cattle or, indeed, his family to higher ground. The average time between a rainstorm or melt event and the resulting increase in streamflow is referred to as the *time of rise* or the *basin lag* and is a variable which depends upon the interaction between precipitation or melt characteristics and the flood intensifying conditions tabulated in figure 1.1. Lag may be measured in a number of ways, only two of which are shown in figure 1.3. These are the time from the beginning of rainfall to the peak discharge (T_1) and the time from the attainment of actual flood conditions, for example bankfull discharge, to the peak discharge (T_2). The second interval may be considerably shorter than the first and in socio-economic terms is normally the more important. This is largely because people generally do not become concerned with flooding until actual flood conditions have been reached, so that the period between then and the flood peak represents the time available for adjusting to the oncoming flood (Sheaffer, 1961). Apart from the time of concentration, which has already been defined, other measures of lag include time from beginning of rainfall to the centroid of runoff, time from centroid of rainfall to centroid of runoff, and time from centroid of rainfall to the peak discharge.

2 Floods Caused by Precipitation: I Rainfall

Following the brief discussion of the causes and conditions of floods in chapter 1, the principal generic flood types will now be discussed in more detail in this and the two subsequent chapters. Initially a distinction is made between floods caused by precipitation acting either directly, by rainfall, or indirectly, by snow and ice melt; and floods which are not essentially caused by precipitation, for example estuarine and coastal floods and those resulting from dam collapse. Such simple categorisation, although helpful in providing a systematic basis for discussion, is demonstrably inadequate when subjected to careful scrutiny, largely because the most important and disastrous floods are the result of complex interactions between many of the possible causal factors. For example, during the flooding of Honduras caused by Hurricane Fifi in September 1974, the town of Choloma was particularly badly hit because the floodwaters running through the town were ponded back by high sea levels built up by the hurricane force winds. As a result, the floodwaters backed up near the town and eventually undercut a hill which had served as a temporary dam, thereby releasing an additional wave of water and debris.

It is appropriate that the discussion of generic flood types should begin with a consideration of rainfall floods. These are the most important category on the world scale, ranging from the great flood events resulting from semi-predictable seasonal rains affecting areas of sub-continental size, to the dramatic flash floods due to highly episodic, intense storms over very localised areas.

THE FLOOD-PRODUCING PROCESS

The flood hydrograph consists almost entirely of *quickflow* or direct runoff (see figure 1.3), that is, water which reaches the stream channel very quickly during and immediately after precipitation. According to the runoff model propounded by Hewlett (1961*a*), and discussed in detail by Ward (1975) most of this quickflow derives from limited, hydrologically responsive *source areas* within a catchment which may otherwise be regarded as predominantly hydrologically passive. These source areas may vary in size according to drainage basin, storm and antecedent conditions – hence the normal usage of the term *variable* source areas.

At the beginning of a flood-producing storm, quickflow may be generated only by the stream surfaces themselves, since these are the only areas within the catchment where all the falling precipitation cor tributes directly to an increase

13

in streamflow. Eventually, however, the already moist riparian and valley-bottom areas become waterlogged and as the water table reaches the ground surface the effective infiltration capacity over these areas drops to zero. After this, all precipitation falling on these expanded source areas contributes directly and substantially to streamflow. The wetting-up of riparian and valley-bottom lands is, in part, a continuous hydrological process resulting from the downslope movement of soil moisture (unsaturated interflow), which may be a major factor sustaining the flow of some streams during dry weather (Hewlett, 1961b), and from deeper, saturated groundwater movement. During storm periods, however, the process is greatly accelerated by the downslope movement of saturated interflow and by infiltration. It is believed that the speedy contribution of inter-flow to slope-foot wetting is facilitated by a process variously referred to as translatory flow or the push-through mechanism, whereby each new increment of precipitation infiltrating the slope soil profile displaces a similar amount of previously infiltrated moisture in both a downward (vertical) and a downslope direction.

In this way the wetted source areas will gradually expand upslope, outside the immediate valley-bottom areas, as downslope moisture movement through the slope material, aided by infiltration, saturates the slope-foot zone. At the onset of a storm the source areas for quickflow may frequently represent less than 5 per cent of the drainage basin area, expanding to 20–25 per cent of the area as precipitation continues and resulting, thereby, in an approximate fivefold increase in the volume of quickflow generated by a given rate of precipitation. Clearly the greater the amount of precipitation which falls the greater will be the expansion of the source areas contributing quickflow to the stream channels until, after prolonged heavy rainfall of many days' duration, most of the catchment area may be contributing. This helps to explain why even comparatively gentle rains, provided they are sufficiently prolonged, may result in quite severe flooding.

Source areas may develop in other parts of the catchment than the valley bottoms and lower slopes. Thus Hewlett and Nutter (1969) suggested that source area expansion would reach quickly into areas with shallow soils and bare rock surfaces, while Kirkby and Chorley (1967) postulated that hollows and slope-profile concavities, in addition to the base of slopes and areas of thin or less permeable soils, would rapidly become saturated during storm precipitation. In fact, however, only those wet patches which are connected directly to the stream channels and adjacent floodplain areas will contribute directly to quickflow.

Not all the quickflow produced during a storm results from precipitation falling directly on to expanding, hydrologically responsive source areas. The downslope movement of saturated interflow, for example, is capable not only of accelerating the saturation of the slope-foot zone but also, in some circumstances, of contributing directly to streamflow during storm periods. This view, supported by Hewlett, accords with the earlier findings of Hursh (1944) and with later experimental evidence, particularly that of Whipkey (1965; 1967; 1969). The role of macro-cavities, in particular of pipes, in the rapid downslope movement of subsurface water was investigated in some detail by the Institute of Hydrology (1972) who concluded that pipeflow represents a dominant storm runoff process in some areas; by the same token, artificially constructed under-drainage represents an important factor in many other areas.

In extreme hydrological conditions over-the-surface movement of water may result not from the wetting process described above which involves infiltration and interflow, but from the inability of the ground surface to absorb precipitation as rapidly as it is falling, in other words where rainfall intensity exceeds infiltration capacity. This mode of quickflow generation, originally propounded by Horton (1933), was formerly thought to be widely applicable but is now seen to relate only to conditions of low infiltration capacity, as in areas of bare rock, impermeable soils or surface compaction resulting from human interference with the soil and vegetation cover, or areas of very high rainfall intensities, particularly where these are maintained over several hours. It is not uncommon in the humid tropics, for example, for rainfall intensities to reach 200 mm per hour or for 400 mm of rain to fall in one day.

The flood-producing process outlined here will result in more or less severe floods according to the operation of certain flood-intensifying conditions described in chapter 1 (see figure 1.1) and particularly those variable basin and network conditions which together affect the size and disposition of the quickflow-producing source areas. In this respect, antecedent precipitation conditions play an extremely important part. Precipitation during the period before a flood event will either lead to a wetting-up of potential source areas, thereby permitting their rapid expansion soon after the onset of storm rainfall, or will actually be sufficient to lead to substantial source area expansion before the onset of storm rainfall (see figure 1.2b). The effect of antecedent precipitation conditions often leads to a marked seasonal variation in source area expansion and, therefore, in flood response from the same catchment. Harvey (1971) described seasonal flood behaviour in the Ter catchment in eastern England, noting that summer floods required higher rainfall intensities and that their short duration and rapid rise suggested that quickflow was occurring from only a limited part of the catchment, whereas short duration storms in winter, even those having low peak intensity and fairly low rainfall totals, produced substantial floods, their general consistency of form suggesting that quickflow occurred from a fairly uniform area and probably from the catchment as a whole.

Frozen ground is another important flood-intensifying factor, especially in high latitudes, which may effectively expand the source area to 100 per cent of the catchment. Its effect is seen most dramatically in catchments which normally show a rather sluggish flood response. Figure 2.1a depicts flood hydrographs from a limestone catchment in conditions of frozen and non-frozen ground.

Quite apart from factors accentuating source-area expansion, rainfall characteristics themselves may affect considerably catchment flood response and in this respect rainfall distribution, in both space and time, is particularly important. The effect of storm location within the catchment is shown schematically in figure 2.1b, with the steepest flood hydrograph associated with the storm located closer to the basin outlet. With regard to the distribution of rainfall with time, figure 2.1c illustrates that whereas a gentle rain extending over several hours or days may result in only a modest flood peak with a comparatively long time base, the same amount of precipitation falling within a few minutes or hours may produce very high flood peaks of much shorter duration. Illustrating this point, Jarvis (1942) referred to a damaging flood at Colorado Springs where,

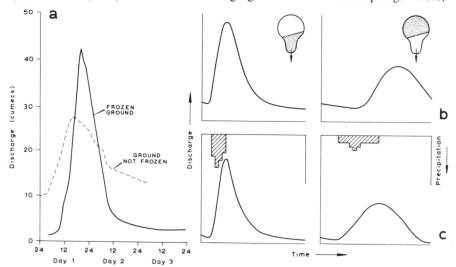

Figure 2.1   Factors affecting flood hydrograph shape: *a*, Conditions of frozen and non-frozen ground, Spring Creek Pennsylvania; *b*, Identical storms differently located within a drainage basin; *c*, Identical rainfall amounts but with markedly different intensities and durations
Source: *a*, White and Reich (1970) pp. 193–8; *b*, De Wiest (1965).

although the total volume of water discharged was only a little over 12 million m³, most of the water passed through the city in the space of 2 hours. The stream channel, normally dry for most of the year, would have carried the entire volume in 20 hours with no appreciable damage.

TYPES OF RAINFALL FLOOD

In view of the markedly varying flood response to different rainfall conditions, it is perhaps inevitable that many attempts have been made to classify rainfall floods on the basis of the storm event itself. Thus Colman (1953) recognised four types of flood, related to different causal factors, of which two were pluvial – flash floods and long-rain floods. *Flash floods* are often the result of convectional storms or of high-intensity rain cells associated with frontal storms; *long-rain floods* are associated with several days or even weeks of low-intensity rainfall, usually of the cyclonic type, and are the most common cause of major flooding. Lambor (1956), in a sevenfold classification of floods recognised three pluvial types, namely, those caused by *local convectional* storms, *frontal* storms, and *orographically reinforced frontal* storms. Of these, the third type is normally responsible for the most damaging, long duration floods. By way of contrast, in a review of Texas flood conditions, the flood-producing characteristics of three major weather disturbances, *easterly waves, hurricanes* and *thunderstorms*, were discussed by Carr (1966), Morgan (1966) and Orton (1966).

Although helpful in many respects, such classifications suffer from their failure to accommodate the inevitable complexity of most flood-producing rainfall events. Reference has already been made, for example, to the fact that intense rainfall cells may occur within a belt of relatively more gentle frontal rain and may show many of the characteristics of thunderstorm rainfall. Or again, it has been shown that some of the catastrophically heavy orographic storms experienced in the Austrian Alps can be explained only in terms of the dynamics of a jet stream impinging from the south. Similarly, in their analysis of the 1970 Labour Day storm in Arizona, Thorud and Ffolliott (1971) demonstrated that intense-rain thunderstorms resulted not simply from normal daytime heating but also from the eastward advance of surface and upper air troughs.

In many ways, therefore, it is probably more helpful to consider the characteristics of the floods themselves, rather than the characteristics of the flood-producing rainfall, and to recognise not so much a classification as a gradation from a single brief flood peak, at one extreme, to a flood season at the other. Such a gradation may have many or few recognisable stages; for convenience, the following discussion recognises four – *flash floods* of a few hours' duration, *single event floods* of longer duration, *multiple event floods* and finally *seasonal floods* which are often simply an extended form of multiple event flood.

(i) Flash floods

Flash floods (IAHS, 1974) are most frequently associated with violent, convectional storms which tend to be of short duration, often measured in minutes rather than hours. Convectional storms are also normally of small areal extent, the modal diameter for the United States being 3 km and the mean diameter 8 km (Morgan, 1966). Such storms, therefore, generate floods only on small headwater streams, on minor tributaries or in inadequately drained urban areas. Expectedly, flash flood hydrographs have sharp peaks, the floodwaters rising and falling almost equally rapidly; indeed, it was their sudden appearance and disappearance in headwater streams which led to the term 'flash flood'. Flash floods may also result from other kinds of very intense rainfall over small drainage areas and are, for example, commonly experienced on headwater streams in the Appalachians as hurricanes move northward into the eastern United States.

Convectional rainfall, in particular, has a virtually global distribution so that examples of flash floods occur almost everywhere in the world. In the British Isles one of the most dramatic of these resulted from the cloudbursts of 18 June 1930 which fell on part of Stainmore Forest in the Pennines. A series of intense convection cells yielded 60 mm of rainfall in an hour at one gauge located about one km from the storm centre and resulted in a series of short-lived flood peaks which swept away bridges and field walls (Hudleston, 1933). Thunderstorms are particularly common in continental interiors during the summer and literally hundreds of flash floods resulting from them are recorded each year in the United States alone. One of the most intense small-area short-duration storms of this type ever recorded occurred near D'Hanis, Texas on 31 May 1935 producing a world record of more than 550 mm in $2\frac{3}{4}$ h (Jennings, 1950). It is, however, with deserts that most people associate flash flooding. Certainly, it is most dramatic when a normally dry landscape is suddenly subjected to torrential rain which results in sheet floods and stream floods often lasting only 10 or 15 minutes.

Reliable quantitative data on desert floods are, almost inevitably, sparse although some excellent studies in the essentially semi-arid area of Utah were presented by Woolley (1946). Schick (1970;1971) discussed desert floods in southern Israel and provided valuable examples. He found that the great differences in flow characteristics between various storms for a given watershed, and between various watersheds for a given storm, could be related to physiographic diversity, rainfall intensity, relative timing of effective rainfall over the watershed, antecedent moisture conditions and existing alluvial storage. Conditions for incipient runoff are satisfied by a variety of combinations of rainfall intensity, rainfall amount and antecedent moisture and, thereafter, runoff hydrographs exhibit exceedingly sharp peaks (see figure 2.2a). All the rising limbs have at least one vertical segment which indicates an instantaneous increase in discharge, perhaps in the form of a bore; some of the hydrographs show two or three such vertical segments separated by moderate to steep rises. The duration of rise from 10–90 per cent of the peak discharge, the steepest part of

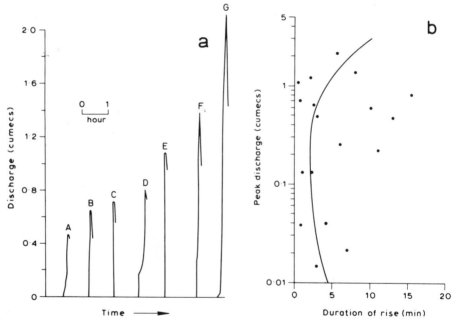

Figure 2.2   Flash floods: *a*, Hydrograph rises for Israeli desert floods (time datum is independent for each flood event); *b*, Relationship between duration of rise and peak discharge
Source: Schick (1970)

the rising limb, is plotted against peak discharge in figure 2.2b; the median line drawn with reference to several clusters of flood peaks, shows the duration of rise exceeded in 50 per cent of cases. The nearly vertical fronts typical of so many desert floods (see plate 1) may be associated with high concentrations of suspended solids or with the rapid abstraction into the channel-bed alluvium of the leading part of the flood wave, thereby enabling the following part of the wave to glide over the now saturated surface. Schick (1970) suggested that the way in which an initially shallow flow front would so steepen would depend on the infiltration and roughness characteristics of the channel but, provided there is a balance between rate of infiltration and replacement of water from upstream, the front can be maintained indefinitely during travel downstream.

(ii) Single event floods

Single event floods may be regarded as those floods with a single main peak and, therefore, a relatively simple hydrograph but having a substantially longer duration than flash floods. This is the most common type of flooding in most parts of the world and may result from a variety of rainfall conditions in which widespread rains of several hours' or days' duration move over a drainage basin. Such rains are commonly associated with cyclonic storms which may or may not have a well-developed frontal system. In Britain, for example (Manley, 1952), periods of excessive rain of several days' duration are often associated with slow-moving depressions in which the fronts are nearly stationary, especially in the summer months when the moisture content of the air is high. Thus the severe flooding of the Whitby Esk in 1930 occurred when some 300 mm of rain fell from 20–23 July on the North Yorkshire Moors around Castleton. In central America, and in eastern North America, the major flood-producing rains result from hurricanes; in recent years devastating floods resulted in the eastern United States from Hurricane Camille in 1969 and Hurricane Agnes in 1972. In the case of Hurricane Camille, the heaviest rains exceeded 700 mm and occurred as the storm's remnants suddenly intensified and moved eastwards over the state of Virginia. It is believed that the rainfall approached the Probable Maximum Precipitation for that part of the world. In other world areas severe single-event flooding may result from individual storms associated with monsoonal conditions.

It has already been suggested that rainfall is notoriously difficult to classify. In particular, the meteorological conditions which favour heavy frontal rainfall also frequently favour both the substantial intensification of rainfall by orographically induced instability and also convectional storm development resulting from daytime intensification of instability. A brief discussion of two case studies will illustrate some of the most important characteristics of single event floods.

(a) The Lynmouth, Devon flood of 15 August 1952

The small tourist resort of Lynmouth in North Devon was decimated during the night of 15–16 August 1952 by a flood wave in the River Lyn after one of the three heaviest 24-hour rainfalls ever recorded in the British Isles. Approximate isohyets are shown in figure 2.3a; 230 mm was recorded at Longstone Barrow

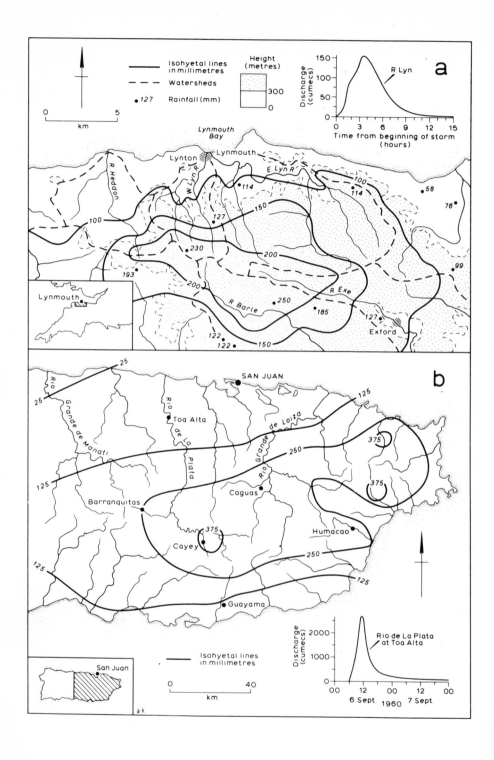

Isohyetal lines in millimetres

Watersheds

•127 Rainfall (mm)

Height (metres)
300
0

Discharge (cumecs)

R.Lyn

a

Time from beginning of storm (hours)

Lynmouth Bay

Lynton   Lynmouth

R Heddon   W Lyn   E Lyn R

•114

127

•58

76•

100

150

•230

•193

200

200

99•

R Exe

R Barle   •250

•185

•127

Exford

122•
122•   150

Lynmouth

b

25   125

SAN JUAN

Rio Grande de Manati

Rio de La Plata

•Toa Alta

Rio Grande de Loiza

375

25

250

375

125

Caguas•

Barranquitas•

375

Humacao•

Cayey•

250

125

125

Guayama•

Isohyetal lines in millimetres

Discharge (cumecs)

2000

1000

Rio de La Plata at Toa Alta

00   12   00   12   00
6 Sept.   7 Sept.
1960

San Juan

0   40
km

a k

and as much as 280–300 mm fell in some places (Bleasdale and Douglas, 1952).

The storm resulted from an Atlantic depression which had moved to the western English Channel by midday on 15 August. Although this depression initially had no clearly defined frontal system, warm air from France appears to have been drawn into its circulation as it approached Brittany, thereby creating a new warm sector which quickly occluded (Bleasdale and Douglas, 1952; Marshall, 1952). The steep temperature lapse rates and the high moisture content of the air masses comprising the depression clearly favoured both the orographic intensification of precipitation and thunderstorm development. Examination of figure 2.3a suggests that both factors may have played a major part. In addition, the heavy rainfall was accentuated by the occlusion and by the slow movement of the system as a whole.

Flood response was greatly intensified by antecedent and drainage basin conditions. Rain, amounting to some 90 mm, had fallen on all but two of the preceding fourteen days so that the ground was unusually wet. This, together with the typically thin soils underlain by bedrock found over much of this area, particularly in the headwaters of the West Lyn, must have favoured a rapid and massive expansion of the quickflow contributing areas immediately after the onset of the flood-producing storm. Certainly, post-storm surveys of erosion and damage suggested that at some time during the evening of 15 August large tracts of Exmoor must have been literally awash to a depth of almost 10 cm, the water pouring directly into the main channels through any convenient surface conveyance (Bleasdale and Douglas, 1952). By the time the rain had reached its greatest intensity, the rate of runoff was probably almost equivalent to the rate of rainfall over the high ground, a state which may have been maintained for some hours (Bleasdale and Douglas, 1952). The large volumes of water moving over the moorland plateau flattened the usually long, tough bog grass and effectively 'thatched' the ground surface, before pouring off the moor and into the deeply incised, steeply sloping valleys.

Within the valleys it seems clear that temporary dams developed when trees and boulders piled up behind bridges and other obstructions and that the sudden breaching of these dams greatly intensified the devastating nature of the floods (Kidson, 1953).

The flood hydrograph was not recorded although local residents described the flood's advent as resembling a 'wall of water' or a 'tidal wave' (Marshall, 1952). After the event Dobbie and Wolf (1953) attempted to reconstruct the hydrograph from basic meteorological and hydrological principles, after careful field examination of evidence, including wrack lines and valley-side damage. Their estimated hydrograph, illustrated in figure 2.3a, suggests that the peak flow probably occurred about $3\frac{1}{2}$ hours after the beginning of the storm and may well have attained a value of 570 000 m³ per hour. Kidson (1953) found that if the

---

Figure 2.3   Single event floods: *a*, Lynmouth flood – storm isohyets and reconstructed hydrograph; *b*, Puerto Rico floods – storm isohyets and discharge hydrograph for the Rio de la Plata at Toa Alta
Source: *a*, Dobbie and Wolf (1953); *b*, Barnes and Bogart (1961).

rate of flow from the entire drainage basin is calculated on the basis of two-thirds of the storm rainfall falling in a five-hour period it would have amounted to 510 m³ per second (cumecs) over a period of a few hours, in other words almost as great as the highest daily discharge for the Thames at Teddington. It has been calculated that a flood of this magnitude would have a return period of almost 50 000 years.

(b) The Eastern Puerto Rico floods of 6 September 1960
The floods of 6 September 1960 in the eastern half of Puerto Rico rank among the most disastrous floods ever experienced on the island. Approximate isohyets are shown in figure 2.3b for the period 5–7 September. The largest rainfall total reported was 475 mm in the north-east but high-intensity rain, amounting to more than 250 mm, fell over an area about 25 by 65 km, extending from Barranquitas, in the central interior, to the east coast of the island. Over parts of this area, particularly in the mountains between Cayey and Humacao, the total rainfall may have been considerably higher than that indicated by the map (Barnes and Bogart, 1961).

The heavy rainfall resulted from the passage of Hurricane Donna off the north-east coast of Puerto Rico. Hurricanes are notoriously unreliable variable weather systems and it is difficult to find a 'typical' example. They normally develop over warm tropical seas when an existing stable tropical disturbance is triggered into unstable cyclonic action and then intensifies, thereby drawing more and more moisture and heat energy into the system. On 2 September 1960 Hurricane Donna was located some 1900 km east-southeast of Puerto Rico but by the evening of 5 September had moved to a position about 160 km north of San Juan. Heavy rains began falling on the island at this time and continued until the early hours of the following morning (Barnes and Bogart, 1961).

The resulting floods were widespread and damaging and rose so rapidly in many places that people were unable to escape to safety even after being warned of the danger. The flood hydrograph for the Rio de la Plata at Toa Alta, draining an area of about 520 km², is shown in figure 2.3b. The peak flow of about 2700 cumecs was attained at 1130 hours, some five and a half hours after the beginning of storm runoff, and represents a discharge rate of more than 5 cumecs km². Analyses of peak discharges at 24 other sites on the island showed that this value was exceeded in all but two cases and that, in some of the smaller drainage basins, discharge rates exceeded 30 cumecs km². In the upper Rio de la Plata basin a drainage area of 108 km² (approximately the size of the combined East and West Lyn basins) yielded 1450 cumecs at the flood peak. Such values have been only rarely exceeded (Barnes and Bogart, 1961).

(iii) Multiple event floods

Some of the most troublesome flooding occurs when successive flood peaks follow closely on each other in response to a more complex weather situation than is normal in the case of single event floods. In such cases, although the individual flood peaks may not exceed or even closely approach previous maxima, the flooding is often severe because its duration extends over a period of several weeks or months. On rare occasions, record peak discharges combine with the extended duration of flooding to make multiple event floods the most disastrous of all flood occurrences. In this context Manley (1952), referring to the August 1829 Moray floods on the Findhorn and the Spey, concluded that a series of active depressions crossing southern Britain is one of the worst meteorological events that can occur in the British Isles.

Sometimes complex weather systems give rise to multiple event floods on smaller headwater streams which then combine to produce only single event floods farther downstream on the major rivers. This was well illustrated in the December 1961 floods in Mississippi described by Shell (1962), which resulted from a series of frontal storms associated with low-pressure systems moving across the state. Figure 2.4a shows the multi-peak response of the small Sowashee Creek compared with the single-peak response to a similar precipitation sequence of the much larger Pearl River. In other cases even large rivers exhibit multiple event characteristics. This was well illustrated by the ephemeral Finke River in the central Australian desert during the February–March 1967 floods which resulted from three separate southward incursions of monsoonal weather that, together, yielded rainfalls of between 120 and 350 mm (Williams, 1970). The Finke at Hermannsburg (see figure 2.4b) drains an area of several hundred km², while at Finke itself the river drains an area of many thousand km², but at both locations multiple flood peaks were recorded.

One of the most noteworthy of multiple event flood situations in recent years occurred in Texas between April and June 1957. These floods were outstanding not only because of the large geographical area which experienced flood conditions but also because of the large volume of runoff produced. The Texas Board of Water Engineers (1957) reported that all streams in the state were in flood for much of the three month period during which, if the Red River and the Rio Grande are excluded and only the interior Texan streams considered, more than 46 000 million m³ of runoff were generated. Despite this enormous total, peak flows which exceeded previously known flood maxima occurred on only a few streams.

The Texas floods were produced by a series of frontal storms which occurred over almost the entire state between 18 April and 5 June following a period of moderate rainfall during the first half of the month. These storms were noteworthy because of the large areas which they covered, their persistent recurrence during the period and the severe weather that often accompanied them. In addition Hurricane Audrey produced heavy rainfall in some areas of southeast Texas on 27 June. Scattered minor flooding occurred early in April. More serious flooding began on 19 April, developed into major and widespread flooding by 24 April and then continued for about six weeks (Texas Board of Water Engineers, 1957). During the three-month flood period most of the major rivers exceeded their mean annual discharge by a factor of between two and four. Typical hydrographs, for the Brazos and Colorado rivers, are shown in figure 2.4c.

(iv) Seasonal floods

In many parts of the world multiple-event flooding recurs annually in the wet season on a massive scale, with the period of high water often extending over several months and with the area of inundation counted in tens of thousands of

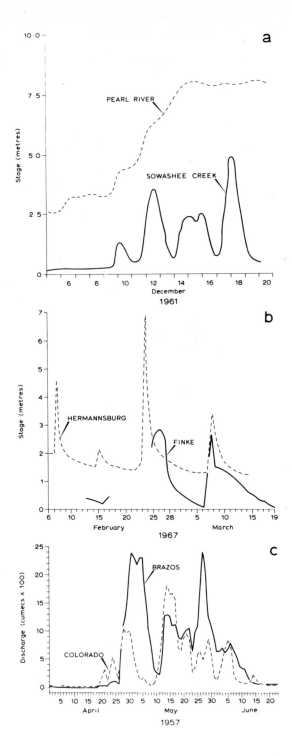

square kilometres. According to the level of man's adaptation to them, these seasonal floods may bring great benefit or catastrophe. Thus in the Nile valley, for thousands of years, the rising river levels during summer were observed with satisfaction and the moment eagerly awaited when the dikes could be breached allowing the water to flood the land and assure adequate crop yields for the coming year (Biswas, 1970). Monsoon floods in the densely populated lower Ganges and Brahmaputra basins in India and Bangladesh regularly cause great distress and loss of life. Again in contrast, massive flooding in the relatively un-inhabited upper Amazon basin, resulting largely from the influx of rain-swollen tributaries from Ecuador and Peru, inundates thousands of square kilometres of forest for several months, causing temporary asphyxia of some of the trees, but even these burst into leaf again as the floodwaters recede. Brief discussion of two examples of seasonal floods should illustrate their main characteristics.

The summer flood on the River Nile is one of the best-known and most fre-quently documented of all seasonal floods. Mean minimum discharge occurs in May (570 cumecs) and mean maximum discharge in September (8440 cumecs) at Wadi Halfa. It can be seen in figure 2.5a that for eight months the mean dis-charge is below 2000 cumecs, rising sharply to very high values in August, Sep-tember and October. The seasonal flood experienced on the Egyptian Nile is a complex phenomenon resulting from the combined influx of water from many tributaries, only the most important of which are illustrated in figure 2.5a.

The Blue Nile and Atbara are two of the principal tributaries draining the Ethiopian Highlands and, as Hurst and Phillips (1931) observed, have the char-acteristics of mountain streams. That is, they rise rapidly and flashily during the rainy season, decline equally rapidly afterwards, and in the case of the Atbara, cease to flow at all for half of the year. The remaining tributaries drain into the White Nile whose flow, moderated by its passage through vast areas of swamp, shows only a muted seasonal regime. Peak discharge (1400 cumecs at Khar-toum) is delayed until October, partly because of the lag imposed by the swampy areas and partly because the rapid rise of the Blue Nile holds up the White Nile discharge which can only be released later when the Blue Nile falls (Hurst and Phillips, 1931). During the peak of the main Nile flood in September the Blue Nile contributes approximately 69 per cent of the total flow, the Atbara 17 per cent and the White Nile 14 per cent.

Analysis of the long period of recorded Nile floods provides one of the first examples of the phenomenon known as persistence, the tendency for above-average and below-average rainfall and discharge conditions to be grouped to-gether. Thus Hurst and Phillips (1931) reported that over considerable periods, sometimes as long as 50 years, the Nile floods are above average, while over other periods they are below average, although very low floods may occur in a

---

Figure 2.4 Multiple event flood hydrographs: *a*, On Sowashẹe Creek, Meridian, Miss. (drainage area 133 km²) and Pearl River, Edinburg, Miss. (drainage area 2300 km²); *b*, On Finke River at Hermannsburg and Finke; *c*, The Brazos River near Glen Rose, Texas (drainage area 63 600 km²) and the Colorado River near San Saba, Texas (drainage area 78 300 km²) from 1 April – 30 June 1957
Source: *a*, Shell (1962); *b*, Williams (1970); *c*, Texas Board of Water Engineers (1957).

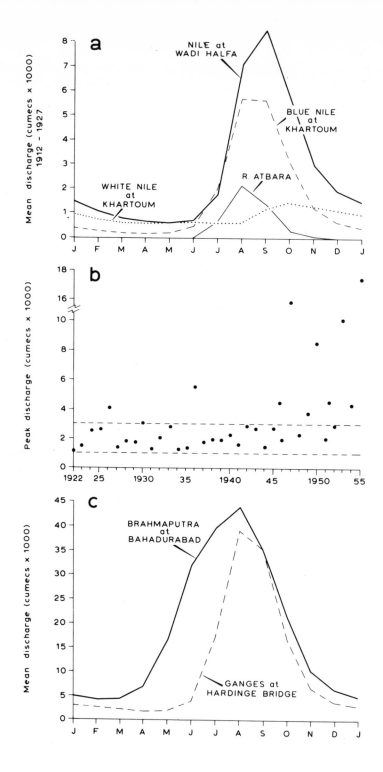

Figure 2.5   Seasonal floods: *a*, Mean monthly discharge – Nile and its major tributaries; *b*, Annual peak discharges – River Ravi, 1922–55 (broken lines at 1000 and 3000 cumecs enclose 74 per cent of annual flood peaks); *c*, Mean monthly discharge – Brahmaputra at Bahadurabad and the Ganges at Hardinge Bridge
Source: *a*, Hurst and Phillips (1931); *b*, Uppal and Sehgal (1956) pp. 14–21; *c*, Rogers (1969).

---

high series and vice versa. This phenomenon is also illustrated by the seasonal floods on the River Ravi in the Punjab (see figure 2.5b). In this case, during the period from 1922 to 1955, 74 per cent of the flood peaks were between 1000 and 3000 cumecs. However, the last nine years of the record contains six floods exceeding 3000 cumecs, while the preceding 25 years contains only three.

The lower Ganges and Brahmaputra join in Bangladesh to form one of the major rivers of the world, with a combined annual discharge of more than 96 000 million m³. Seasonal flooding here is by no means as well-documented as that on the Nile but has, during recent years, become tragically familiar to the rest of the world. On both rivers the peak flow is reached in August as a result of heavy monsoon rain which starts in June and continues until October. The mean August discharge for the Ganges at Hardinge Bridge is 39 224 cumecs and for the Brahmaputra at Bahadurabad is 43 955 cumecs (see figure 2.5c).

In Bangladesh and the neighbouring portions of India the pressure of a largely agricultural population on resources is extreme. As Rogers (1969) observed, the agriculture of the region is dominated by the monsoon, with rice being virtually the only crop grown during the wet season. It is ironical that in an area through which flows the discharge from the second largest river system in the world, flood is followed by drought because the floods, which assume such vast proportions often inundating one-third of the total land area of Bangladesh, are not adequately controlled. Destruction by flood is thus followed by drought-provoked famine in a vicious and, as yet, unended circle.

3 Floods Caused by Precipitation: II Snowmelt, Rain-on-snow and Icemelt

Floods resulting from the melting of snow and ice, with or without an additional increment from rainfall, are a major component of the hydrological regime in the high latitude areas of Canada, the United States and Russia, in parts of Europe and at high altitudes in the major mountain areas of Europe, Asia and North and South America. Meltwater floods are essentially seasonal floods in which a substantial increase in river discharge takes place every year in the same season in corresponding geographical and altitudinal zones. Such floods normally occur only once each year, resulting in a single flood wave which may have several peaks (Snyder *et al.*, 1971) and although caused indirectly by precipitation, their principal direct cause is the increasingly positive radiation balance of the snowpack or glacier which results in melt.

The two most crucial factors determining the severity of snowmelt floods are the depth of snow accumulation and the rate of melting. Thus, referring specifically to the United States, Hoyt and Langbein (1955) suggested that where the annual snowfall exceeds 1·5 m, for example in the north-east and around the Great Lakes, snowmelt alone may produce floods, whereas in areas where the annual snowfall ranges from 0·5 to 1·5 m snowmelt alone is rarely sufficient and often does little more than accentuate the effects of spring rainfall. However, even deep snows, particularly in mountainous areas, may melt so gradually that flooding is averted and instead a period of high runoff is maintained over several weeks. Some of the most severe floods occur when several factors combine to produce a maximising effect. Nelson and Byrne (1966), investigating floods on the Bow River in Canada, found that the most severe floods had occurred when copious precipitation in a short period, high temperatures, deep snow-cover, and high ground-moisture levels coincided.

Icemelt normally takes place more slowly than snowmelt and by itself is rarely responsible for severe flooding. Floods do occur, however, when the melting of glacier ice suddenly releases large volumes of ponded meltwater or when the break-up of an ice pack results in an ice-jam which may hold back large volumes of water before suddenly giving way.

SNOWMELT

Snowmelt refers to the conversion of small ice crystals to liquid meltwater at the melting point (0 °C) and is essentially a thermodynamic process, the amount of meltwater produced being dependent on the net heat exchange between the snowpack and its environment. The main components of the snowpack energy budget which are involved in the snowmelt process are: (1) absorbed shortwave (solar) radiation; (2) net longwave (terrestrial and atmospheric) radiation; (3) condensation from the overlying air; (4) convective or turbulent heat transfer from the overlying air; (5) the heat content of rain falling on the snowpack; and (6) the conduction of heat from the ground beneath the snowpack, although this is normally only a minor item. The relative importance of these components and their combined influence on the snowpack energy budget depends upon a number of meteorological, snowpack and drainage basin characteristics.

Thus the intensity of incoming shortwave radiation reaching the snowpack will increase with the angle of inclination of the sun's rays (which in turn depends upon latitude, season and time of day) and will also increase in response to other atmospheric conditions such as decreasing cloud and pollution. Atmospheric conditions will also affect the availability of net longwave radiation on the snow surface, the amount increasing with increasing cloud cover and humidity. Similarly, condensation from the overlying air will increase with increasing humidity and may be an important factor in foggy conditions, as evidenced by the Russian saying 'fog eats snow' (Chebotarev, 1962), while convective or sensible heat transfer will increase with increasing windspeed and the associated turbulence. The heat contribution of rain falling on the snowpack will depend largely on the temperature difference between the two (1 cal/g/ °C difference) and with a snowpack close to melting point is generally small. Where, however, rain falls on a sub-freezing snowpack and itself becomes frozen, a considerable amount of heat (80 cal/g) is released to the snowpack as the latent heat of fusion. As a result, even deep sub-freezing snowpacks may be 'ripened', that is brought to isothermal conditions at the melting point, by heavy rainfalls.

Apart from its temperature, the main snowpack characteristic to affect the energy budget is the albedo, which directly determines the relative proportions of the incoming shortwave radiation which is reflected and absorbed. Figure 3.1a shows how albedo changes with time, decreasing from values of 80 to 90 per cent for freshly fallen snow to values of 40 per cent after several weeks of atmospheric and biotic contamination.

Finally, the snowpack energy budget is greatly affected by drainage basin characteristics. Some of these operate quite simply – for example, the effects of slope and aspect on the intensity of incoming solar radiation. In other cases, however, several drainage basin characteristics may interact in a complex way to affect the snowpack energy budget. One such interaction involves the varied landscape mosaic comprising areas of snow, open water, snow-free vegetation (especially in forested areas) and bare soil (particularly as the melt season progresses). Each landscape element has different albedo, evapotranspiration and temperature characteristics with the result that some of them will act as sources of, and others as sinks for, sensible heat and moisture. Generally speaking forested areas tend to act as sources of, and barren snow surfaces as sinks for, advected heat and moisture. The presence or absence of vegetation, and particularly of a coniferous forest cover, may substantially modify the snowpack energy budget. The dark, snow-free canopy projecting above the snow surface will intercept and absorb incoming shortwave radiation and thereby decrease that

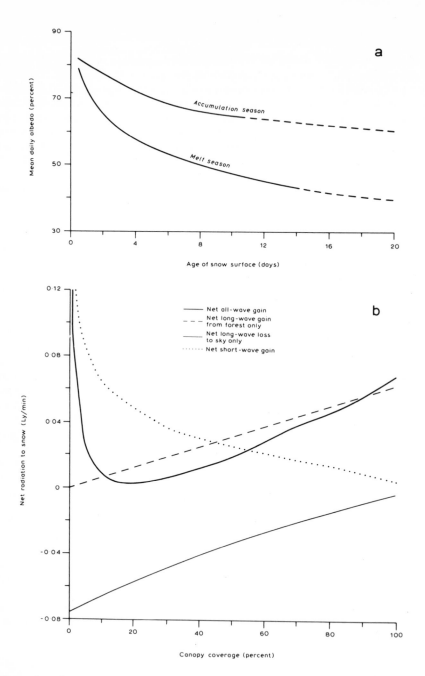

Figure 3.1   Snowpack energy budget: *a*, Variations in snow surface albedo with time; *b*, Calculated net gains and losses of radiation to a snowpack related to canopy coverage for a spruce–fir forest

Source: *a*, U.S. Corps of Engineers (1956); *b*, Reifsnyder and Lull (1965).

radiation total at the snowpack surface. The absorption of incoming shortwave energy, however, warms up the tree crowns and often increases their rate of transpiration. In this way longwave radiation to the snowpack is increased, as is also the transfer of moisture and, therefore, the related transfer of latent heat. The degree of compensation between reduction in shortwave flux and increase in longwave flux to the snow surface, resulting from the presence of a forest canopy, depends largely on the canopy density (see figure 3.1b). Net shortwave gain and net longwave loss decrease progressively with increasing canopy cover, while net longwave gain increases. As a result, the net radiation gain to the snow surface decreases up to a canopy coverage of about 20 per cent and increases thereafter, although even with total canopy coverage the net radiation gain at the snow surface is little more than 50 per cent of that in the open.

The production of snowmelt by means of the energy transfers described above represents only the first stage in the production of snowmelt floods because floods will result only if substantial quantities of meltwater are routed rapidly into the stream channels. This, in turn, will depend on a number of factors including the rate of melt, various snowpack characteristics, and the location and extent of variable source areas within the catchment.

Since the rate of melt depends on energy balance conditions, it may vary considerably within a given drainage basin from one year to the next. The most severe floods tend to occur in areas of heavy snowfall when the temperature rises rapidly after a long cold period and then stays high for several days or even weeks. Generally speaking there is a distinct contrast between the snowmelt floods produced on rivers draining plains and mountains. Average conditions for a number of rivers are shown in figure 3.2 and indicate that melting takes place earlier and more rapidly on the plains, especially when Fohn or Chinook wind conditions occur, and later and more gradually in the mountains. Thus flood peaks on plains rivers are commonly at least four times greater than the mean annual flow, while on mountain rivers they are normally between two and three times the mean annual flow. Some of the Russian rivers provide classic examples of plains snowmelt floods, with rapid thaws producing spectacular flows so that, for example, the mean June flow of the lower Yenisey at Igarka is 78 000 cumecs, which is exceeded only on the Amazon (Beckinsale, 1969). Although, as figure 3.2b indicates, the snowmelt floods on mountain rivers are generally more subdued, there are occasionally dramatic exceptions, as in the case of the 1948 Fraser River flood in British Columbia which was one of the worst flood disasters in Canadian history. In this case, there had been a heavy snowfall during the previous winter and the spring was late in coming. Then, suddenly, at the beginning of May, temperatures began to rise and remained high for several weeks leading to rapid snowmelt and disastrous flooding in the lower valley for more than a month (Sewell, 1969).

Various snowpack characteristics also significantly affect the character and magnitude of the floods produced by snowmelt. The water equivalent, or rainfall equivalent, of a dry snowpack will clearly determine the total magnitude of meltwater which will eventually be generated, as also will the thermal quality of the snowpack – the quantity of water produced by the melting snow as a ratio of the quantity of water produced by the melting of the same amount of pure ice –

especially in the immediate pre-flood situation. Thus, a dry sub-freezing snowpack may have a thermal quality of less than 100 per cent, requiring a substantial input of heat energy to bring it to an isothermal condition at melting point, whereas a ripe snowpack, isothermal at melting point and holding the maximum possible amount of liquid water in pores and interstices between the ice particles, may have a thermal quality considerably in excess of 100 per cent, and will thus produce substantially greater quantities of meltwater for a given input of energy. Other snowpack characteristics likely to affect the meltwater flood include porosity and permeability, which largely determine the amount of liquid water retained in the snowpack and the rate of movement of meltwater through it. Permeability at the onset of melting may be very low, particularly where lenses and layers of ice have formed within the pack, and as a result runoff may lag considerably behind melting. However, as soon as adequate channels are opened up in the snowpack by the action of percolating meltwater,

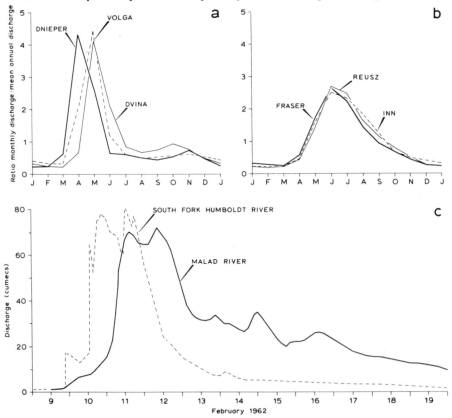

Figure 3.2 Snowmelt floods: *a*, Plains snowmelt regimes; *b*, Mountain snowmelt regimes; *c*, Flood hydrographs for Malad River at Woodruff, Idaho and South Fork Humboldt River, near Elko, Nevada, from 9–19 February 1962
Source: *a* and *b*, Parde (1955); *c*, Thomas and Lamke (1962).

permeability rises substantially and the lag of runoff behind melting is correspondingly reduced.

Finally, the character of meltwater flooding will be partly determined by the location and extent of variable source areas within the meltwater basin. In terms of meltwater runoff the variable source area concept needs some slight modification from that outlined in chapter 2, although the essential features remain unchanged. Thus quickflow will be produced only from those areas beneath the snowpack where meltwater is either unable to infiltrate or is able to infiltrate only the surface layers before moving laterally beneath the ground surface as interflow. The theoretical maximum contributing area is, therefore, the area of the snowpack itself, which may completely cover the drainage basin at the onset of melting but which gradually reduces in areal extent as the melt period continues. Normally, however, quickflow is produced only from that part of the sub-snowpack ground surface which is frozen or ice-crusted or which has become saturated during the initial phases of melting.

It will be clear from the foregoing discussion that the generation of a snowmelt flood is a complex process in which climatological, drainage basin and snowpack characteristics combine to produce, from superficially similar snowpacks, meltwater outputs which may vary enormously. This, in turn, poses considerable problems of flood forecasting in snow-covered areas, which are considered in chapter 7.

RAIN-ON-SNOW

The situation is even more complex in the case of rain-on-snow floods than it is with snowmelt floods alone. In the rain-on-snow case the snowpack may either temporarily store and detain the rainfall and any meltwater generated, or the rain and meltwater may pass straight through the snowpack, in which case the meltwater effectively adds an increment to the flood runoff generated by the rainfall event. Clearly, therefore, identical rainstorms can result in very different flood hydrographs simply because of the different characteristics of the snowpack on which the rains fall.

A considerable quantity of rainfall may be stored within a dry subfreezing snowpack, some remaining as liquid water between ice particles, the remainder becoming frozen into the matrix of the snowpack. In addition, ice layers in the snowpack will initially encourage a predominantly lateral, rather than vertical, movement of percolating rainfall and may also result in the formation of perched water bodies. Finally, a snowpack of this type effectively chokes off the natural surface drainage channels for high rates of streamflow (U.S. Corps of Engineers, 1956). In all these ways the runoff, even from heavy rainstorms, may be effectively retarded and delays of as much as two days have been recorded. Flood investigations in Scotland showed that a blanket of snow up to 30 cm thick may have completely absorbed a heavy rainfall and stored it for several hours before collapsing to cause a flood peak some 35 per cent greater than would otherwise have been expected (Wolf, 1952).

Alternatively, falling rain may pass through the snowpack without depletion or delay. This is the likely situation where previous melting has rendered the snowpack isothermal at 0 °C and may have satisfied its liquid water-holding capacity, established percolation paths through the pack and melted and scoured adequate surface drainage channels beneath the pack. In such cases, not only is there virtually no delay in runoff due to the snowpack, but meltwater from the pack may actually increment the resulting flood waters. The U.S. Corps of Engineers (1956) referred to such an event in the Sierra Nevada, where intense rains falling on a relatively shallow snowpack passed through the pack without delay and were, in fact, abetted by melting snow. This resulted in a record peak discharge of 33·7 cumecs from a small 10 km² drainage basin. Similarly, Manley (1952) observed that in Britain some of the worst floods, as in the Fenlands in 1947, are caused by a combination of heavy warm rain falling on a deep snow cover with an underlying saturated or near-saturated ground surface.

As in the case of floods caused by rainfall alone, rain-on-snow flood conditions may be intensified by the presence of frozen ground. For example, the severe (100-year recurrence interval) flooding in Idaho and Nevada in February 1962 resulted from prolonged low-intensity rain falling on moderate depths of snow in low-altitude areas during a period of warm weather, with a glaze of ice over deeply frozen ground (Thomas and Lamke, 1962). Daytime temperatures were above freezing and rose to as much as 10°C or more. These warm conditions, together with the rain, were sufficient to melt most of the low-altitude snow, although snow at altitudes above 2000 m did not melt. The rain plus the melted snow ran off rapidly over the frozen ground and resulted in floods with high peak discharges and very rapid rises (see figure 3.2c).

ICEMELT

As far as flood formation is concerned, ice may be considered to occur in two main ways: as quasi-permanent ice-sheets and valley glaciers, and as the result of the seasonal freezing of rivers. In most cases ice tends to melt much more slowly than snow so that icemelt alone is rarely the direct cause of severe flooding. Glaciers, for example, are essentially reservoirs for both liquid and solid precipitation, retaining winter precipitation and releasing it gradually during the summer when low albedo and high temperatures encourage maximum melting. Typical runoff regimes of glacier-fed streams are shown in figure 3.3a and emphasise the very low winter outflows and the comparatively rapid increase in flow through May and June to a July or August maximum. Indirectly, however, icemelt may trigger off flood conditions either through the release of liquid water held on or within a body of ice, or through the formation of ice jams during ice break-up on rivers.

Sudden releases of water from glaciers are known as glacier floods, although sometimes the Icelandic team *yökulhlaup* is used, and may represent the outflow either of water which had been held within the ice body or of surface lakes on the ice, or dammed back by the ice in tributary valleys. Particularly in the latter case, when damming results from the periodic advance of a mobile glacier, the floods may show a marked periodicity. In other cases flood occurrence may depend on

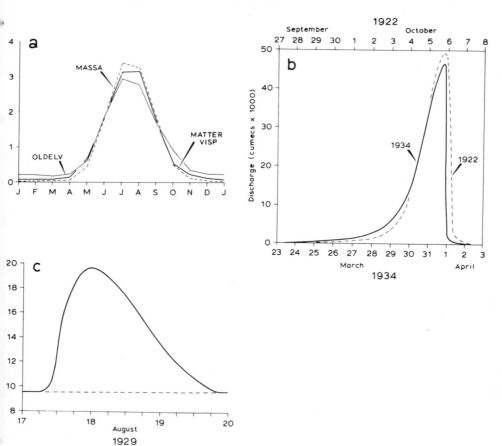

Figure 3.3 Glacial floods: *a*, Glacial melt regimes; *b*, The Grimsvotn glacial floods, 1922 and 1934; *c*, Flood hydrograph at Attock, 560 km below breach of glacial dam on Indus River
Source: *a*, Pardé (1955); *b*, Thorarinsson (1953); *c*, Khan (1969).

the attainment of a given head of water which, in turn, depends on the relationship between water inflow and outflow. In such cases periodicity is less marked. In still other instances glacier floods appear to be sporadic, isolated events with no predictable return period.

One of the most dramatic examples occurs at Grimsvötn in Iceland, where periodic releases of up to 7500 million m³ of water have produced flood peak discharges of almost 50 000 cumecs (Thorarinsson, 1953). In the Argentine, Lago Argentino discharges between 2000 and 5000 million m³ of water every year or so (Meier, 1964). Isolated events include the sudden release from the Tête Rousse glacier, south of Mont Blanc, of some 198 000 m³ of water on the night of 12–13 July 1892 (Pardé, 1964) and a glacier flood in August 1959 in Kashmir which caused a rise in water level of more than 30 m at a distance of over 40 km from the point of outburst (Meier, 1964).

The flood hydrographs of the 1922 and 1934 glacier floods at Grimsvötn are shown in figure 3.3b and their shapes may be considered fairly typical. In comparison with the normal stream flood hydrograph, the glacier flood hydrograph appears to be reversed (Meier, 1964). The flow starts at quite low rates, then increases exponentially as the water-transmitting channels through the ice are enlarged by the flowing water until peak flow is reached, after which so little storage water remains that discharge falls off abruptly. Another example of very sharp initial flood peak is the flood hydrograph of the River Indus at Attock, some 560 km below the glacial dam breach which caused it (figure 3.3c). Even at this distance, the river rose rapidly from a base discharge of about 9500 cumecs to a peak discharge of 19 500 cumecs in 18 hours, the volume of the surge being about 1230 million m^3 (Khan, 1969).

Major floods occur on some rivers, often in advance of the main period of meltwater generation, when river ice breaks up into large blocks during the early stages of spring melt and piles up to form ice jams (see plate 2). Floods may occur upstream as the level of ponded water rises and/or downstream when the jams break and the impounded ice and water are released. These jams happen most frequently in shallow sections of a river channel or at a constriction point such as a sharp bend, gorge or bridge. They also occur where the channel gradient flattens out or a stream discharges into a lake (Burton, 1969). The problem is enhanced in rough, irregular channels because ice formation begins earlier producing greater spring ice thicknesses and because there are more obstructions on which ice blocks can lodge than in the smoother channels. The situation is intensified in long northward flowing rivers such as those in North America and Russia. In Siberia, for example, the upper and middle courses usually thaw out between late April and mid-May, whereas their mouths remain frozen until early June.

After a jam develops the water level behind it rises, often quite rapidly, until eventually the obstruction gives way, releasing great volumes of water and debris into the downstream channel. Therefore, the flood hydrograph close to an ice jam is often extremely sharp-peaked until the flood wave moves down the channel, when its form moderates (see chapter 7).

Some spectacular ice-jam floods have occurred in the past. Pardé (1964) mentions the disastrous flood on the Rhine in January 1784 when the water level was at least three metres higher than in any known iceless floods, and the March 1838 floods on the Danube, which were two metres higher than any previous or subsequent recorded levels, and in which over half the buildings in Pest were destroyed. Burton (1969) described conditions at Belleville, Ontario where the Moira River enters Lake Ontario. Here the river ice frequently breaks up first, jamming against the still frozen lake and causing the water to back up and flood the city. Finally, Hoyt and Langbein (1955) described a number of examples, including the flooding of the Missouri River in the Dakotas in the spring of 1952. Warm weather upstream in Montana caused ice in the tributaries to break up and move downstream to jam against the firmly frozen Missouri. Eventually the ice jam gave way and at Bismarck, North Dakota the discharge rose from

2120 cumecs to a peak of 14 200 cumecs within a few hours. Today bridge, dam and power plant designs minimise any damage and explosive charges used during the ice jam formations safely disperse many jams which threaten damage or danger to life.

4 Floods Not Caused by Precipitation

The floods discussed so far resulted directly or indirectly (for example through melting) from a precipitation event within a drainage basin. It was shown in the discussion of figure 1.1 that other types of flooding may occur, primarily outside the context of the drainage basin system, and it is these which will be examined in this chapter. Most occur at the margins of existing bodies of fresh, brackish or saline water due to unusually high water levels, or surges of water level, in those water bodies. Thus high tides, storm surges and tsunamis cause flooding in estuaries and along coasts, and landslides can produce flooding along the shores of lakes and reservoirs. Failure of dams or other water control systems may, however, simply result in extra severe flooding in drainage basin areas which, in the absence of such structures, normally would have been subjected to precipitation induced flooding.

Although, in some cases, these flood events may be intensified by the effects of precipitation, they are not themselves the result of precipitation. Some, like estuarine and coastal floods, usually occur after extreme climatological events while others, such as tsunamis and dam collapse, are normally unrelated either to climatological events in general or to precipitation events in particular.

ESTUARINE FLOODS

Flood problems in estuaries result primarily from the interaction of the seaward flow of freshwater discharge from the river and the alternating seaward ebb and landward flow of saline water in the estuary caused by the tidal oscillation, in an approximately twelve-hour period, from low to high tide and back to low tide again. The estuary is the only part of a river channel in which freshwater discharge encounters an opposing landward water flow and, by the same token, estuaries are the only portions of a coastline where the normal tidal currents meet a concentrated seaward flow of freshwater.

This interaction results in an asymmetrical modification of the normal tidal curve (see figure 4.1a), in which the duration of the incoming rising tide is shortened by the effects of gravity and the opposing freshwater discharge, and the duration of the outgoing falling tide, aided both by the gradient of the estuary bed and the freshwater discharge, is lengthened. In extreme cases this asymmetrical modification leads to the development of a bore – the incoming rising tide is so shortened that it literally becomes a 'wall' of water. Tidal bores having a vertical height of five metres have been described for the Amazon River and

38

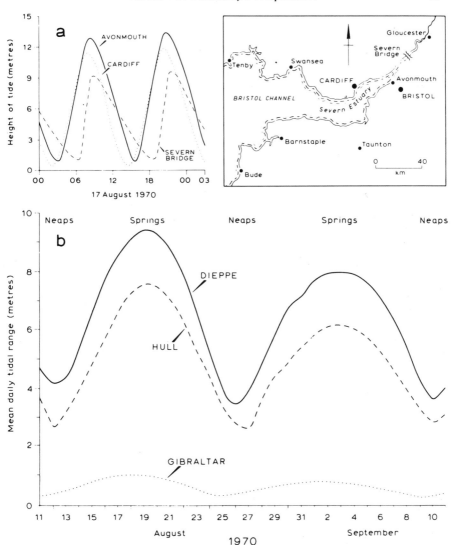

Figure 4.1 Tidal characteristics: *a*, Increasing asymmetry of tidal curve upstream in Severn estuary. *Inset* location map; *b*, Variation of tidal range from spring to neap tides at Hull, Dieppe and Gibraltar

Source: *b*, Admiralty Tide Tables (1970) vol. 1.

even greater heights have been reported for the Tsientangkiang in northern China. In the British Isles, the best-known examples are the Severn bore, which attains a height of one metre at spring tides, and the egre or aegir on the River Trent. Since the seaward flow of freshwater is impeded by the rising tide, river stage in the tidal reach increases during the period of the incoming tide and falls during the period of the outgoing tide. Furthermore, because of their shallow depth and constricted shape, estuaries normally experience a greater tidal range from high to low tide than do sections of open coastline or the open sea. In the open ocean, for example, mean tidal range may be less than 1 m but at Hull on the Humber estuary it is about 5 m and at Avonmouth, on the Severn estuary, about 10 m.

For most of the time, the pattern of interaction described above occurs uneventfully and without flooding, although it must be emphasised that this is often because of the presence of flood protection works in estuarine areas. For example, substantial areas of the city of Hull, on the north bank of the Humber estuary, lie well below the mean height of high tides and this situation is repeated in virtually all estuaries where land has been reclaimed from former fringing salt-marshes and mudflats. However, in both protected and unprotected areas it is only in particular circumstances that floods occur. Of the two main circumstances, the first concerns the tidal range, from low to high tide, which varies in a regular periodic way from a minimum at neap tides to a maximum at spring tides two or three days after the new and full moon. Figure 4.1b illustrates that at Hull on the east coast of England, tidal range varies from less than 3 m at neaps to more than 7 m at springs, and at Dieppe and Gibraltar the corresponding figures are 4 m and 0·5 m at neaps and 9 m and 1 m at springs. The second potential flood-producing circumstance is that freshwater discharge into estuaries may change markedly both in the short term, for example during a storm event, and in the long term, as it does seasonally throughout the year.

Either of these two circumstances may be sufficient to cause flooding. Thus, very high spring tide levels can so reduce the storage capacity of an estuary that even modest freshwater inflow during the rising tide can exceed the channel's remaining storage capacity and produce flooding. Or, very high river discharges may do this even though the high tide levels are only average. Therefore, the particular danger periods in estuaries are at spring tides in the high discharge season, as during winter spring tides in the British Isles, and exceptionally high spring tides due to storm surge effects (which will be discussed later in the chapter), especially if these occur during the wet season. Two illustrative examples are the River Rother in Kent, where exceptional flooding in November 1960 inundated more than 70 km² as heavy rainfall coincided with very high spring tides, and the Neva River where periodic estuarine flooding in the Leningrad region results from wind-induced surge effects in the Gulf of Finland, substantially increasing high-tide levels (Labzovskii, 1966). Clearly, estuaries which are regularly exposed to surge-producing strong winds are particularly at risk, for example rivers draining to the east coast of Japan, or the Humber and the Thames on the east coast of England.

It has been remarked that the funnel shape characteristic of many estuaries normally accentuates the increase in high water level in the upper narrow reaches, and that this is particularly noticeable during tidal surges. Exceptions do occur, however, and Edwards (1953) reported that during the 1953 storm surge in the North Sea, which was one of the worst on record, tidal levels at successive locations up the Humber estuary showed no evidence of surge effects.

One of the most striking examples of the combined effects of high freshwater discharge and high spring-tide levels intensified by a storm surge was the Thames estuary flood of 1928, detailed by Brooks and Glasspoole (1928). A heavy snow accumulation melted rapidly during a fast thaw on 2 and 3 January, causing widespread flooding in the Thames valley above London which was further exacerbated by exceptionally heavy rainfall during that week. By 7 January the flow of the Thames at Teddington (the tidal limit) was a near-record 499 cumecs, in effect more than twice the normal bankfull discharge. At the same time, a deep depression moving rapidly across Scotland on 6 January gave rise, in the evening, to southerly gales over the North Sea which produced a surge effect on the Thames estuary spring tides the following morning. The combined effect of storm surge, spring tide and near-record river discharge was an increase in water height in the estuary to nearly two metres above the predicted level with attendant widespread flooding of riverside land, much of which lay downstream of London well below the level of spring high tides.

Delta areas are also zones of conflict between river and sea water. Because of their high agriculture potential compared with most estuaries, they tend to attract large populations and therefore experience even more severe flood problems, as in the deltas of the Nile, the Yellow River in China, and the Red River and the Mekong in Vietnam. Gentle freshwater floods with a slow rise to peak flow have normally proved beneficial, as in the Mekong delta, but rapid river flooding is harmful as is, of course, high-tide or storm-surge-induced sea flooding, particularly in the effects of saline water on agricultural land and crops.

COASTAL FLOODS–STORM SURGES

Like estuaries, the intervening portions of open coastline are subjected to a normal tidal rhythm of two high and two low tides each day, with tidal amplitude or range reaching a maximum at spring tides and decreasing to a minimum at neap tides (see figure 4.1a b). There are, however, a few special areas, such as the Gulf of Mexico and the seas around the Philippines and parts off the Alaskan and Chinese coasts, which experience diurnal tides with only one high and one low water every 24 hours. In no case does the normal range of tidal behaviour result in flooding, either because the coastal land surface is well above spring high tide level or because low-lying coasts, such as those of the Netherlands (see figure 4.2), are protected by systems of embankments, walls and dykes (see chapter 10). As with estuarine floods, it is the unusual event which causes problems although, in the case of open coasts, the situation is not complicated by freshwater discharge interacting with tidal behaviour. Coastal flooding, except where caused by failure of protection works, is almost always the result of severe meteorological conditions producing abnormally high sea levels, known as storm surges, at about the time of spring tides.

For convenience, a storm surge may be expressed as the difference in height between the predicted and the observed tide. In the example illustrated in figure 4.3a, the 1953 storm surge at Dover is shown as a dotted line and represents the actual, minus the predicted, tide. This method is not entirely accurate since there is a coupling of ordinary tides and the storm surge itself whereby, because the

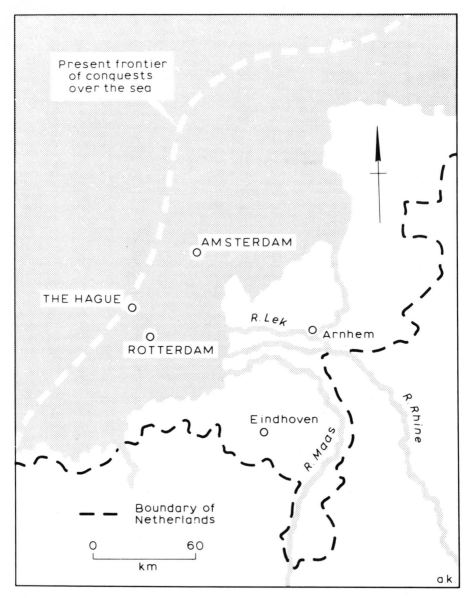

Figure 4.2   The coastline of the Netherlands in the absence of coast protection works
(broken line indicates approximate position of protected coastline)
Source: Graftdijk (1960).

water depth is increased by the storm surge, the ordinary tide will arrive earlier than expected and will be lower in amplitude, although the total tide will be higher (Bretschneider, 1967a). Two major types of storm surge may be distinguished. First, there are surges on open coastlines, for example on the Atlantic coast of the United States, which travel as running waves over very large areas of sea. Damaging surges of this type are mainly confined to those caused by intense storms such as tropical cyclones, hurricanes and typhoons. Secondly, there are surges in more or less enclosed seas (or lakes), for instance in the North Sea and the Adriatic Sea. Here the sea area is small in comparison with the horizontal dimensions of the atmospheric disturbance and thus the surges affect more or less the whole sea at any one time, and may be both frequent and severely damaging (Groen and Groves, 1962).

Since the storm surge results essentially from the stresses of the atmosphere on the sea, it is not surprising that the main influencing factor is storm intensity which, for most tropical and extra-tropical storms, can be expressed in terms of the central low pressure and the pressure gradient across the storm and its associated windspeed (Harris, 1967). Windspeed is a major factor in both piling up the sea against the coastline and generating large-scale turbulence and waves which further add to the maximum height of water, enhancing its destructive effect upon reaching the shore. Tropical storms are considered to have attained cyclone intensity when the maximum windspeed has reached 120 km/h, although it is not uncommon for windspeeds in excess of 240 km/h to be experienced (see figure 4.3b). A rise in sea level normally accompanies localised reductions in atmospheric pressure and is a noticeable feature of surges produced by intense storms, particularly of the tropical type. The threshold windspeeds of 120 km/h are generally associated with a central pressure drop of about 34 mbar, which is equivalent to about 36 cm of hydrostatic head. Bretschneider (1967a) noted that the lowest central pressure for an American hurricane was 891.85 mbar recorded off the Florida coast in 1935. If normal pressure is taken to be 1013·20 mbar this gives an anomaly of 121·35 mbar and is equivalent to a sea-level rise of 125 cm. The lowest central pressure recorded in a typhoon was 886·56 mbar some 740 km east of Luzon in 1927. In this case the anomaly was 126·64 mbar, equivalent to a 131 cm rise in sea level (Bretschneider, 1967a). Figure 4.3c shows empirical relationships between peak storm surge height for the eastern United States and the central pressure of the associated hurricanes.

The severity of a surge is also related to the size and track of the storm and particularly, in the case of open coastline surges, to the proximity of the storm track to the coastline. Further important factors are wind direction and fetch. If wind direction remains consistent for a sufficient period of time, which may be only a few hours for shallow coastal water, it may initiate large-scale drifting of the surface layers of an underlying water body. The effect of the earth's rotation, in certain circumstances, is to deflect the wind-drifted water up to 45° from the wind direction (to the right in the northern hemisphere). Bretschneider (1967b) showed that maximum water level rise along the coast resulting from wind drift was achieved at low windspeeds when the wind direction is parallel to the coast and at very high windspeeds when the wind is perpendicular to the coast. Wind direction is also directly related to fetch, which is the distance of open water over which the wind has blown. Fetch, in association with windspeed, determines the magnitude of water piling up at the downwind end of the ocean basin and the height and energy of the waves driven on to the shore. In the northern hemisphere the ocean areas around Iceland in the Atlantic and the Aleutians in the Pacific are frequently origins of intense storms which, if they move away south-eastwards, may produce persistent gale-force and hurricane-force winds

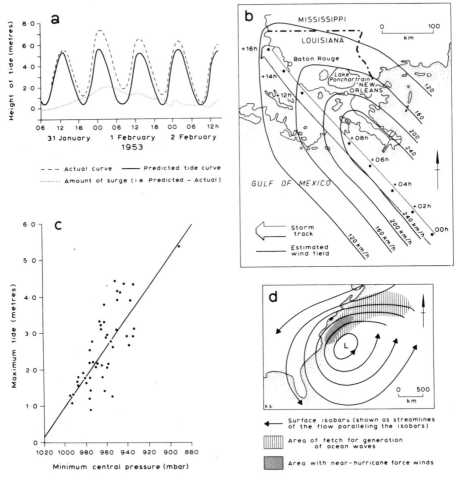

Figure 4.3   Storm surges: *a*, Predicted and observed tides and the 1953 storm surge at Dover; *b*, Track of Hurricane Betsy through Louisiana, showing areas affected by high wind speeds; *c*, Peak storm-surge height as a function of the central pressure of hurricanes; *d*, Surface streamlines, area of fetch and area of near-hurricane force winds producing storm-surge effects from Canada to Florida, 7 March 1962
Source: *a*, Steers (1953); *b*, U.S. Weather Bureau map; *c*, Conner, Kraft and Harris (1957); *d*, Riehl (1965).

blowing without appreciable change of direction for 1500 km or more, their potentially severe surge effects threatening the eastern coasts of the United States and Japan, respectively (see figure 4.3d).

Apart from the meteorological factors which have been discussed so far, the severity of storm surges is also influenced by the shape of the ocean basin both in terms of its bottom topography and its coastal configuration. As might be expected, these influences tend to be more important in the case of surges produced in relatively enclosed seas. Areas having a wide shallow continental shelf are more susceptible to damaging surges than those where the shelf slopes steeply. Roughness, apart from coastal irregularities, is also important. In the case of low-lying coasts, vegetation has a marked effect because now both the rate at which water can be transported across coastal marshes and the effect of bottom friction on the water surface slope are decisive (Bretschneider, 1967a). Coastal configuration exerts its major effect where converging coastlines create a funnel shape into which the storm surge moves and inevitably intensifies. This phenomenon occurs in the Gulf of Mexico, for example, where the coasts of Louisiana and Mississippi create a funnel, and it occurs 'par excellence' in the North Sea which is open at its northern end and almost closed at its southern end, the Flemish Bight. Basin shape is also important in terms of its effects on tidal oscillations, particularly where a given combination of basin shape and wind characteristics favour the formation of a standing wave oscillation which may intensify the effects of the wind-driven surge. In the case of the North Sea, the shape of the basin is such that the normal tidal oscillation, about three amphidromic points, results in the progressively southward movement of high or low water along the east coast of Britain. Since this is also the direction often followed by a storm surge, it is frequently found that, where the peak of the surge coincides with high tide, its effects are felt along virtually the whole length of the east coast of Britain.

From the preceding discussion it is apparent that although storm surges can affect almost any coastline in the world, there are certain combinations of meteorological and physiographic factors which make some coastlines more susceptible to large surges of a particularly damaging nature. In general, the most dangerous situation is that of a low-lying, semi-enclosed coastline exposed to the effects of cyclones or other intense storms. Thus the Bay of Bengal with its cyclones, the Gulf and Atlantic coast of the United States with its hurricanes, the east coast of Japan with its typhoons, the North Sea with its deep Atlantic depressions and the northern Adriatic, where sudden storms pose a continuing threat to the city of Venice, are all prime examples which are well documented in the literature. It is undoubtedly in the Bay of Bengal that the most devastating loss of life occurs. Smith (1975) estimated that as many as 300 000 people died in the surge-induced flooding of Bangladesh in November 1970 and that more than two million people were directly affected over an area of almost 7500 km^2. However, other coasts experience a similar frequency of flooding, some of it of great severity. In the fifty years from 1916 to 1965, for example, the Japanese coast was affected by five particularly severe typhoon surges having a maximum departure above normal of more than 2 m (Miyazaki, 1967). Between 1900 and 1960 the coast of Florida experienced forty *major* hurricanes, while even as far north as

Maryland on the Atlantic coast there is an average of one hurricane per year with direct or fringe effects upon the shore (Truitt, 1967). Two of these coastlines prone to surges, those of the southern North Sea and the Atlantic coast of the United States, will now be considered in more detail in order to illustrate, by specific examples, some of the general principles already discussed.

(a) Surges in the southern North Sea
As previously mentioned, the semi-enclosed funnel shape of the southern North Sea makes it particularly susceptible both to surge effects entering from the North Atlantic and to those generated by strong wind systems moving over the North Sea itself – and of course to a combination of both factors. In addition, the fact that this part of the North Sea is fringed by low-lying coastlands, where the ground surface is often several metres below the spring high tide level, means that when substantial surges occur the results are normally disastrous. Most of the severe surges of the recent past, for example 1825, 1894, 1897, 1906, 1916, 1921, 1928, 1936, 1942, 1943, 1949, 1953, 1969 and 1976, appear to have been associated with strong north-westerly winds accompanying the passage of especially deep depressions moving from the Atlantic towards the west coast of Norway. The circumstances of the January–February surge in 1953 were particularly severe.

A depression began to form south-west of Iceland on 29 January and to move north-eastwards. The position of its centre at 6-hourly intervals from 0000h on 30 January is shown in figure 4.4a. The central pressure fell from 996 mbar to less than 968 mbar at 0600h and 1200h on 31 January. During this initial period the intensifying winds had a strong westerly and south-westerly component which is believed to have caused a flow of water from south to north out of the Flemish Bight, thereby resulting in abnormally low tides at Southend on the morning of 31 January (Robinson, 1953). From 0600h on 31 January to 0000h on 1 February the depression continued to move south-eastward and to partially fill to 976 mbar. Behind it, however, a strong ridge of high pressure had built up over the Atlantic so that the steep pressure gradient over the North Sea in the rear of the depression was maintained. Significantly, the winds had now veered to north-west and north while continuing to blow with gale force or storm force strength (see figure 4.4b), thereby enormously increasing the fetch and reversing the flow of water previously expelled from the southern areas. This encouraged a southward movement of water along the east coast, as the wind drift was deflected to the right by the Earth's rotation (Robinson, 1953).

Maps of the increase in sea surface elevation (see figure 4.4c) show that these northerly winds raised the level of the entire southern part of the North Sea by more than two metres south of the Humber estuary, and by more than three metres off the Netherlands coast. Soon after 0000h on 1 February, the peak of the surge had reached the Thames and the Scheldt and then slowly, throughout the following day, the 'external' water flowed back out of the North Sea as the winds moderated, but again, owing to rotational deflection, most of the movement took place along the coasts of the Netherlands, Germany and Denmark.

Some authorities attributed the 1953 surge almost entirely to the influx of external water and Rossiter (1954) estimated that some 422 000 million m^3 of

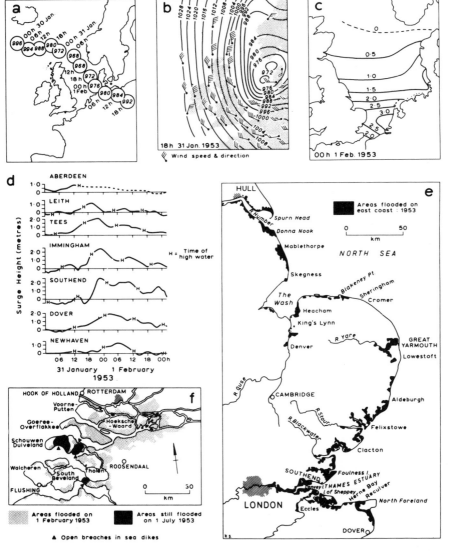

Figure 4.4 1953 North Sea storm surge: *a*, Track of the surge-forming depression 30 January – 1 February (central low pressure in mbar); *b*, Synoptic chart for 1800 h on 31 January; *c*, Sea surface disturbance (height in metres) at 0000 h on 1 February; *d*, Surge graphs for selected locations on the U.K. east coast, 31 January – 1 February; *e*, Flooded areas on the east coast of England; *f*, Flooded areas in the south-west Netherlands, 1 February and 1 July

Source: *a*, Robinson (1953); *b*, Meteorological Office *Daily Weather Report*; *c*, Groen and Groves (1962); *d*, Robinson (1953); *e*, Steers (1953); *f*, Edwards (1953).

water was forced into the North Sea from the Atlantic, thereby raising the mean level of the North Sea by more than 60 cm. Others – following the pioneering work of Corkan (1948; 1950), who distinguished between surges of external origin resulting from disturbances well to the north of Scotland and surges of internal origin caused by local effects within the North Sea basin itself and showed that for a surge of external origin its rate of progression around the coasts of the North Sea was identical to that of the diurnal tide – have suggested that residual graphs of the surges, derived as in figure 4.3a, indicate clearly that this was not the case. Figure 4.4d shows surge graphs for a number of east coast locations in Scotland and England and relates these to the time of high water. Robinson (1953) argued that, even allowing for the known limitations of surge graphs derived in this way, it is clear that the rates of progression of the surge and the diurnal tide are not identical and that indeed the peak of the surge occurred approximately simultaneously over a long stretch of coastline. Furthermore, the surge was maintained at a high level for five or six hours at some locations. These facts led Robinson to the conclusion that the greater part of the surge originated internally, within the North Sea basin itself, and was accompanied by abnormal sea surface gradients established directly by the gale force winds.

The magnitude of the storm surge along the east coast of the United Kingdom is well illustrated in figure 4.4d and for most locations was of the order of 2 m or slightly more. Along the Netherlands coast, however, the magnitude was substantially greater, averaging 3 m along the open coastline and reaching almost 4 m in some inlets (Robinson, 1953; Van Ufford, 1953). Minor oscillations, which show up on most of the surge graphs, are believed to reflect a standing wave oscillation, developed in the North Sea by the combination of wind strength and wind reversal, to which reference has already been made.

Inevitably, with actual tide levels so far in excess of the predicted levels, extensive flooding occurred (see figure 4.4e and f and plate 3). In England the majority of the flooding took place between the estuaries of the Humber and the Thames. Some was natural flooding, as when the sea broke over the dunes near Easington and flowed across the neck of land north of Spurn Head to make its exit into the Humber, but in most cases flooding occurred because sea defences were overtopped and then breached, often by erosion from the rear on the relatively unprotected landward face of a wall or embankment. In such cases, the water flowed into low-lying areas where it caused much damage and loss of life and where it remained in some cases for many months. In total, more than 850 km² were inundated and 307 people lost their lives (Steers, 1953). The situation was even worse in the Netherlands where the higher surge levels resulted partly from the funnelling effects of the Flemish Bight and partly from the fact that at the height of the surge the winds were blowing directly onshore. Altogether some 1600 km² were flooded, equivalent to six per cent of the arable land surface of the Netherlands, and 1800 lives were lost (Volker, 1953). The worst affected areas were concentrated between Rotterdam and the Scheldt and, as figure 4.4f indicates, substantial areas still remained flooded five months later.

The 1953 storm surge was a particularly severe example of a frequently experienced phenomenon; Rossiter (1954), for example, referred to the investigation of 85 surges which occurred at Southend between 1928 and 1938. Despite its severity however, several authorities have emphasised that it could have been much worse if it had coincided with flooded rivers, particularly in the low-lying fenland areas, and with the equinoctial spring tide, whose predicted level for Dover was some 61 cm higher than that predicted for the beginning of February and for Immingham in the Humber estuary was 136 cm higher (Robinson, 1953; Steers, 1953).

(b) Surges on the Atlantic coast of the United States

The Atlantic coast of the United States has already been mentioned as particularly prone to storm surges. As in the North Sea, this is partly due to the physiographic situation, with a wide shallow continental shelf and a number of coastline embayments which give rise to a funnelling effect, and partly to the meteorological conditions, which expose the coast to the tropical storms moving from the south-east and the mid-latitude storms moving south-westward from the north Atlantic. Extensive studies, particularly of the effects of hurricanes and other tropical storms, have resulted in determinations of storm surge potential for various sections of the coastline. Figure 4.5a shows relative storm-surge potential in terms of a topographic variable (θ) which is based on the distance of the 50-fathom submarine contour from the shore and which, in conjunction with data on the central pressure of a hurricane, can be used to provide a quantitative estimate of storm surge magnitude. A brief discussion of two surges, one produced by a tropical and the other by an extra-tropical storm, will serve to illustrate the Atlantic coast situation.

In September 1944 one of the most violent hurricanes recorded in the United States, the Great Atlantic Hurricane, moved northward along the coast from Puerto Rico, via Cape Hatteras and Long Island, and into New England. Enormous damage was done and the coast of New Jersey was particularly badly hit, with Atlantic City taking the brunt of the storm (Truitt, 1967). Surge graphs for Atlantic City and for five other Atlantic coast locations are shown in figure 4.5b and indicate average surge values of about 2 m. These graphs are very typical of hurricane-produced surges along the Atlantic coast which, according to Redfield and Miller (1957), show three distinct successive stages: the forerunner, the hurricane surge and the resurgences. The forerunner is the gradual, slow change in water level which takes place many hours before the storm itself arrives and which appears to result from the windfield over a more extended region than that of the hurricane proper. The forerunner may be either a rise or a fall in sea level, depending on whether the hurricane is moving northwards or southwards along the coast. The hurricane surge is the sharp rise in water level that occurs when the hurricane centre approaches the coast. This stage is usually of short duration, lasting up to five hours, although peak surges of as much as four metres have been recorded. Finally, the resurgences are oscillations occurring after the passage of the hurricane and the hurricane surge and are well illustrated by the Atlantic City graph. The resurgences can be particularly hazardous, partly because they often arrive unexpectedly as the storm appears to be subsiding and partly because coincidence with the astronomical tide may result in one or more of the resurgence peaks being higher than the original hurricane surge itself. Munk *et al.* (1956) regarded the resurgences as a 'wake' of waves in the

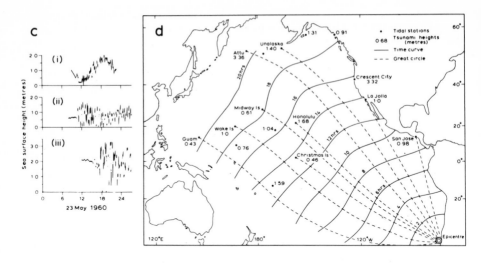

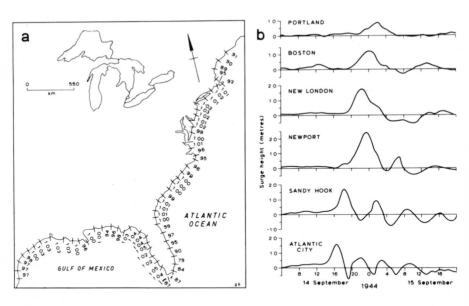

Figure 4.5   Atlantic surges and Pacific tsunamis: *a*, Relative storm surge potential on Atlantic and Gulf coasts of the United States; *b*, Surge graphs for six Atlantic coast locations, 14–15 September 1944; *c*, Tide gauge records of Pacific tsunami at (i) San Francisco, (ii) Honolulu and (iii) Attu Island; *d*, Isochrones of arrival times (in hours) of the initial tsunami wave after the earthquake in Chile

Source: *a*, U.S. Weather Bureau (1959)p. 8; *b*, Redfield and Miller (1957); *c* and *d*, Robinson (1961).

trail of a hurricane (analagous to the wake of a ship). These 'wakes' progress along the coast but are little affected by the hurricane once they have been generated.

The Great March Storm, alternatively known as the Ash Wednesday Storm, of 1962 was not a hurricane, nor, except locally, did its windspeeds attain hurricane strength, and yet its effects were more severe than those produced by many tropical storms. Indeed, this was the most destructive extra-tropical storm ever recorded in America (Truitt, 1967), leaving in its wake, from Florida to New England, some $250 million worth of damage and more than 30 deaths, and yet its origins were sudden and unexpected. As Burton *et al.* (1969) observed, the prevailing weather pattern over the eastern half of the United States on 4 March 1962 gave no cause for alarm. A small, cold front storm between Florida and Bermuda was expected to move harmlessly out into the Atlantic and another storm centre in the Mississippi Valley was filling and moving slowly northwards. Both storms, however, behaved unexpectedly. The Florida storm moved northwards along the coast and the Mississippi Valley storm moved eastwards until, eventually, the two met near Cape Hatteras, increased in strength and produced the Great March Storm of 6–7 March 1962. The storm intensified rapidly but then stagnated, producing the situation illustrated in figure 4.3d, whereby windspeeds of 80 to 100 km/h developed along a fetch of about 2000 km. A storm surge of between 0.5 and 2 m was produced along the entire east coast from Canada to Florida, accompanied by very high waves, and persisted during three successive high tides (Riehl, 1965; Truitt, 1967). It was this persistence which proved so serious because although offshore bars, barrier beaches, sand dunes and artificial coastal defences survived the first high tide in many places, the repeated attack of waves and tide during a second and third high tide caused numerous breakthroughs and often spectacular damage.

COASTAL FLOODS – TSUNAMIS

Some of the most spectacularly disastrous coastal flooding results from tsunamis which are waves produced by submarine earthquakes, volcanic eruptions, or landsliding and slumping (Thornbury, 1969). Similar effects have also been caused by the explosion of nuclear bombs at the sea surface (Bascom, 1959). Tsunamis normally comprise a train of waves triggered off by the rapid motion or subsidence of the ocean floor along a submarine fault or by submarine slumping associated with earthquakes. These waves have enormous dimensions in comparison with ordinary wind-generated waves which are only rarely 300 m from crest to crest and travel at maximum speeds of about 100 km/h. A tsunami often extends more than 150 km, sometimes reaching 1000 km, from crest to crest and since, even in the deep Pacific Ocean, water depth is less than one-half the wavelength their speed is proportional to depth and may reach as much as 700 to 800 km/h. Because tsunamis are so shallow in comparison with their length they are normally barely detectable in the open ocean, where their amplitude rarely exceeds 0·5 m, or even in deep water close to the shore. Bascom (1959), for example, quoted the case of the captain of a ship standing off the port of Hilo, Hawaii watching in astonishment as the harbour and much of the city was demolished by waves he had not noticed passing beneath his ship. This type of circumstantial evidence together with more rigorous evidence provided, for example, by spectral analysis – by which the spectra of different tsunamis at any one station generally look alike, but an individual tsunami exhibits at different positions no reproducible spectral features (Munk, 1962) – points clearly to the dominant effect of coastal configuration and bottom topography on the character of the tsunami waves which reach the shore. On reaching shallow coastal water the velocity and wavelength of the tsunami rapidly diminishes but as the period remains unchanged there is a marked increase in wave height. Tsunami waves are therefore much more dangerous on flat shores, where they may range from 6 to 18 m, than on steep ones but when they pour into a funnel-shaped inlet or harbour they can rise to mountainous proportions (Bernstein, 1954).

Because of the wavelengths involved, tsunamis commonly have a period (the time interval between successive waves in the train) of between 15 minutes and an hour or more, and the wave succession may continue for many hours. This is illustrated in figure 4.5c for the Pacific tsunami of 22 May 1960, although the sequence of events experienced on this occasion was fairly typical of many tsunamis. The first few waves are not usually the largest and before the arrival of each large wave there is a marked drawdown of sea level, leaving reefs and other offshore features high and dry.

Certain coasts near zones of instability in the Earth's crust are particularly prone to tsunamis, especially the shores of the Mediterranean, the Caribbean and the west coast of Asia (Bascom, 1959). For the globe as a whole the average occurrence exceeds one a year and in the Pacific 270 damage-causing tsunamis were listed by Heck (1947) for the period 279 BC to 1946. The ancient Greeks recorded several catastrophic inundations by huge waves (Bernstein, 1954) and an Arabian Sea tsunami in 1945 prompted further thoughts about the biblical stories of the Flood and of the parting of the waters described in Exodus. One of the most damaging tsunamis on record followed the famous Lisbon earthquake of 1 November 1755; its waves persisted for a week, crossing the Atlantic as well as affecting the English coast. Another famous tsunami, well documented by Baird (1884), was associated with the explosion of the volcano Krakatoa in the Sunda Strait in August 1883. In this case waves at least 30 m high swept away the small town of Merak, over 50 km distant from the volcano, and carried the man-of-war *Berow* 3 km inland depositing it some 10 m above sea level. A train of about a dozen waves crossed the Pacific and Indian Oceans at speeds between 550 and 700 km/h and then traversed the Atlantic Ocean and some 32 hours after the initial explosion was recorded in the English Channel as disturbances a few centimetres high (Robinson, 1961).

Of the numerous Pacific tsunamis, that of 1 April 1946 is described as the most thoroughly investigated in history (Bernstein, 1954), mainly because of the large number of oceanographers who were in the area to observe the effects of the atom bomb test at Bikini atoll. The tsunami, which originated with a landslide in the Aleutian submarine trench, struck particularly hard at Hawaii causing 159 deaths and property damage of $25 million (Bernstein, 1954). The same waves caused considerable destruction throughout the islands of Oceania, 6400 km from the epicentre, and on the coast of South America, but their effects were most spectacular at Scotch Cap in the Aleutian Islands of Alaska, where a light-house whose base was 10 m above sea level and a radio mast whose foundations were 30 m above sea level were both demolished (Bascom, 1959; Shepard, 1948). The Pacific tsunami in May 1960 resulted from an exceptionally severe earth-quake which affected southern Chile on 22 May and caused a large area of the sea-bed to founder off the Chilean coast. The resulting wave progression, recon-structed by Robinson (1961), is shown in figure 4.5d. Despite the tsunami warn-ing system, which had been introduced largely as a result of the 1946 disaster, there was still considerable damage and loss of life around the Pacific coastlands as far as ten thousand miles from the earthquake epicentre. As the tsunami was only a little over one metre high at Hawaii it was not considered a threat to Japan, but in fact the waves attained heights of up to 10 m along the coasts of Hokkaido and Honshu where many lives were lost (Robinson, 1961). This clearly illustrates the failure, at that time, to appreciate the effects of bottom topography on wave characteristics.

The highest tsunami-type waves are the result of landslides into more or less enclosed water bodies. By far the largest recorded event occurred when a rock-slide associated with the Alaskan earthquake of July 1958 caused an estimated 30·5 million m³ of rock to fall from an altitude of almost 1000 m into the waters of Lituya Bay (Miller, 1960). This rockfall caused a surge of water on to the opposite shore of the bay which reached to the incredible height of 524 m!

Bascom (1959) warned that, in view of the continuous increase in the popula-tion of the world's coastlands, the worst tsunami disaster is yet to come and pre-dicted that within the next century there will be a tsunami which will at least equal the one which swept the shores of the Bay of Bengal in 1876, leaving 200 000 dead.

DAM COLLAPSE FLOODS

Although, fortunately, major dam disasters are comparatively rare events, more than 300 were referred to by Biswas and Chatterjee (1971) and in 1976 alone the failure of the newly-built Teton dam in Idaho in June was followed in July by the failure of the floor of the newly-built Elbe canal at a viaduct near Luneburg, West Germany. When dam disasters do occur the accompanying violent flood-ing normally causes considerable damage and loss of life. The earliest known dam failure is that of the Sadd-el-Kafara dam near Cairo which apparently failed during its first flood season, sometime between 2950 and 2750 BC, through a combination of design and construction faults (Biswas, 1970). In modern times early dams, particularly those built before the development of grouting techniques, frequently failed due to water undermining their foun-dations. Walters (1971) referred to more than 100 such disasters in America alone which could be attributed to this cause, including the failure of the St Francis dam in California. This massive concrete dam, some 60 m high, failed suddenly on 12 March 1928, drowning 400 people and causing damage of £4 million.

The comparatively few English dam failures have never been entirely satis-factorily explained. According to Walters (1971) the collapse of the first Wood-head embankment in 1850 was probably due to percolation through the underlying bedrock, while the Bilberry dam near Huddersfield which burst on 4 February 1852, causing great loss of life and almost completely destroying the village of Holmfirth, probably failed because of water forcing its way through fissures in the bedrock and by upward pressure rapidly washing away the earthen embankment. Again, undermining by water and embankment slipping following saturation probably caused the Dale Dyke reservoir disaster at Bradfield, near Sheffield, on 11 March 1864 when 245 lives were lost, nearly 800 houses destroyed and more than 4000 flooded (Brooks and Glasspoole, 1928). The last dam disaster to occur in Great Britain was at Dolgarrog, north Wales, in 1926 when 16 people were drowned (Walters, 1971).

A particularly dramatic dam failure happened on 2 December 1959 when the left foundation of the 66·5 m high Malpasset dam near Fréjus in southern France gave way releasing 25 million m³ of water which swept down the valley of the River Reyran, partly destroying the town of Fréjus and causing the loss of 421 lives (see plate 4). The collapse of the Malpasset dam seems to have been due entirely to geological causes, probably a plane of weakness in the bedrock be-neath the left foundation (Walters, 1971). Undoubtedly the most disastrous dam floods in recent times took place on the night of 9 October 1963 when a landslide deposited about 115 million m³ of rock into the reservoir above the Vaiont dam in Italy generating a wave which ran up the reservoir shore some 270 m above the still water level and overtopped the dam. In spite of cracks in the abutments (strengthened after the Malpasset failure) the Vaiont dam did not fail although the overtopping resulted in a 70 m wave of water which passed downstream des-troying everything in its path and causing the loss of 3000 lives (Biswas and Chatterjee, 1971; Davidson and McCartney, 1975).

A particularly dangerous situation results when there is an excessively high inflow of water, either from rainfall or snowmelt, upstream of a partially com-pleted dam. Scott and Gravlee (1968) described the failure of the partly com-pleted Hell Hole dam on the Rubicon River in California on 23 December 1964 after a torrential five-day rainfall of approximately 560 mm in the basin upstream from the dam site. The flood surge was released over a period of one hour during which the mean discharge was 7400 cumecs and the peak flow reached at least 8500 cumecs, which was probably the highest discharge attained in any part of the Rubicon River within the past 10 000 years. Fortunately this flood surge occurred in a remote valley in the Sierra Nevadas where its major effects were geomorphological.

With the improved design of major dams the worst flood disasters of this type now tend to result from failure of more minor structures such as those built for industrial purposes, for example as settling ponds. An especially dramatic example was provided on 26 February 1972 when after heavy rainfall a coal-waste dam collapsed on Buffalo Creek in West Virginia releasing some 495 000 m³ of water which swept 24 km down the valley as a 3 to 6 m high flood wave, travelling at just over two metres per second, and reaching the town of Man at the mouth of Buffalo Creek on the Guyandotte River some three hours after the dam failure. During those three hours at least 118 lives were lost, 500 homes destroyed, 4000 people left homeless and damage exceeding $65 million was done (Davies *et al.*, 1972). In this case coal-waste banks were not engineered as dams but were simply waste dumps used to impound waste water from a coal washing plant and as porous filters to cleanse that water before its recycling to the washing plant. Stricter controls over the design and maintenance of such structures have since been recommended.

The failure of natural dams can have disastrous consequences similar to the failure of man-made structures. Some rivers, particularly those flowing in deep narrow valleys, are subject to periodic obstruction by landslides. The Indus is a good example of this type of river. Two of its highest and most disastrous floods resulted from landslides in 1841 and 1858 (Khan, 1969). In 1841 a side of Hatu Pir mountain slipped into the Indus downstream of Bunji in Gilgit district and completely blocked the river for about six months causing the formation of a backwater lake nearly 60 km in length and more than 100 m deep. When the barrier burst after the spring thaw the resulting floodwave caused colossal damage, sweeping away everything in its path including an entire Sikh army that had encamped in the valley bottom below Attock.

Most dam-collapse floods are, inevitably, examined after the event in a more or less empirical way. Recently, however, mathematical simulation techniques have facilitated the theoretical study of the hydrological effects of dam failure (Balloffet and Balloffet, 1974; Fread and Harbaugh, 1973).

5 Floods as Geomorphological Agents

Landforms change as a result of the combined processes of erosion, transportation and sedimentation which involve the removal of material from one part of a drainage basin and its deposition in another. Although, in the past, it was customary to separate considerations of erosion–sedimentation processes in stream channels from those within the remainder of the basin, it is now recognised that such a separation is geomorphologically unrealistic. Just as there is a continuum of water movement from all parts of the basin to the stream channels so too is there a continuous movement of weathered material from all parts of the drainage basin towards and through the stream channels. In addition, the processes of detachment, transportation and deposition of material may take place at any point within the drainage basin system. In our examination of floods as geomorphological agents, it will be convenient to reimpose the earlier divisions and to consider 'normal', that is fluvial, processes as operating on two distinct units, the hillslopes and the combined channel and floodplain. This division recognises first that, hydrologically, stream channels and their adjacent floodplains are complementary and inseparable and *together* form the proper conveyance for the transmission of floodwaters (a view emphasised in chapter 1) and second, that since most of the floodwaters will be transmitted via the channel–floodplain unit it is within this unit that the main interaction between floods and geomorphology occurs.

On hillslopes the movement of material results from gravity-induced and water-lubricated mass movement and from the effects of water running below the surface as interflow and pipeflow and on the surface as anastomosing and sheet flow. Within stream channels material moves in solution and suspension and as bedload. For much of the time these processes operate gradually and almost imperceptibly; even so, considerable volumes of material are involved. Holeman (1968) listed the average annual suspended loads carried by the Nile, Mississippi and Yellow Rivers as 111, 312 and 1887 million tonnes (or 37, 97 and 2804 tonnes km²) respectively. In mountainous areas, as might be expected, the equivalent values are somewhat higher. Thus McPherson (1971), investigating a small basin in the Canadian Rockies, observed during one summer the removal in suspension of 11 655 tonnes (or 1295 tonnes/km²) which closely approximates the 0.51 mm/yr average denudation rate found by several other workers in mountainous areas. Furthermore, Gibbs (1967) found that 85 per cent of the total dissolved salts and suspended solids discharged by the Amazon is eroded from the 12 per cent of the basin comprising the Andean-type environment.

In both mountainous and non-mountainous environments average values of erosion may be greatly exceeded during specific flood events. For example, substantial hillslope erosion may accompany rapid snowmelt or torrential rainfall, particularly in steeply sloping areas having thin soils. Over much of the Appalachian area for instance most large floods are accompanied by landslides and slope failure on a massive scale; Williams and Guy (1973) estimated that in Nelson County, Virginia during the Hurricane Camille floods of August 1969 almost one-half of the 44 000 m^3/km^2 of erosion took place in the form of debris avalanches on upland hillslopes. Similarly in peat-covered areas heavy rainfall, particularly following a wet period, may cause peat slides or bog bursts. These have been recorded from time to time in the English Pennines. An example, described by Crisp *et al.* (1964), occurred in Teesdale in July 1963 and involved the movement of a sheet of peat some 230 m long, 36 m wide and up to 1.5 m deep having an approximate volume of 4000 m^3. Again, within stream channels, both the movement of bedload and the carrying of material in suspension are controlled largely by turbulence and therefore tend to increase with discharge during the passage of a floodwave. An analogous situation occurs along the coast where the normal range of wind and tides results in the gradual erosion and redistribution of material but where, during a single storm surge, the erosive work of centuries may be performed.

Inevitably erosion increases with the magnitude of the event, large floods and high waves and tides producing the most spectacular erosion. Large-magnitude events, however, occur comparatively infrequently whereas small floods and modest wave–tide combinations, although individually causing less erosion, occur frequently. This has led to considerable debate as to the relative effectiveness of events having widely different magnitude–frequency relationships. Leopold *et al.* (1964) argued cogently, from the evidence of rivers in widely different climatic and physiographic situations, that in terms of the transportation of suspended load '. . . the major work is accomplished during the more modest but relatively frequent floods rather than during the larger but rarer catastrophic floods'. A major problem is that since catastrophic events *are* rare there are very few data from which to generalise although occasionally events, such as the 50-year flood in the Cypress Hills of Alberta in 1967, seem to support the view that rare extreme events are less important geomorphologically than their magnitudes appear to suggest (McPherson and Rannie, 1969). Other workers feel that catastrophic events have a much greater geomorphological importance than was suggested by Leopold *et al.* (1964), particularly in environments where rapid mass movement of slope material is a major factor in landform modification and where the debris produced by a single storm may take many years or many decades to be removed or obliterated. Supportive examples have been derived from upland areas in England (Gifford, 1953), New Zealand (Pain and Hosking, 1970) and the United States (Williams and Guy, 1973).

To some extent the geomorphological importance of catastrophic events will depend upon their distribution in time. Although they are, by definition, rare they are not necessarily evenly spaced through time and it seems likely that two high-magnitude floods occurring in quick succession, with little time for the basin to 'recover' from the first event, will have a greater geomorphological effect than the same floods widely separated in time. A similar effect is seen when either climatic or human factors produce flood-intensifying effects during a particular time period. Haggett and Chorley (1969) observed that the period of arroyo cutting in the south-western United States between about 1880 and the late 1920s resulted from the combined effects of human intervention and climatic fluctuation. Thus low winter rainfall, decreasing grass cover, and overgrazing combined to produce overland flow and the headward extension of arroyos like that of the Rio Puerco in New Mexico which cut back well over 150 km during this period of relative aridity.

In the remainder of this chapter the main geomorphological processes at work during floods and some of the more important morphological changes produced will be discussed in the context of the stream channel, the floodplain and the coast. Hillslope processes which may or may not result from flood-producing events will not be considered further.

STREAM CHANNELS

Since, as has already been observed, the load carried by a stream is controlled largely by turbulence, which in turn is associated with discharge, it is to be expected that total streamload, and indeed the individual contributions of the dissolved, suspended and bedload components, will increase in relation to discharge. On an annual basis this relationship is often very clear and figure 5.1a, for example, indicates a good correlation between suspended load and discharge for the Colorado River at Grand Canyon. On a shorter-term basis, as for example during the passage of a flood wave, the relationship between load and discharge may be more complex. Figure 5.1b illustrates the situation during the May 1967 flood on the Graburn Creek in Alberta and shows that although maximum bedload discharge coincided with maximum stream discharge, maximum suspended and dissolved loads were attained before the discharge peak occurred. This is a fairly commonly observed relationship which is illustrated more clearly for suspended loads in figure 5.1c. The non-coincidence of the peaks of suspended load and flood discharge may be explained in part by the fact that at the beginning of many storms the water moving towards and through the stream channels may find much more loose material ready to move than at the end of the storm (Einstein, 1964) and partly by the breaking up of the protective layer of coarse material on the channel bed. Once this (often imbricated) armouring is broken by the rising floodwaters, large quantities of smaller particles underneath enter into suspension. However, in some cases the relationships between the peaks of suspended load and discharge are reversed with the rise in river discharge preceding the rise in sediment concentration (see Figure 5.2a). Heidel (1956) explained this type of lag on the Bighorn River as due to the fact that many flood waves approximate to a kinematic wave, and thus have a travel velocity substantially larger than the mean water velocity at which the suspended load is transported downstream. In such cases, the lag between the arrival of the discharge peak and the subsequent peak concentration of suspended solids will increase with distance downstream.

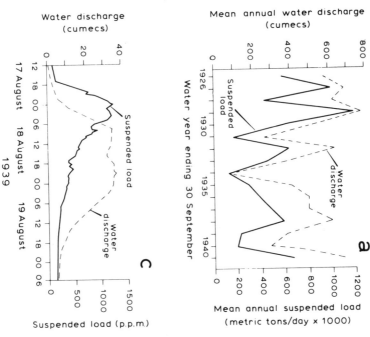

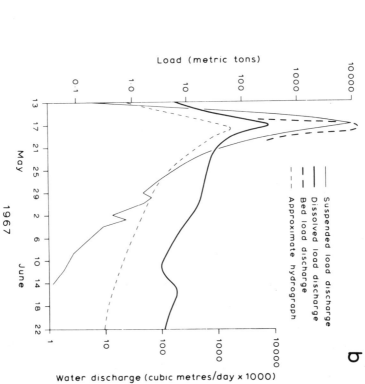

Figure 5.1 Stream channel loads: *a*, Mean annual discharge and suspended load for the Colorado River at Grand Canyon, Arizona; *b*, Variations of discharge and load on Graburn Creek, Alberta; *c*, Discharge and suspended load variations during passage of a flood wave on the Enoree River, South Carolina

Source: *a*, Howard (1947); *b*, McPherson and Rannie (1969); *c*, Einstein, Anderson and Johnson (1940) pp. 628–32.

Floods

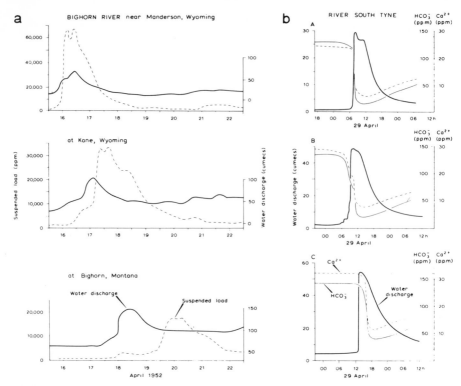

Figure 5.2 Stream load lagging water discharge: *a*, Discharge and suspended load during downstream passage of a flood wave on the Bighorn River in Wyoming and Montana; *b*, Discharge and the concentration of calcium and bicarbonate during downstream passage of flood wave on the River South Tyne
Source: *a*, Heidel (1956); *b*, Glover and Johnson (1974).

A similar kinematic wave effect has been observed in the relationships between dissolved loads and discharge (Glover and Johnson, 1974). In such cases, however, the nature of the dissolved load variation depends very much on whether the dissolved component represents a baseflow contribution to streamflow, which is therefore diluted by an influx of quickflow, or whether it represents a periodic flushing-out by quickflow of the residue of chemical weathering since the last major flood episode. In the latter case concentrations of dissolved matter may increase with stream discharge. The former situation is illustrated in figure 5.2b which shows how the diluting effect of a flood rise on the River South Tyne progressively lags behind the flood rise itself as the flood wave moves downstream.

Relations between bedload movement and flood discharge are noteworthy for a number of reasons. First, movement of large material takes place only at high discharges and there is normally a clear threshold discharge below which no movement occurs (see figure 5.1b). This results in a direct relationship between bedload movement and flood discharge. Once flow drops below the threshold value, bedload is simply 'dumped' and will normally remain virtually undisturbed until the next flood of equal or higher magnitude occurs, which may be several months, years or even decades later. Second, the contribution of bedload to total streamload is often remarkably high despite the comparatively short travel-distances of the individual particles. Again this is indicated in figure 5.1b and Schick (1970) found that for a number of desert streams the volume of bedload moved downstream during individual floods exceeded the suspended load by a factor of between two and ten. Third, the size of individual bedload particles ranges widely between coarse sand at one extreme and boulders several metres in diameter at the other. Furthermore, because the movement of large bedload particles is possible only at high discharges (and therefore high stages) there is frequently a substantial introduction into the channel of material derived from the valley sides and also a deposition of coarse material, not only in the channel but also on the higher margins of the floodplain, and in exceptional circumstances even beyond that. (See plate 5)

Clearly, during the passage of a flood wave the total amount of material in movement in the channel increases significantly, although this amount can vary enormously from virtually clear water flowing over a rock bed to massive mudflows having up to 60 per cent of their total volume comprised of solid materials (Gagoshidze, 1969; Kherkheulidze, 1969). Part of this increase in load is derived from outside the channel and part from within. As a result, channel form exhibits an adaptation to flood discharge. This adaptation takes the form both of changes in bed configuration, such as the appearance and disappearance of dunes and ripples, and modification of the depth and width of the channel through the processes of scour and deposition. Over a period of time these relationships may be reflected in the hydraulic geometry of the channel system (Leopold and Maddock, 1953) whereby channel depth and width and the velocity of flow at a given cross-section increase with stream discharge in accordance with simple power functions. In the short term, however, much of the adaptation of channel form is temporary. Thus, width increases rapidly with discharge as water spills from the channel on to the floodplain and reduces again as overbank flow ceases. Similarly, depth may be increased by scour during the period of increasing discharge to the flood peak and may be reduced again by fill during the subsequent reduction in discharge after the flood peak has passed (see figure 5.3a and b). Scour at one point will normally be accompanied by deposition elsewhere either within or outside the channel. Miller (1951), for example, noted that one of the first effects of a flood is to move bedload into hollows from which it is not readily removed. Major floods can cause impressive changes, particularly in the form of channel widening by bank scour and slumping, but over the succeeding weeks and months this damage is gradually 'repaired' as deposition causes the enlarged channel to adjust to the smaller flows. Only when high-magnitude floods occur with sufficient regularity, thereby preventing the repair processes referred to above, do they leave a permanent imprint on the landscape (Gupta and Fox, 1974).

Thus, it is only in rare circumstances that channel form is adjusted to major

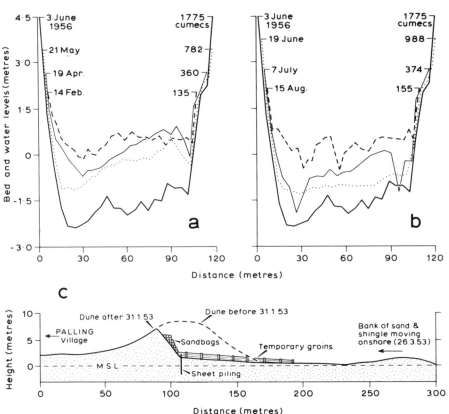

Figure 5.3 Erosional and depositional effects: *a*, Scour and *b*, Fill, during passage of flood wave on the Colorado River at Lees Ferry, Arizona; *c*, Erosion of dune belt at Palling, Norfolk during storm surge and subsequent position of onshore-moving bar Source: *a* and *b*, Leopold, Wolman and Miller (1964); *c*, Grove (1953).

flood discharges. In most cases channels adjust to peak events having a recurrence interval of one to two years (Wolman and Leopold, 1957). It is clear that major flood events result in the sporadic influx to the drainage system of large quantities of eroded material. Since, however, the effects of such large inputs are felt within the actual channels for only very brief periods it is pertinent to look elsewhere for their lasting effects, particularly in the complementary part of the flood conveyance, the floodplain.

FLOODPLAINS

Although frequently thought of as features produced by major rivers such as the Mississippi, floodplains are common depositional forms produced by streams and rivers of all sizes. Essentially, the floodplain may be regarded as a store of sediment across which channel flow takes place and which, in the long term, is comparatively unchanging in amount. In the short term, however, quite dramatic changes can take place. Floodplain morphology frequently indicates an apparent adjustment to flood discharge in the sense that different floodplain or terrace levels are significantly related to different frequencies of flood discharge, the higher levels being inundated only by very rare flood events. Although such adjustment normally takes place over a considerable period of time, it is brought about by the continuous interplay of erosion and depositional events having a wide range of frequencies, which operate both within and outside the stream channels, sometimes very gradually and sometimes very rapidly.

Since the peak concentration of suspended load usually occurs before the discharge peak (see p. 58), there is a tendency for much of a stream's load to be contained within its channel and for the water which does overflow on to the floodplain to be less heavily laden with suspended solids. This means that within-channel processes resulting in lateral accretion are normally the most important in floodplain formation, compared with overbank flows which result in vertical accretion, and in many cases account for between 60 and 80 per cent of the deposited sediment (Leopold *et al.*, 1964). The eventual result of point bar and channel bar deposition in migrating channels (for example meandering or braided) is the formation of a single sheet of gravel, sand or silt which in the past was often wrongly assumed to be a genuine flood (in effect, overbank) deposit.

Although lateral accretion is the most important factor in floodplain development, overbank flows which cause the inundation of the floodplain often result in more marked topographic features such as levees, crevasse-splays and flood-basins. As floodwaters overtop channel banks and spread out, their ability to transport material in suspension is reduced. The coarsest debris is dropped near the edge of the channel, where the rate of deposition is at a maximum, while finer material is transported farther and laid down as back-swamp deposits. Levees thus slope away from the channels into the floodbasins which are the lowest parts of the floodplain. At high stages, breaks and low sections in the levees may result in a concentrated outflow of water from channel to floodplain which rapidly erodes a crevasse and leads to the deposition in the floodbasin of a crevasse-splay or delta. The floodbasins themselves act as stilling basins in which suspended fines from overbank flows settle out after the coarser debris has been deposited on levees and as crevasse-splays.

Lateral accretion deposits seem to be common to all floodplains, although vertical accretion features may be only weakly developed or even absent and in some cases, particularly in upstream sections of a valley, it is often difficult to distinguish the two. To a large extent the morphological characteristics of a floodplain and the degree of morphological response of the floodplain to individual flood discharges depends on the relative importance of lateral and vertical accretion features. These, in turn, depend on the discharge regimes of both water and solids, channel characteristics and the effect of 'external' factors such as base-level changes due to subsidence and uplift. There is, for example, a substantial difference between the situation where relatively steep braided streams with coarse loads rapidly shift position across the whole width of the floodplain, thereby keeping overbank deposition and floodplain relief at a minimum, and the situation in the floodplain of a large meandering river such as the Mississippi, where the levees may be 2 km wide and stand more than 7 m above the adjacent floodbasins. Where levee development is pronounced and has resulted in the meander belt being raised substantially above the surrounding floodplain level, a major flood may cause avulsion – the sudden abandonment of a part or the whole of a meander belt as the river breaks through the levees and adopts a new course at a lower level on the floodplain. In such cases the process of levee development will begin again at the newly adopted lower level. With more simple and subdued floodplain relief even major floods will cause relatively little morphological change, the floodwaters spreading out more or less uniformly across the floodplain and draining back into the channel after the passage of the flood peak. In such situations, the effect of vegetation is important. Where conditions favour the development of vegetation, particularly bushes and trees, erosion by floodwaters tends to be reduced, deposition increased and generally the floodplain morphology stabilised (Schumm and Lichty, 1963). However, a commonly observed effect of major floods is the destruction of floodplain vegetation and the tendency, therefore, for vegetation height on the floodplain, particularly that of bushes and trees, to be associated with the recurrence interval of large floods (Gupta and Fox, 1974). Once again the frequency of occurrence is an important factor and closely spaced major floods can denude a floodplain of vegetation and expose it to large-scale erosion and morphological change.

The usual balance between erosion and deposition may be substantially

Although so far deposition has been stressed, erosion also occurs. Indeed, in the long term, erosion must equal deposition or the height of the floodplain surface and the total volume of floodplain deposits will consistently increase or decline, and the channel bed and the local floodplain will not maintain a constant relative elevation. Within the floodplain subaerial erosion, particularly by raindrop impact, may cause a rapid downslope redistribution of newly deposited and therefore unvegetated material and a fairly rapid reduction in the local amplitude of relief. However, large-scale removal of sediment from the floodplain can only be achieved by running water, and Leopold *et al.* (1964) suggested the principal mechanisms. First, channel migration removes part of the floodplain, thereby obliterating its pre-existing topography and limiting the elevation of its surface. Second, floodwater velocities over the surface of the floodplain are often irregularly distributed and may, in places, be high enough to produce scour rather than deposition. The hydrodynamic characteristics of floodplain currents are difficult to investigate and Popov and Gavrin (1970) suggested that the use of aerial photography might improve our understanding of this phenomenon. A third factor, which has already been discussed, is that the water which does overflow on to the floodplain may contain relatively little material in suspension so that deposition, even in the slack-water areas of the floodplain, is often negligible. Costa (1974) noted that in floods generated by Hurricane Agnes considerable erosion of floodplain surfaces was caused by coarse gravels being moved along the surface by the floodwaters.

The usual balance between erosion and deposition may be substantially distorted by external factors, either natural or induced by man. Thus, a combination of subsidence and rising base level has led to deep alluviation in the lower valley of the Mississippi and other rivers flowing into the Gulf of Mexico, while isostatic uplift after glaciation in higher latitudes has created terraced floodplains which are in general characterised by little or no overbank deposition (Douglas, 1975). Again, the height of floodplain surfaces in some estuarine areas has been significantly increased by warping.

A major conclusion from this brief survey of the interaction between floods and floodplains is that just as stream channels show the effect of floods only in the short term so floodplains show them for only slightly longer, geologically speaking. In other words, in the long term, the role of the floodplain as a 'temporary' store for sediment moving out of a drainage basin is reflected in an equilibrium whereby the net inflow of sediment equals the net outflow (Leopold *et al.*, 1964). Seen in this light, floods are simply part of the complete range of hydrogeomorphological events operating within the drainage basin. Of course, on the much shorter time-scale of man's adaptation to floods the morphological changes produced by an individual flood may, like those in coastal areas, assume a considerably greater significance (Lewin and Manton, 1975). These will, therefore, be discussed again later.

COASTS

In this final section the theme developed in relation to the geomorphological role of floods in stream channel and floodplain development, that flood events cause 'damage' of a more or less ephemeral nature which is gradually 'repaired' by smaller events of higher frequency, will again be briefly pursued in the context of coastal features. Such ephemeral changes are seen when beach material is stripped off overnight by destructive waves only to be restored in the succeeding weeks by the action of constructive waves.

The analogy is not, however, perfect. Thus, we may liken the beach to the floodplain, that is the sediment store through which debris is gradually passed from areas of net erosion to areas of net deposition, but the stream channel on the one hand and the coast on the other have no strict analogy. Beach development takes place over a wide range of normal tidal heights from spring high tide level to spring low tide level and indeed continues underwater below the latter. Flood surges may greatly extend the area of operation of these normal processes on a lowland coast where breaching of natural or artificial coast defences results in extensive flooding, but they have no spatial expression where massive vertical cliffs are washed by the normal range of tides. Again, morphological changes along the coast are obviously more irreversible than those on the floodplain. For example, the rapidly eroding boulder-clay cliffs of East Yorkshire can never be replaced by marine deposition and while some parts of the coastline show evidence of 'permanent' erosion others show evidence of 'permanent' accretion by continual deposition. In some ways, therefore, the often substantial morphological changes which result from flood surges may appear to have a more lasting and significant erosional or depositional effect on the coastline than do rare stream floods on their floodplains. Ultimately, however, catastrophic events must be viewed as but one, and not necessarily the dominant, part of a continuum of events, both large and small, which constitute coastal processes.

In the following brief discussion an understanding of the 'normal' range of coastal geomorphological processes is assumed and we will concentrate on examples illustrating the role of storm surges in the two areas previously chosen for detailed discussion, the east coasts of Britain and the United States.

During the 1953 North Sea storm surge, the greatest damage to the British coast occurred south of the Humber. Throughout most of its length this is essentially a lowland coast where a predominantly sandy beach is backed by shingle ridges, sand dunes, saltmarshes or low clay cliffs. In terms of coastal erosion, the beach is the first natural line of defence but its effectiveness varies considerably depending on its width and height and on the offshore topography. Wide gently sloping beaches, rising to high levels on which the waves can expend their energy, afford the best natural protection. Surveys carried out before and after the 1953 storm surge showed that where such beaches occurred coastal erosion was minor or non-existent. Steeper, narrower and lower beaches are easily over-ridden by big waves breaking upon them and the resulting seaward scour of the sand further reduces their height as well as frequently exposing the underlying bedrock. Once this has been achieved, the backing dune belt or cliff is exposed to direct wave action and may be rapidly eroded.

In the case of sand dunes this is often of considerable geomorphological importance. Barnes and King (1953) concluded that the most geomorphologically stable coast was a broad belt of high, well-vegetated dunes, fronted by a wide high beach. While beach destruction during the surge may be rapidly rectified afterwards – Grove (1953) noted that within two months some parts of the east coast had already gained more by accretion than they had lost by erosion during the storm – the regrowth of dunes is much less certain and inevitably much slower. Dunes grow and are maintained by sand blown from the adjacent beach. On wide high beaches there is a sufficient supply of dry sand above low tide level to permit the development of high well-vegetated dunes, but in areas of severe wave erosion beach material is in short supply and normally wet so that either dune and vegetation growth are retarded or windblow causes a net loss of sand from the dunes (Barnes and King, 1953). Steers (1953) referred to the overrunning and complete destruction of belts of low sand dunes and to the erosion of up to 10 m from the seaward face of high dune belts. Grove (1953) described the situation at Palling in Norfolk where the sea advanced inland on a wide front by as much as 40 m, eroding two-thirds of the high dune belt and leaving only a razor-back ridge of sand (see figure 5.3c) which would probably have been entirely demolished if the surge had been more prolonged.

Beach erosion also exposes the backing cliffs to intensified wave activity. While highly resistant cliffs of hard rock appear to show no immediate response to the effects of a single storm surge, the soft clay cliffs typical of the English east coast can be drastically affected. Average cliff retreat here is of the order of a metre or so per year but, as a result of the 1953 storm surge, cliff retreat of 10 m was common and in some places as much as 30 m was observed. Cliff erosion initiated by a storm surge may continue for many weeks or months afterwards.

Thus wave attack may cut away the base of the cliff, causing instability and initiating slumps which give many east coast cliffs a scalloped form (Grove, 1953).

Surge-induced beach and dune removal normally results in a seaward movement of debris, some part of which eventually returns to the beach either in a diffuse manner or as a well-defined offshore bar which moves steadily landwards (see figure 5.3c). In some cases, however, and particularly where shingle ridges are backed by marshland or other low ground, sand and shingle may be swept over the crest to form lobes on the inland side, thereby permitting the ridges to advance inland *en masse*. For example, Steers (1953) noted that the main shingle beach at Blakeney had been pushed inland throughout its length and that the shingle bank at Aldeburgh was similarly displaced by approximately 45 m. Other inland deposition occurs when major breaching of dune belts or sea walls takes place. One of the most spectacular examples during the 1953 surge occurred in the form of a 300 m breach between Sutton and Sandilands in Lincolnshire behind which an extensive sand delta more than one metre thick was formed.

In several respects, not least the extensive sandy beaches backed by dunes, conditions along the eastern coast of the United States are not dissimilar to those on the east coast of England, although their scale is considerably larger and there is a much more extensive development of offshore bars and islands backed by lagoons. The greatly intensified wave energy accompanying major storm surges is largely expended on these bars and islands resulting in frequent if minor changes in coastal configuration as islands merge or new inlets are created. In the absence of offshore bars and islands the mainland beaches and dunes receive the full brunt of wave attack and may be destroyed on a major scale.

In summary, then, storm surges are geomorphologically most immediately effective on lowland coasts where large-scale beach and dune destruction occurs, and least effective on massive vertical cliffs of hard rock. In the post-surge period, however, much or all of the beach damage and some of the dune damage is repaired while weakened and undercut cliffs, particularly those composed of unresistant rocks, continue to retreat until quasi-equilibrium conditions are again established. To a large extent this confirms the earlier stated view that surges are responsible for a high magnitude but low frequency erosional increment which forms part of the continuum of events involved in coastal processes.

6 Flood Prediction

There are many situations in which an estimate of future flood conditions is required and many different categories of individual investigator, industry, government agency or other group requiring such information. Essentially, however, this information is needed for either design or forecasting purposes. In the design situation engineers (involved in the design of, for example, dams, spillways, river channel improvements, storm sewers, bridges, and culverts), planners, farmers, etc., need information on flood magnitude and frequency. In other words, what is the maximum flood which is likely to occur at a given place and what is the probability that a flood of a certain magnitude will be exceeded at a particular place once in any given number of years? In the forecasting situation local government agencies, industrialists, farmers and home-owners require more immediate information on flood magnitude and timing so that appropriate evasive action may be taken. It is necessary to forecast that a flood of given volume, depth and duration will occur within a specified time.

This difference between flood prediction (for design purposes) and flood forecasting (for warning purposes) has been emphasised frequently in the literature and developed in terms of the necessity to understand the relevant physical processes. In practice, however, design predictions often involve a consideration of hydrograph shape (the timing) and the change in hydrograph shape as a flood-wave moves downstream (flood routing). Flood forecasting may involve considerations of probability – the probability of comparatively low-magnitude floods recurring several times a year. Again, although a detailed understanding of the runoff processes involved in the catchment and stream channels is necessary for the development of a general flood forecasting method and is less necessary for long-term prediction purposes, there has been a strong development of interest in process-based flood prediction procedures as a complement to the non-process-based statistical approach. A further point of contrast is that whereas flood predictions may be required for catchments having no streamflow data and/or no meteorological data, flood forecasting is almost invariably based on current hydrometeorological data, often of an extremely detailed nature. In the present work the distinction between flood prediction and forecasting, albeit blurred at times, is preserved in the separate but related discussions in this and the next chapter.

THE DESIGN FLOOD

In terms of prediction for design purposes, a fundamental question concerns the design flood, that is the maximum flood against which protection is being designed, whether in relation to the spillway capacity of a dam, the waterways through a bridge or embankment, the height of a floodwall or the diameter of a sewer. Much will depend on the design life of the structure, the degree of risk which is considered acceptable and whether or not human life is likely to be lost in the event of the structure failing. Van der Made (1969) stressed that the starting point in determining the design flood must be the design life of the structure. In the simple case of a small coffer dam this might be only one year. Then if Q_{10} is the flood magnitude which is on average exceeded once in a period of 10 years the chance of its being exceeded in any one year is 0.1 (or expressed differently, 10 per cent). If this level of risk is acceptable then the design discharge will be Q_{10}. Obviously, for more permanent structures a much longer design life will be appropriate, say 50 or 100 years or more. Van der Made (1969) noted, for example, that for river flood dikes in the Netherlands a 100-year design life and a 3 per cent risk were considered acceptable and that in this case the design flood would have a return period of 3000 years. The important point to stress is that for the normal range of acceptable risk the design flood will invariably have a return period much greater than the design life of the structure involved (see figure 6.1).

This return period may be greatly increased if there is a risk that human life may be lost. A commonly held view where human life is at risk is that structures should be so designed that '. . . the maximum possible flood can be discharged without risk of . . . failure . . .' (Wolf, 1966). Some of the problems of defining this maximum are discussed later in this chapter but the clear implications are that no design should deliberately expose human life to risk and that, as Wisler and Brater (1959) so categorically stated, 'It is impossible to place a monetary value upon human life'. Attitudes are changing, however, and, as in traffic engineering where monetary values *are* attached to human life for design purposes, so may this become standard practice in hydraulic engineering. This was the view expressed in a recent re-evaluation of spillway design by an ASCE Task Committee (ASCE, 1972) and reiterated by Benson (1973b).

Other considerations which normally play a part in design-flood calculations are damage values, including both direct damage to property and indirect damage resulting, for example, from the inconvenience caused by severed rail or road links, and such factors as the inflation of property values in areas 'protected' from flooding. These and other largely economic considerations are incorporated into a benefit–cost assessment of the design flood which is often highly arbitrary and in which 'judgement' and 'experience' inevitably tend to play a dominant part. Over the years a number of more or less arbitrary specifications of design-flood magnitude, or more usually frequency, either for specific structures or for more general application have emerged. Thus Schnackenberg (1949) recommended minimum design-flood return periods for various categories of dam, ranging from 1000 years in the case of major earth dams where life is at risk to 20 years for minor dams. In the United States a hierarchy of design floods has been adopted. The *Intermediate Regional Flood* is defined as a major flood having a minimum average recurrence rate of 100 years at a particular location. The *Standard Project Flood* represents the flood which would be rarely exceeded

Floods

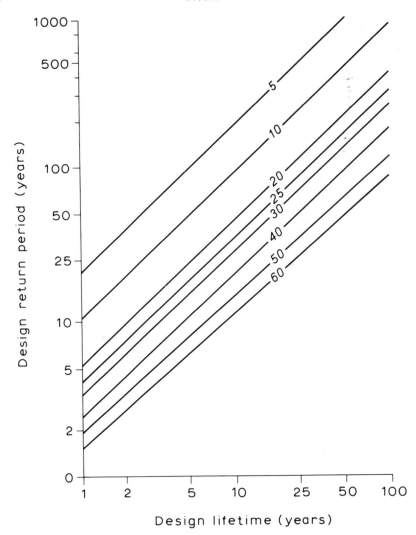

Figure 6.1.   Relationship between design flood and return period, design lifetime of the structure and level of risk (diagonal lines equal percentage probability of failure during the design lifetime)
Source: Hershfield and Kohler (1960) pp. 1737–46.

and although assigned no specified frequency, it is a useful design standard providing a high degree of protection. It is defined as a flood that can be expected from the most severe combination of meteorological and hydrological conditions, excluding extremely rare ones, characteristic of the geographical area in which the drainage basin is located. It is thus substantially smaller than the

Maximum Probable Flood which would result from the worst combination of meteorological and hydrological conditions. The Maximum Probable Flood (see p. 77) thus represents an extreme situation which is highly unlikely to occur and against which it is seldom economically feasible to provide complete protection.

Because of the large return periods explicit or implicit in these and many other design floods, it is frequently extremely difficult to substantiate the validity of the design flood adopted. If, for example, a structure designed against a 100-year flood fails because it encounters a 500-year flood, it does not follow that the original design was in error. On the other hand, as Linsley (1967) observed, if a structure does not fail after a long period of time, it does not ensure that the design was correct – the design flood may have been far too large and the resulting structure, therefore, far too substantial. Occasional failure of even properly designed major structures is inevitable if one accepts the reasoning advanced by Alexander (1969) on a cumulative probability thesis based on the fact that there are approximately 10 000 major dams in the world and the assumption (optimistic) that these were all designed against the 1000-year flood.

Various methods are available for estimating design floods and some of these will be discussed in the remainder of this chapter. Broadly speaking these methods fall into two main categories: those which are deterministically based, which treat floods as the product of specified precipitation falling upon a specified catchment area, and those which are probabilistically based, which treat floods as almost purely random events susceptible to statistical analysis. Subsequent discussion will show that neither approach is entirely satisfactory. Many authorities recommend using both approaches and comparing the results and indeed many standard flood prediction procedures incorporate elements from each method. Most of the available methods have been developed in the context of rainfall floods and comparatively little work has been done on snowmelt or coastal flooding. This imbalance is reflected in the discussions which follow although an attempt is made to indicate the application, where appropriate, of both deterministic and probabilistic approaches to these other types of flooding.

DETERMINISTIC APPROACH

The basis of the deterministic approach is that floods are physical phenomena which result from an input of precipitation into a drainage basin, the flood magnitude varying with the nature of both the precipitation and the drainage basin. There have been many attempts to relate precipitation and catchment variables in order to estimate maximum flood discharge.

Empirical methods

Some authors (for example Linsley, 1967) have referred to the age of empiricism as if this were a thing of the past – in fact, in terms of flood prediction, the age of empiricism is still with us. Chow (1957) has reported 107 empirical formulae still in use, although there are other similar techniques involving envelope curves, tables and simple rules of thumb. Largely because of an inevitably inadequate data base, early attempts to relate maximum flood discharge to catchment and precipitation characteristics were simple approximations, but the continuing, more intense collection of hydrometeorological data has meant that more sophisticated relationships can now be formulated, many of which incorporate an estimate of the occurrence frequency of the calculated flood discharges.

(A) The simplest empirical formulae for flood discharge use the single parameter of drainage area and take one of the following forms (Gray and Wigham, 1970)

$$Q_m = CA^n \qquad (61.)$$

$$Q_m = CA^{mA-n} \qquad (6.2)$$

$$Q_m = \frac{CA}{(a + bA)} m + dA \qquad (6.3)$$

where Q_m is the maximum flood discharge, A is the catchment area, n and m are exponents and C, a, b, d are coefficients which must be evaluated for an area depending upon its geographical and climatological characteristics. There are many formulae of this type (more than thirty were tabulated by Gray and Wigham, 1970) and only a few selected examples will be used for illustrative purposes here. For the United Kingdom, Bransby Williams proposed

$$Q_m = 2700A^{0.75} \qquad (6.4)$$

for catchments smaller than 10 square miles (26 km²) and

$$Q_m = 4600A^{0.52} \qquad (6.5)$$

for catchments greater than 10 square miles. In both cases discharges are in cusecs and area in square miles. One of the earliest of such formulae in the United States was proposed by the railway engineer Major E. T. D. Myers and first published in 1879. As subsequently modified by Jarvis (1926) it takes the form

$$Q_m = 10\,000pA^{0.5} \qquad (6.6)$$

where Q_m is the maximum flood discharge in cusecs, A is the catchment area in square miles, and p is a coefficient expressing the relationship of the estimated flood peak for a particular river to an assumed maximum possible of 10 000 for all rivers (Wolf, 1966). A formula which is still widely used in the United States, particularly in the west, was devised by Talbot for determining the waterway area of culverts

$$w = CA^{0.75} \qquad (6.7)$$

where w is the required waterway in square feet, A is the catchment area in acres and C is a coefficient depending on the physical characteristics of the catchment.

In some cases formulae were not specifically stated but instead envelope curves based on previous flood experience were used to estimate future flood magnitudes for different sizes of catchment. Such curves were embodied in the 1933 Interim Report of the Institution of Civil Engineers' Committee on Floods which has since formed the basis of flood prediction procedures in the United

Kingdom, now (hopefully) to be superseded by the recommendations in the 1975 NERC Flood Studies Report (NERC, 1975). The use of envelope curves for a wide range of conditions was discussed in some detail by Francou and Rodier (1969).

Often the type of simple empirical formula discussed so far contains no specification of the expected frequency of the calculated flood, although sometimes a subjective estimate is incorporated, as in the Kuichling formula which is differently stated for 'frequent' and 'rare' floods. In some cases, however, an explicit frequency term is included to yield formulae of the general type

$$Q_t = CA^nT \tag{6.8}$$

where Q_t is the flood discharge having a return period of T years. One of the best known formulae of this type is that of Fuller (1914)

$$Q_t = CA^{0.8}(1 + 0.8 \log t) \tag{6.9}$$

where Q_t is the maximum 24-hour flood discharge in cusecs having a return period t, C is a coefficient and A is the catchment area in square miles.

(B) Other, more elaborate, empirical formulae relying on a broader or more detailed data base have incorporated characteristics in addition to area, such as precipitation characteristics, hydrograph shape, and mean catchment slope, and have often also included an explicit frequency term. One of the oldest and certainly one of the most widely used formula in this category is the so-called *rational formula* which, although having long ago fallen into disrepute both in Europe and North America among theoretical hydrologists, maintains much of its popularity among practising engineers, particularly in terms of flood discharges into urban storm sewers and from small, relatively homogeneous rural catchments. The origins of this method are somewhat obscure. Chow (1964) pointed out that it was first mentioned in American literature by Kuichling (1889), although some authors believe that the principles may be ascribed to the earlier work of Mulvaney (1851), while in England the rational formula has often been referred to as the Lloyd-Davis method (Lloyd-Davis, 1906). The method assumes that the maximum flood discharge from a catchment will occur when the entire area is contributing to runoff and may be expressed in the form

$$Q_m = CIA \tag{6.10}$$

where Q_m is the maximum flood discharge, C is a runoff coefficient indicating the percentage of rainfall which appears as quickflow, I is the mean rainfall intensity during the period of concentration, T_c, that is, the time required for the most distant part of the catchment to contribute to outflow from the catchment, and A is the area of the catchment.

The U.S.D.A. Soil Conservation Service (U.S.D.A., 1957) proposed a formula incorporating area, rainfall characteristics and a time parameter to describe a simple, triangular flood hydrograph

$$Q_m = \frac{CAR_e}{T_p} \tag{6.11}$$

where Q_m is the maximum flood discharge in cusecs, C is a coefficient, generally 484, A is the catchment area in square miles, R_e is rainfall excess in inches, and

T_p is the time to peak or the time of rise of the hydrograph which can be estimated empirically from catchment characteristics.

There are a number of formulae in category (B) which take the same general form by including a catchment area factor, various morphometric characteristics and usually some index of rainfall intensity and frequency. Among the better known are the U.S.D.C. Bureau of Public Roads method devised by Potter (1961) and in the United Kingdom the formula presented by Rodda (1969), which will serve as an illustration. Rodda combined various catchment and precipitation characteristics in regression analyses and found that the most satisfactory prediction of the mean annual flood was obtained from

$$Q = 1.08A^{0.77}R^{2.92}D^{0.81} \tag{6.12}$$

where Q is the mean annual flood, A is catchment area in square miles, R is the mean annual daily maximum rainfall and D is drainage density in miles per square mile. Regression analysis was repeated to determine the T-year flood using daily maximum rainfalls for the appropriate recurrence intervals and assuming equality between rainfall and discharge recurrence intervals (this assumption is discussed in more detail later on pp. 91–92 to give

$$Q_{10} = 1.22A^{0.69}R^{1.63}D^{1.06} \tag{6.13}$$

$$Q_{50} = 1.24A^{0.51}R^{2.02}D^{0.94} \tag{6.14}$$

One of the most detailed empirical approaches to flood prediction was presented by Rostomov (1969) in a comprehensive paper which included full details of each component term, with tables and nomograms where appropriate, together with a fully-worked example. In summary form his equation is

$$Q_m = 16.67CBSA^R_{R_d} \tag{6.15}$$

where Q_m is the maximum flood discharge, C is a runoff coefficient, B is a rainfall distribution coefficient, S is a catchment shape coefficient, A is catchment area, R is rainfall amount and R_d is rainfall duration.

Most empirical formulae suffer from a number of basic defects. Thus little direct account is taken of the hydrometeorological processes involved in the production of flood peaks. The formulae adopt an essentially 'black-box' type of approach and may even incorporate unrealistic general assumptions about processes as, for example, in the rational formula where the assumed simple relationship between rainfall intensity and runoff could, in fact, only apply to very small areas. Accordingly, the resulting flood predictions are only approximations, sometimes of the grossest sort, and wide discrepancies result from applying different empirical methods. For example, Francis (1973) used 37 such methods (20 of type (A) using only catchment area, and 17 of the more elaborate type (B)) to predict the maximum flood from an imaginary circular catchment of 129 km² in Britain. The simple formulae gave a mean result of 410 ± 240 cumecs, while the complicated formulae gave 387 ± 258 cumecs. Furthermore, since these methods are based on data for specific areas, they are rarely applicable generally without considerable manipulation of the various coefficients. Those few which seem to have more general applicability (for example the rational formula) have inevitably attracted widespread popularity. Again, their close reliance on limited experience means that some of the techniques are not even internally consistent over a wide range of flood magnitudes.

Despite such obvious weaknesses, however, empirical methods are still widely used, receiving strong support at the Leningrad Symposium on Floods and their Computation in 1967 (IASH/UNESCO/WMO, 1969). Sokolov (1969*b*), for example, contended that they should yield results as reliable as other methods provided that '. . . their parameters are sufficiently well grounded and the influence of climatic and morphological factors are taken into account'. Heras (1969) advocated their use in regions of homogeneous meteorological conditions where the relationship between catchment area and maximum discharge may be more reliable. The use of such methods in small, homogeneous catchments, particularly those having a large percentage of paved or impervious surface, is probably more acceptable and is certainly supported by the widespread use of the rational formula in such conditions. In many developing countries, of course, the sparsity of hydrological data reproduces the conditions which encouraged the early development of empirical methods elsewhere and makes their use virtually inevitable, if temporary.

Process based methods

Although a general weakness of empirical methods is their 'black-box' approach and their failure to incorporate a proper understanding of flood producing processes, the more sophisticated empirical formulae utilise so much detailed information that, in fact, processes are reasonably well modelled, for example the Rostomov formula. Much of the impetus for more realistic process based attempts to predict flood peaks was undoubtedly given by the work of Sherman (1932) on the unit hydrograph and Horton (1933) on the role of infiltration in the runoff process. Full discussion of both these contributions are found in standard hydrological texts (for example Ward, 1975) and although the fundamental thesis of each has since been superseded their contribution to subsequent flood prediction methods was substantial. In the case of the unit hydrograph some of the most valuable work concerned the development of the instantaneous unit hydrograph and synthetic hydrographs, particularly in terms of flood predictions from ungauged catchments (see also p. 97). Horton's infiltration theory has subsequently manifested itself in flood prediction methods both directly, in the form of infiltration indices, and indirectly in the form of indices of antecedent precipitation, soil moisture and the proportion of the catchment under different land-use types – all of which are in accord with more recent ideas on runoff formation involving the generation of quickflow from source areas of variable size and location within the catchment (see Ward, 1975, for detailed discussion).

The Flood Study Project of the Institute of Hydrology (1974) led to the development of an excellent process based empirical method of determining flood discharges from specified rainfall and catchment conditions which can serve as a useful illustration. This method involves two main steps, in the first of which the proportion of precipitation appearing as quickflow is calculated from

$$P_q = 95.5S + 0.12U + 0.22(C - 125) + 0.1(P - 10) \qquad (6.16)$$

where P_q is the percentage of rainfall appearing as quickflow, S is a soil index related to the winter rate of rain acceptance, U is the percentage of urban development, C is a catchment wetness index calculated from soil moisture deficit and antecedent precipitation, and P is storm rainfall. The second step involves distributing this volume of quickflow according to the ordinates of the synthetic unit hydrograph to determine the flood peak. In common with many other flood prediction methods a simple triangular flood hydrograph is assumed. It was found that the peak discharge was inversely proportional to the time to peak

$$Q_m = \frac{220}{T_p} \qquad (6.17)$$

where Q_m is the peak discharge in cumecs/100 km² and T_p is the time to peak in hours and can be calculated from catchment characteristics. The time base of the hydrograph (T_b) is controlled by the assumptions of a triangle and unit volume

$$T_b = 2.525 \, T_p \qquad (6.18)$$

By making assumptions, discussed later in the chapter, about the relationships between the return periods of rainfall and discharge, the Institute of Hydrology method (fully explained in the *Flood Studies Report,* (NERC, 1975)) permits the prediction of Q_t for a selected return period. However, there has long been an interest in the prediction of the maximum flood possible in a given catchment, particularly in relationship to the design of major structures where large-scale risk to life and property is involved.

Probable Maximum Precipitation

Logic dictates that there must be an upper limit to the amount and the rate of precipitation in a specified time at any one location. As Wilson (1968) pointed out 'the speed of light must place an upper limit on the rate at which a solid mass of water can fall to Earth', however, 'the maximum conceivable intensity is far less than this . . .' if only because of the limiting effect of air resistance on raindrop size and rate of fall. One fundamental problem is that to estimate the maximum conceivable intensity a large number of assumptions must be made. This is emphasised by Horton's often quoted half-truth that 'a small stream cannot produce a major Mississippi River flood, for much the same reason that an ordinary barnyard fowl cannot lay an egg a yard in diameter; it would transcend nature's capabilities under the circumstances'. The question is begged by limiting the size of the fowl to 'ordinary' – and the problem of estimating the maximum possible flood is to determine the effects not of ordinary but of extraordinary meteorological events. The principal upper limits on precipitation which must be quantified are those of the humidity concentration in the air, the rate at which the humid air can move into an area and the proportion of the inflowing water vapour which can be precipitated.

It cannot be overemphasised that in our present state of knowledge estimates of the maximum possible precipitation for a given catchment area are inevitably approximations involving a number of untestable assumptions. This weakness is implicit in the change in terminology from the initial usage of the term 'maximum possible precipitation' to the present *probable maximum precipitation*

(PMP) which, although having the same meaning, is more 'descriptive and realistic' (U.S.W.B., 1960). Further assumptions must be made to convert the estimated PMP to the *probable maximum flood* (PMF), in other words, that flood which will result from the PMP falling upon a catchment area when it is in its least receptive (maximum quickflow-producing) condition. Myers (1969) incorporated the PMF concept into his definition of PMP which was '. . . that magnitude of rainfall over a particular basin which will yield the flood flow of which there is virtually no risk of being exceeded'. Some modification of this definition would be needed for those climatic conditions in which a high rate of snowmelt was an additional factor in producing the PMF.

The PMP concept has attained greatest acceptance in the United States, where it originated in the mid-1930s (Miller, 1973), and numerous U.S. Weather Bureau publications have followed the initial PMP publication in 1941 (U.S.W.B., 1941).

The process of deriving a PMP estimate involves three main steps: first, the identification of the maximum recorded rainfalls for the specific catchment and for the other comparable areas; second, the transposition of those storms, where this is appropriate, to the catchment under consideration; and third, the upward adjustment of the transposed rainfall values (maximisation) on the basis of meteorological conditions over the catchment area. Transposition is a device to broaden an inevitably narrow data base but must be used with care. Ideally it should be restricted to relatively homogeneous regions, having no significant topographic barriers, in which major storms of the same type have an equal chance of occurring – a tropical cyclone should not be transposed to polar latitudes, but a major thunderstorm could probably be safely transposed anywhere within the Great Plains area of North America. Analysis of actual major storms permits the derivation, for specified areas, of the maximum average depth of rainfall and its duration (depth–area–duration curve) which can then be maximised on the basis of our understanding of the precipitation process. Precipitation results essentially from the lifting of moist air, and the rate of precipitation depends on the rate of lift and the amount of moisture present. Although the lifting processes are complex and not easily measured, atmospheric moisture content (precipitable water) is highly correlated with surface dewpoint, which can be measured. Maximisation therefore, is normally achieved by an adjustment for moisture content or precipitable water using the ratio of the maximum moisture content observed over the problem catchment and the moisture content actually observed in each storm. These procedures are well described by Miller (1973) and Wiesner (1970).

The transposition and maximisation of actual storms is reasonable for extensive areas of low relief, where storm types can often be transposed over large distances and large amounts of representative data are available. The method is less suited to mountainous areas where data will be more sparse and where orographic effects tend to dominate the precipitation distribution. In these circumstances methods have been devised (U.S.W.B., 1961) to separate the storm (for example, frontal) component of precipitation from the orographic component by using precipitation moisture ratios so that non-orographic storms are transposed to mountainous areas and then maximised. Normally, however, the PMP for mountainous areas is estimated using storm models to simulate the movement of moisture into the catchment and its release as precipitation. Storm models are discussed in detail by Miller (1973) and Wiesner (1970). The main types are the upglide model, which describes forced ascent over a topographic barrier or frontal surface, and the convergence model, which describes the dominantly convective mechanisms in thunderstorms and tropical cyclones.

Hershfield (1961; 1965) suggested a statistical method of estimating the PMP as an alternative to the more conventional techniques which have already been discussed. Hershfield used the generalised frequency formula proposed by Chow (1951)

$$X_{max} = \bar{X} + K\sigma \tag{6.19}$$

where $\bar{X}$ is the mean of the observed values of X, K is a frequency factor or reduced variate which depends on the statistical distribution used, the number of years of record and the return period, and σ is the standard deviation. Since it is reasonable to expect that for the PMP there is a value of K which will not be exceeded the PMP may be expressed as

$$PMP = \bar{P} + K\sigma \tag{6.20}$$

where $\bar{P}$ is the mean precipitation for a specified duration. Analysis of daily rainfalls from 2645 stations in the United States led Hershfield to the conclusion that $K = 15$. In other words, the PMP is the mean plus 15 standard deviations for a given duration of rainfall. Myers (1969) suggested that Hershfield's method is a convenient way of getting a quick approximate answer in a situation where the order of magnitude of the PMP is unknown but that it fails to yield a precise answer (whatever that may mean in the context of PMP estimates!) because no one value of K is universally transposable.

Generalised isohyetal maps of PMP are now produced by the U.S. Weather Bureau for the United States (see figure 6.2). These not only provide a useful source of readily available data, particularly useful in the initial stages of project planning, but also ensure some consistency of PMP estimates from one project to another and at the same time provide a basis for comparing individual project estimates of PMP.

Conversion of PMP values to values of the Probable Maximum Flood (PMF) is normally achieved by applying unit hydrograph procedures and by taking into consideration the physical characteristics of the catchment area in question. The assumptions which must be made and the problems faced are identical with those involved in the conversion of statistically derived maximum rainfalls to discharge values and will therefore be discussed in the next section of this chapter.

One of the greatest attractions and potential strengths of the PMP/PMF approach is that one is trying to estimate the worst possible flood on the basis of an understanding (albeit partial) of rainfall and flood producing processes both in the atmosphere and in the catchment itself. Certainly the technique has proved a useful benchmark procedure by defining a practical upper limit to the flood potential of a catchment. This information is of value to the theoretical hydrologist and also serves as a starting point for the design engineer – a starting point

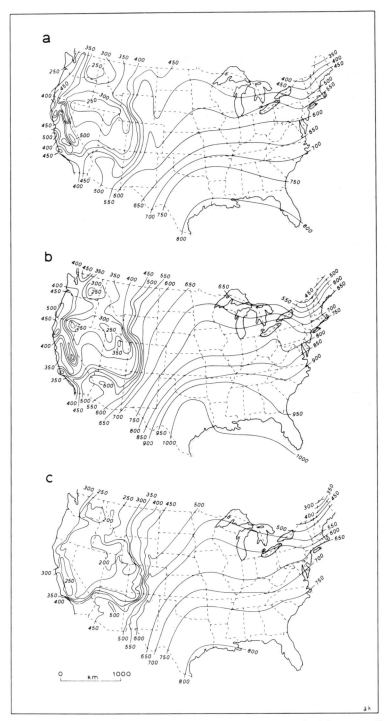

Figure 6.2 Probable maximum precipitation (PMP) for the United States: *a*, For 24 hours and 500 km²; *b*, For 24 hours and 25 km²; *c*, For 6 hours and 25 km²
Source: U.S. Weather Bureau.

from which he must normally step down to an economically viable proposal!

Despite its long history of development and application, however, there is still a large gap between the theory and practice of estimating PMP values and the technique has been strongly criticised, especially by stochastic hydrologists. As Benson (1973a) pointed out, despite the claims of many PMP proponents that the maximum rainfall theoretically possible is being established, in fact the determined values can only be based on experience and that experience is minimal. Furthermore, many of the assumptions and simplifications inevitably made in the transposition, maximisation and modelling procedures contain inherent weaknesses which diminish the value of the final estimate. There is no space to detail these here, but Biswas (1971), for example, drew attention to the problems of maximising dewpoint and to the high degree of precision required if the results are to have practical value. Again, the PMF derived from the PMP is itself an estimate and subject, like any other estimate, to inaccuracies and limitations of data and methods.

In short, it must be recognised that PMP values are merely estimates, which may be grossly inaccurate. On the one hand there are many areas for which the PMP estimates exceed present comparatively conservative design values by a considerable margin, and on the other hand there are areas in which the PMP estimate has already been equalled or exceeded. Newton (1973) called for a recognition that the PMP and PMF are not impossible but rather extremely rare occurrences. The problem then is to determine how rare and to define the likelihood of their recurrence. In the final analysis, as Benson (1973b) observed, this can only be done in terms of economics and acceptable risk. It is significant that the ASCE, which for so long opposed the use of statistical methods to predict major floods, recently published through its Task Committee (ASCE, 1972) the suggestion that further research is required to better define the probability of the PMP and the PMF, and that in the meantime an arbitrary return period of 10 000 years should be assigned to the PMF for the purpose of making economic estimates of spillway design. This apparent convergence of viewpoint between proponents of deterministic and probabilistic methods of flood prediction leads us conveniently to the next section.

PROBABILISTIC APPROACH

The probabilistic approach regards floods as random streamflow events whose distribution can be identified and whose probability of occurrence during a given period of time can be calculated using standard statistical techniques. Clearly, the longer the period under consideration the larger is the maximum flood experienced likely to be and the more frequent is a flood of modest magnitude liable to occur. The average time elapse between two events which equal or exceed a particular level is the *return period*, T_r, or recurrence interval. Thus the N-year flood, a flood which is expected to be equalled or exceeded on average every N years, has a return period of N years. Naturally, the 100-year flood could occur within fifty years, five years or even one year, but the probability of its occurring during 100 years is obviously much greater than during a five-year period, and greater still during one thousand years of record. The relationship between probability (expressed as a percentage), return period and the length of the period under consideration is shown in table 6.1. The statistical relationships between the magnitude of a flood and the frequency with which it is likely to occur can be investigated in two ways. First, given a return period, which for most design purposes will be of several hundreds or several thousands of years, the instantaneous flood peak which will be equalled or exceeded once on average during that time period can be estimated. Secondly, given a particular flood magnitude the average frequency with which it will be equalled or exceeded (that is, the return period) can be estimated.

Chow (1956) noted that graphical techniques of probability analysis involving

TABLE 6.1

PERCENTAGE PROBABILITY OF THE *N*-YEAR FLOOD
OCCURRING IN A PARTICULAR PERIOD

Number of years in period	N = Average return period, T_r, in years							
	5	10	20	50	100	200	500	1000
1	20	10	5	2	1	0.5	0.2	0.1
2	36	19	10	4	2	1	0.4	0.2
5	67	41	23	10	4	2	1	0.5
10	89	65	40	18	10	5	2	1
30	99	95	79	45	26	14	6	3
60	—	98	95	70	31	26	11	6
100	—	99.9	99.4	87	65	39	18	9
300	—	—	—	99.8	95	78	45	26
600	—	—	—	—	99.8	95	70	45
1000	—	—	—	—	—	99.3	87	63

Where no figure is inserted the percentage probability >99.9.

the use of flow–duration curves were in use in the United States during the latter part of the nineteenth century, although the sparsity of adequate data hindered development for some decades. It was really during the 1920s and 30s that the probability approach became most popular in the United States, with standard methods based upon either the Gaussian or Galton (log-probability) laws. Later, Gumbel (1941) began to apply the Fisher–Tippett theory of extreme values to flood frequency studies. Gumbel's numerous publications in this field culminated in the appearance of the first book devoted entirely to the statistics of extremes (Gumbel, 1958). Subsequently, other workers have developed and refined the statistical analysis of flood data, succinctly reviewed by Zelenhasic (1970).

Despite the increasing sophistication of techniques, however, the probabilistic approach fell into decline in the United States after the 1930s. This was largely due to a number of tragic floods – not only disastrous to the people directly involved but also highly embarrassing to the hydrologists – which vividly demonstrated the continued inadequacy of streamflow records and the failure of hydrologists to recognise the extent of sampling error (Biswas, 1971). Elsewhere, the approach has remained popular and it is widely used in Europe and Asia. An indication of this was that most of the papers presented at the

Leningrad symposium on *Floods and their Computation* (IASH/UNESCO/ WMO, 1969) concerned with rainfall flood prediction dealt with flood frequency studies, which was the topic which aroused most controversy and discussion.

Despite the often vociferous claims of its protagonists, the probabilistic approach to flood prediction has no intrinsic advantage over the deterministic approach other than its greater convenience of application. Floods are obviously both deterministic *and* probabilistic in nature and to claim that one description is truer than the other is as pointless as claiming that beer is brown rather than wet. Indeed both probabilistic and deterministic approaches tend to fail for the same basic reasons; for example, existing flood data may represent a non-homogeneous sample, including melt and non-melt events, or climatic change may mean that conditions during the period of record are not continued into the prediction period or, as is commonly the case, the run of available data is too short to be reliable. Similarly, just as a lack of understanding of hydrological processes can diminish the effectiveness of the deterministic approach, so ignorance of appropriate statistical techniques will detract from probabilistic flood predictions. In the following paragraphs these basic weaknesses will be discussed in more detail beginning with a brief review of some statistical considerations.

Choice of data and frequency distributions

Most methods used in the probability analysis of flood flows, particularly those concerned with design floods for spillways and culverts, are based on the *annual flood series*, that is, the highest flood in each year of the data period. The main advantage of this data series is that virtually every event is independent since it is most unlikely that the highest flood in one year is affected by that of a previous year. In addition, in the pre-computer era the annual flood series had the merit of restricting the amount of data manipulation required. It is, however, often criticised on the grounds that since in some years more than one major flood peak may occur, the omitted values could conceivably exceed the highest flood recorded in other years. Foster (1949), on the other hand, argued that the annual series is selective and averages somewhat higher than an array consisting of all flood peaks. The *partial duration series* consists of all floods above a specified threshold. This series is particularly useful where the frequency with which a particular flood flow is exceeded rather than the magnitude of the largest flood in the year is important. Relationships between annual and partial duration series have been developed, for example by Langbein (1949). The difference in the return periods of the two series is greatest at low values, for example 14 per cent for a return period of 2 years, decreasing to 1 per cent for a return period of 10 years to very small differences for floods of lower frequency. The main disadvantages of the partial duration series are that the selected flood events may not be strictly independent and since the method includes all high floods and omits the low ones it gives even more distorted results than the annual series. For this reason Foster (1949) argued that for the most accurate results all flood data, that is the *complete duration series*, should be used. Wilson (1969) pointed out that although the complete series events are not independent they are most valuable in design problems where quantity rather than peak values are required.

For a series of flood events the return period, T_r, is normally computed from the Weibull formula

$$T_r = \frac{N+1}{m} \tag{6.21}$$

where N is the total number of items in the series, and m is the order or rank number. The crux of the probability approach then lies in the accuracy with which the listed flood values (Q) and the derived return periods (T_r) can be used to extrapolate the data and infer the return periods of floods rarer than those experienced during the period of record.

The probability approach involves the assumption that there is some underlying distribution that describes the flood population. Both graphical and mathematical methods are used to define this distribution from the available data sample. Different frequency distributions have been advocated by various workers and their merits and demerits vigorously argued, a major criterion of usefulness being that, in the graphical case, the plotted values of Q against T_r lie on or near a straight line. This can be achieved by transforming the data and/or by using graph paper with distorted coordinates, such as probability, log-probability, Gumbel paper, etc. In a mathematical analysis the preselected frequency distribution may be described by two or three statistics such as the mean, standard deviation and skew coefficient, which are computed from the data sample. Of course any set of data can be plotted as a straight line since it is always possible either to fit a polynomial of degree n to an array of $n+1$ data or to scale a graph paper to fit a given data array. As might be expected, virtually all the commonly advocated distributions work well in the case of interpolation, but relatively few have any general usefulness in the more common situation requiring extrapolation when, of course, the greatest care must be taken. The dangers of extrapolation have been stressed by numerous authors, the main problem being the attempt to estimate the tail of a probability distribution curve from a data sample which does not include values within this tail (Melentijevich, 1969). Wisler and Brater (1959) suggested that the five-year flood was the rarest that could be estimated with any real certainty from 50 years of data, although many hydrologists are prepared to extrapolate to perhaps four times the period of record (Wolf, 1966). It is not uncommon, however, to find extrapolation to thousands or even tens of thousands of years from a few decades of data. This procedure will yield valid results *if* the correct distribution has been selected, but unfortunately the streamflow records available to date are not sufficient to test the validity of a distribution and the resulting flood predictions, therefore, must be viewed with extreme caution.

Frequency distributions are often badly selected, with little attempt made to justify a particular distribution on physical grounds. Moreover, individual workers and different flood-investigating agencies, even within the same country, have adopted their preferred techniques, each yielding a different predicted return period. Although the differences in predicted T_r are usually small within the range of observed data (in graphical analysis this depends on the plotting formula used) they may be substantial for rare floods which lie well outside the observed data range. As a result, in recent years there have been a number of detailed assessments of commonly used frequency distributions. One of the best known of these, by Benson (1968), reviewed six distributions, the two-parameter gamma, Gumbel, log-Gumbel, log-normal, log-Pearson Type III and Hazen. Comparison of these distributions, applied to selected American runoff data, led to the conclusion that all work equally well and that statistically there is nothing to choose between them, although on administrative grounds the log-Pearson Type III was selected pending further study and research. A subsequent similar study by the Institute of Hydrology (1974) concluded that goodness of fit indices alone could indicate only a group of best fitting distributions – general extreme value, log-Pearson Type III, Pearson Type III – but could not point clearly to a single one. Figure 6.3 shows flood data for three Pennsylvania streams plotted using the Gumbel, log-Gumbel and log-Pearson Type III distributions. In log-Pearson Type III analysis the flood data are transformed to logs and the first, second and third moments of these logs are used for determining the shape of the distribution. For short data runs, the most common, there is some uncertainty about the calculated skewness coefficient which controls the shape of the distribution because as few as one or two values can alter the skewness coefficient enough to change the plotted distribution shape from convex to concave or vice versa (Kerr *et al.*, 1970). To some extent this deficiency can be overcome by using generalised skew coefficients of the type presented by Hardison (1974) for the United States (see figure 6.4). Jennings and Benson (1969) described a method of fitting the log-Pearson Type III distribution to a set of data containing zero values, which occurs frequently in arid and semi-arid areas, particularly on small streams.

A new theoretical approach to the problem of flood frequency analysis has been presented by Todorovic and his colleagues (Todorovic and Rousselle, 1971; Todorovic and Zelenhasic, 1970; Zelenhasic, 1970). The Todorovic approach is based on recent developments in the theory of extreme values and is an attempt to develop a more general stochastic model to describe and predict flood behaviour based on the partial duration series and the assumption that in a given period the number of floods above a specified level follows the Poisson distribution.

In spite of Gumbel's (1967) support of the use of extreme value distribution in flood frequency analysis – '. . . the rivers know the theory . . . It remains to convince the engineers . . .' – it must be emphasised that there is no natural reason why flood series should follow a particular mathematical law and every indication that they consistently fail to do so. Whichever distribution is used, observed flood peaks often lie either in a general S-shape, with systematic deviations from the selected line, or in a J-shape with the biggest floods high above the line. Ultimately, therefore, the probability approach to design flood magnitude, like the deterministic approach, results in a value judgement based on hydrological and socio-economic circumstances. Quite apart from intrinsic weaknesses in the probabilistic and deterministic approaches, which have already been discussed, there are other factors which may detract from the reliability of such value judgements and which, although relevant to both approaches, will be discussed largely in the context of the probabilistic approach.

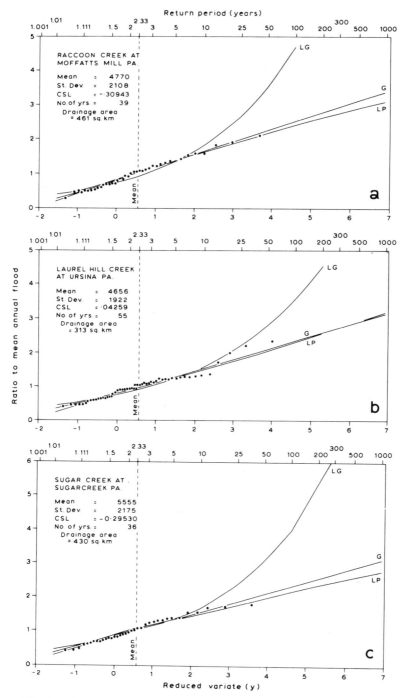

Figure 6.3 Gumbel, log-Gumbel and log-Pearson Type III plots of flood data for three Pennsylvania streams
Source: Reich (1969).

Adverse factors

One adverse factor concerns the nature of the population from which the flood data sample is drawn and the representativeness of that sample. The assump-

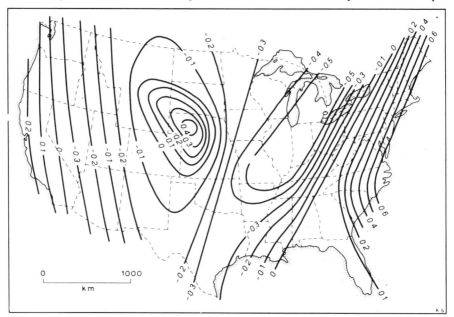

Figure 6.4   General logarithmic skew coefficients of annual flood discharge
Source: Hardison (1974) pp. 745–52.

tion, for example, that various types of rainfall flood, snowmelt floods, rain-on-frozen-ground floods or even floods of widely different magnitudes are all samples of a single population is open to question. A more meaningful approach might be to define the major components of the flood hydrographs, analyse these separately and then combine the results, although the data requirement would be formidable. In any case, as Benson (1969) pointed out, it is only rarely that the storm events responsible for floods can be separated into distinct, independent and truly different populations. If one accepts a mixed distribution as inevitable there is the further need to verify that the data sample includes those phenomena which could be responsible for the rare events. Thus it may well be desirable to take the effects of hurricanes into account in areas marginally affected by hurricanes, even though the available data include no resultant floods.

A second factor relates to a basic assumption of the probabilistic approach – that the probability function of past floods is applicable to future floods. This would clearly not be a reasonable assumption if climate, particularly precipitation, and related catchment characteristics varied in a cyclical or deterministic way. Whether they do or not is a matter of some debate. Still, it seems increasingly clear that although in the long term (for instance the post-glacial period) the broad patterns of climatic change are largely deterministic, in the short term (the duration of most hydrometeorological data) climatic change, although a reality, is largely a stochastic process involving persistence or sequences of similar conditions, such as sequences of wet years or dry years. Even so, if the duration of records is short compared with the periods of persistence, there may be significant changes of statistical parameters from the data collection period to the prediction period. For example, Francis (1973) subdivided ninety years of streamflow data from the River Thames into three 30-year periods and showed that the Hurst coefficient, which indicates the tendency towards persistence, for each of the three periods was 0.51, 0.10 and 0.54. Again, Professor H. H. Lamb, one of the world's leading authorities on climatic change, has remarked that in Britain the first forty or fifty years of the present century, currently accepted as the climatic norm, were probably the most abnormal period for the past thousand years. Clearly flood predictions for south-east England based on any of Francis' three sub-periods, or on the first half of the present century, are unlikely to reflect subsequent reality.

A third factor which, because of its all-embracing nature, is perhaps the most crucial and to which frequent reference has been made in discussions of both the deterministic and probabilistic approaches, concerns the inadequacy of the data base. This is a function not only of the duration of the data period and the quality of the data but also the sampling error. Some of the various procedures which have been devised to remedy the inevitable deficiencies will now be briefly considered.

Extending the data base

The use of old flood marks has often been advocated as a means of extending the duration and range of flood data. These were normally inscribed on walls and buildings to record exceptional flood stages. A major deterrent to their use lies in the problem of converting the evidence of stage to a value of discharge, but the Institute of Hydrology (1973) found that by ranking such marks it was possible to greatly extend the effective record for estimating the return period of recent floods. An interesting modification of this method was described by Levashov (1966) who observed that on many Russian rivers the ice carried along by the high spring floods scored marks in the trunks of trees growing at the rivers' edge. From the observed patterns of scoring Levashov was able to trace six periods of particularly high floods which had occurred between 1786 and the present and to date them approximately by using the ring marks.

Regional analysis has been employed both to make the maximum use of short-period records and to provide a means of estimating flood frequencies in ungauged catchments. Despite the large number of stream gauging stations now in existence these represent only a small fraction of the sites from which flood data are needed for design purposes. In this way, data from within a homogeneous area, which need not be contiguous, are combined to increase the size of a data sample and thus improve the statistical quality of the derived frequency distribution, assuming that the flood frequency curve based on the combined experience of a group of stations has firmer support than one based on the data at a single station.

Floods

A homogeneity test was developed by Langbein (Langbein *et al.*, 1947) to define a homogeneous region based on a study of the 10-year flood, as estimated from the probability curve for each station. Various methods of regional analysis have been devised, the one in most common use was proposed by Dalrymple (1950; 1960) and adopted by the U.S. Geological Survey. Using this method two curves are developed: the first (figure 6.5a) relates the mean annual flood to the size of drainage area, and sometimes other relevant catchment characteristics; and the second (figure 6.5b) shows the relationship of peak discharge, expressed as a ratio to the mean annual flood, to return period. The mean annual flood can thus be determined for any location along a stream within a given region (from the first curve), and from the regional frequency curve the flood magnitude for a number of return periods can be abstracted and plotted to construct a flood frequency curve for any location.

Sometimes factors other than area are included, through the technique of multiple correlation, to improve the estimate of mean annual flood. A recent example was presented in the *Flood Studies Report* of the Institute of Hydrology (NERC, 1975) whereby the mean annual flood for any site within the British Isles can be estimated from   (6.22)

$$\bar{Q} = C.\ AREA^{0.94} STMFRQ^{0.27} S1085^{0.16} SOIL^{1.23} RSMD^{1.03} (1 + LAKE)^{-0.85}$$

where C is a coefficient which varies from region to region, $AREA$ is catchment area in km², $STMFRQ$ is the number of stream junctions per km², $S1085$ is the slope from 10 to 85 per cent of the main stream length in m/km, $SOIL$ is an index based on the winter rain acceptance rate of the catchment, $RSMD$ is the net daily rainfall having a return period of five years in mm, and $LAKE$ is the proportion of the catchment draining through lakes. All the catchment characteristics incorporated in the equation can either be read directly from topographic maps or obtained from standard tables. Regional frequency curves for each of the eleven regions of the British Isles (figure 6.5c) are then used to produce design floods for any return period.

As a basis for prediction, dissatisfaction with the limitations of the historical flood record, with or without the advantages of regional analysis, has led to a growing interest among hydrologists in the development of synthetic streamflow records. Ideally, these would be compiled using a complete theoretical predictive model of the catchment area in question. Unfortunately, at present such models are beyond the reach of hydrologists and are likely to continue so in the foreseeable future. Accordingly, models have been devised that provide stream-flow traces that are *possible*, rather than the actual streamflow for a given stream. Most of these models attempt to accommodate three main assumptions:

(1) the recorded historical sequence of streamflows is extremely unlikely to recur

(2) it is unlikely that the maximum possible flood for a given stream is included within the historical record

(3) streamflow exhibits persistence, sometimes referred to as the Hurst Phenomenon, whereby high flows tend to be followed by high flows, and low flows to be followed by low flows.

A number of types of model are available, until recently the two most important

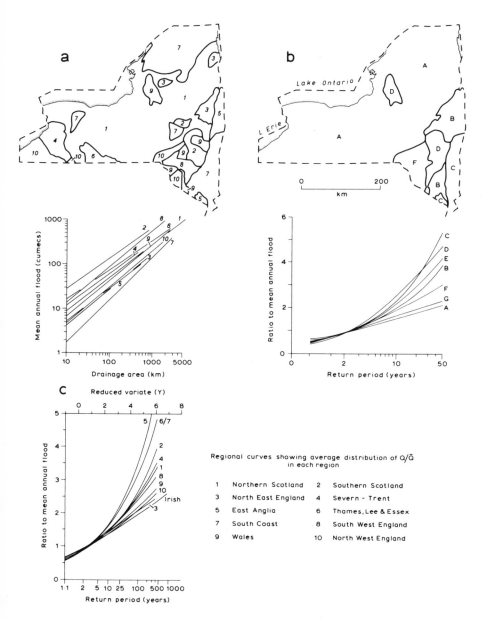

Figure 6.5   Regional analysis: *a*, Variations of mean annual flood with drainage area (graph) in hydrologic areas of New York State (map); *b*, Frequency of annual floods (graph) in regions A–G of New York State (map); *c*, Frequency of annual floods in eleven regions of the British Isles
Source: *a* and *b*, Robison (1961); *c*, NERC (1975).

being the traditional Markovian or autoregressive models and the self-similar or Fractional Gaussian Noise (F.G.N.) models. The Markovian models, in which the present value of the process depends on its own past and on a random component independent of the past, were developed to an advanced state by Thomas and Fiering (1962) and Fiering (1967) but because they are short-memory models they do not represent the Hurst phenomenon particularly satisfactorily. An alternative explanation of this was provided by Mandlebrot and van Ness (1968) and Mandlebrot and Wallis (1968; 1969*a,b,c,d,e*) who described a family of long-memory models, the F.G.N. models, involving a complex correlation structure in which the current value of the process depends on the entire history of the process. More recently another family of long-memory models, based on the broken line process, which also will preserve the Hurst phenomenon, was suggested by a group of workers in Colorado (Garcia *et al.*, 1972; Mejia *et al.*, 1972; Rodriguez-Iturbe *et al.*, 1972).

As Mejia *et al.* (1972) observed, all stochastic models are based on the premise that a streamflow record is only a single realisation in time and that the statistical properties of the recorded streamflow give sample estimates of the possible future long-term streamflow. As has already been pointed out (p. 87), the weakness of this assumption was clearly illustrated by Francis (1973) using data from the river Thames. Accepting the inherent defects of the method, however, the choice of model then depends on which particular statistical properties one wishes to preserve. Most models give a fairly high reproducibility of the historical record over short periods but different assumptions, for example about extreme value distribution, lead to marked differences between model results over long time periods. Despite the great enthusiasm for stochastic modelling among its practitioners, many hydrologists doubt its ability to improve the accuracy of prediction of high-magnitude, long return-period floods.

A fairly common situation is that in which only a short-term record of streamflow is in existence for a given catchment although the rainfall record for the same catchment may be very much longer. In such cases, as well as in those of ungauged catchments, attempts have been made to predict floods from an analysis of the rainfall record. For frequently recurring, low-magnitude flood events it may be possible to convert the existing rainfall record directly into a streamflow record. Kresge and Nordenson (1955), for example, suggested a procedure whereby coaxial rainfall–runoff graphs were developed for the given catchment and used to estimate the volume of direct runoff resulting from the recorded rainfall. Unit hydrograph procedures were then used to determine the flood peaks corresponding to the estimated runoff volumes and finally, a frequency analysis was made of the estimated flood peaks. For estimating rarer floods, with return periods substantially greater than the period of precipitation data, or for ungauged catchments where the derivation of rainfall–runoff graphs is not possible, a direct frequency analysis of the precipitation record itself is normally preferred.

In many cases, this frequency analysis was made with the assumption that the return period of the design flood is equal to the return period of the design rainfall. However, observation indicates that this is not so and that the flood return period is generally very different from the return period of the associated rainfall. Thus, in an analysis of conditions in widely differing locations in the United States, Reich (1968) showed that floods having return periods greater than ten years often occur in response to storms that are smaller than the two-year maxima, while storms with return periods of fifty years or more often produce floods with much smaller return periods. Such differences are only to be expected since the response of a catchment to precipitation depends so much on antecedent moisture conditions, which in turn determine the 'losses' from total rainfall, and on the distribution of total rainfall in time. Clearly, then, antecedent moisture conditions, and/or losses, must be taken into account when attempting to predict flood peaks from precipitation data.

Various methods have been advanced to overcome this problem. Alexander, Karoly and Susts (1969*a,b*) treated floods as a joint distribution of rainfall and losses both of whose probabilities could be calculated from observed data. Thus a 1000-year flood could be conceived of as resulting from the coincidence of a 50-year storm and a 20-year loss rate in a particular catchment. However, they found that only by treating losses as a random variable was it possible to create a satisfactory distribution of floods from rainfall data. For many parts of the world adequate data on loss rates are not available and Pilgrim (1966) suggested the possibility of transposing values from similar catchments in other areas such as between the United States and Australasia. Reich (1971) suggested that the accuracy of flood predictions based on rainfall data could be improved still further if a treatment of joint probabilities of rainfall, antecedent moisture and season were used. Cordery (1971) described a method whereby the estimated rainfall for a given return period is distributed using an appropriate average storm pattern, then reduced by subtracting a median initial loss and continuing loss, before the remaining rainfall excess is convoluted to produce the design hydrograph of quickflow. Finally, investigations by the Flood Study Team of the Institute of Hydrology (Beran and Sutcliffe, 1972) showed that at any location in Britain, and in any season, the rainfall excess for a given return period differs from the rainfall of the same return period by a constant amount, which can be regarded as a mean soil moisture deficit for the given location and season. This means that seasonal maps of mean soil moisture deficit can be used in conjunction with rainfall probability maps to produce estimates for any location of the flood-producing rainfall excess of corresponding probability.

Of the various methods available for converting rainfall excess into a flood hydrograph to obtain an estimate of the peak discharge, the unit hydrograph method is undoubtedly the most popular. The basis of the method, proposed by Sherman (1932), is that since a stream hydrograph reflects many of the physical characteristics of the catchment area, similar hydrographs will be produced by similar rainfalls occurring with comparable antecedent conditions. Thus, once a typical or unit hydrograph has been determined for certain clearly defined conditions, it is possible to estimate runoff from a rainfall of any duration or intensity. In gauged catchments the unit hydrograph is constructed by selecting a recorded hydrograph of a uniform isolated storm, preferably with a fairly large volume of runoff, isolating the base runoff, and dividing the discharge ordinates of the remaining direct runoff hydrograph according to the volume under the hydrograph, thus obtaining the unit hydrograph, that is the hydrograph of

25 mm of runoff. For catchments with few, if any, streamflow records it is necessary to establish the relationships between the physical characteristics of the catchment area and the resulting hydrographs. Snyder (1938) was one of the earliest workers to derive synthetic unit hydrographs and found that the shape of the catchment and its 'lag', the time from the centre of the mass of rainfall to the hydrograph peak, were the main influencing characteristics. Much subsequent work has been done to investigate the main properties of the unit hydrograph and to determine their correlation with catchment characteristics (Gray, 1961; Henderson, 1963; and Nash, 1960). Nash's work enables some properties of the unit hydrograph to be estimated in Britain but there is still a long way to go before sufficiently general rules emerge to permit the synthesis of accurate hydrographs from non-hydrological data in well-mapped catchments (Francis, 1973).

Eagleson (1970, 1972) proposed the use of kinematic wave equations to study the generation of streamflow hydrographs from rainfall and catchment characteristics in ungauged catchments. Various other methods of modelling catchment behaviour in order to generate flood hydrographs from rainfall have been discussed. These range from comparatively simple representations of a catchment as a series of reservoirs which successively delay the passage of water through the catchment from its point of impact as rainfall to its exit as streamflow, to comparatively sophisticated digital-computer models such as the Stanford Watershed Model (Crawford and Linsley, 1966), the USDAHL-70 Model (Holtan and Lopez, 1971) and various flow forecasting models being developed at the Institute of Hydrology (Mandeville *et al.*, 1970; Nash and Sutcliffe, 1970; O'Connell *et al.*, 1970). Some of these will be discussed again in the next chapter.

CATCHMENTS WITH INADEQUATE STREAMFLOW AND RAINFALL DATA

Finally, a brief mention must be made of the problems of flood prediction in catchments where not only the streamflow data but also the rainfall data are inadequate. In such cases it may be necessary to synthesise precipitation sequences as an extension of existing records or to create data where none exist, using similar methods to those for creating synthetic streamflow records.

Snowmelt floods

The techniques for predicting rainfall floods discussed in this chapter are, in general, equally applicable to the prediction of floods in areas where a substantial proportion of the annual precipitation falls as snow. Inevitably, however, the complications of the snowmelt process and the possible coincidence of snowmelt and rainfall present additional problems for both deterministic and probabilistic approaches to flood prediction.

Conditions in many major snowfall areas are such that hydrometeorological data are frequently inadequate in both quantity and quality. The deterministic approach to flood prediction tends, therefore, to involve a high degree of empiricism. A number of empirical formulae in common usage in Russia, as well as new proposals for an improved method, were discussed by Sokolov (1969*a*). In the case of process-based flood predictions, as Hoyt and Langbein (1955) observed, snow complicates the maximising procedures because determination of the PMF depends on an estimate of maximum snow accumulation as well as maximum rates of thaw coupled with heavy rainfall. In addition, since storm types often show marked seasonal variation, it may be necessary to select only those storms from the winter and spring seasons for use in the transposition and maximisation procedures.

In the probabilistic approach the complexity of the problem is little affected if predictions are based on a statistical analysis of streamflow data but it considerably exacerbated if flood prediction is based on precipitation data. Brater *et al.* (1974) showed that the frequency distributions of winter rainfall and rain-plus-snowmelt events differed and that the difference increased with increasing return period. As in the case of flood predictions based on rainfall data, it seems likely that a joint probability approach incorporating snow accumulation and melt, rainfall and losses may eventually yield the most satisfactory probabilistic solution.

A major design problem with snowmelt floods is the variability of hydrograph shape for a given flood peak or volume. Canadian experience has shown that the required spillway capacity for two flood hydrographs having equal peaks but different shapes may differ by as much as 40 per cent. However, improved models of the snowmelt process, such as that reported by Erickson and McCorquodale (1967), enable the shape of the snowmelt hydrograph resulting from specified hydrometeorological and catchment conditions to be estimated with a high degree of accuracy.

Understandably, a major part of the literature and current research effort on snowmelt flood prediction originates in Eurasia and North America. Basic references include the works by Alekhin (1964), Chebotarev (1966), and Gray (1970), U.S. Corps of Engineers (1956) and the collection of papers in Part II of the Leningrad Symposium on *Floods and their Computation* (IASH/UNESCO/ WMO, 1969).

Coastal floods

Finally, and briefly, deterministic and probabilistic methods are also used in the prediction of coastal floods, although the data base is still woefully inadequate. In the case of storm surges, the process-based methods involve the maximisation of major storms, fetch and wave size and tidal level, and, in estuarine situations, the maximisation of freshwater flows as well. Probabilistic predictions, which can incorporate tsunamis as well as storm surges, are based on the probability distributions of coastal water levels, usually calculated from comparatively brief records or from longer records of uncertain quality. The extrapolation of such records to the prediction of rare events, having return periods of 1000 years or more, is inevitably a much more dubious procedure than the extrapolation of data on rainfall-produced river floods. The major uncertainties inherent in coastal flood prediction are, however, to some extent offset by the usually slightly longer time interval available for flood forecasting procedures to operate. Such procedures are discussed in the next chapter.

7 Flood Forecasting

The ability to provide sufficient advance warning of flood occurrence is important in reducing the potentially disastrous effects of floods. It may, for example, save lives by giving floodplain residents time to remove themselves and their possessions to safety, and it may save property by allowing time to effect various structural and other adjustments (discussed in the next chapter). In the early stages, river forecasting was almost exclusively concerned with floods but recently the growing need to utilise water resources more efficiently has encouraged forecasting over the full range of streamflow for the purposes of navigation, hydroelectric power generation, pollution control and so on. Not surprisingly, flood forecasting has benefited from the attention given to forecasting the complete flood hydrograph rather than simply the flood crests.

Hoyt and Langbein (1955) referred to the idea of flood forecasting as 'quite ancient' although, in fact, it was not until 1871 that a regular river and flood forecasting service was started in the United States by the Weather Service branch of the Army Signal Service. This work was later taken over by the U.S. Weather Bureau upon its establishment in 1890. Britain was even slower to develop this service, and despite (or because of) the early development of raingauging, streamflow measurement was largely neglected – as late as 1936 there were only twenty-seven gauging stations in Britain. The need for reliability in flood forecasting has been frequently stressed. Hoyt and Langbein (1955), for example, drew attention to the fact that a forecast that is too low discourages proper preparation, and an over-estimated forecast results in unnecessary expense and anxiety, and may detract from the credibility of subsequent forecasts. However, the inevitable unreliability of many early forecasts was due to the limitations imposed by inadequate understanding of hydrological processes, minimal instrumentation networks, poor communication systems and slow data processing. Improvements in all these fields have resulted in substantial advances towards the two main objectives of flood forecasting: accurate forewarning of the *height* of floodwaters in the area concerned, and the longest possible *advance warning time* of critical flood heights.

At the present time it is still not possible to forecast several months, or even weeks, in advance the occurrence of specific flood-producing storm or melt events. In fact, only rarely are such forecasts made with reasonable accuracy several *days* in advance. This means that generally the most reliable flood forecasts are based on data from precipitation and melt events which have just occurred or are still taking place. Thus advance warning time is normally measured in hours and days, rather than weeks or months, and depends on the type of flood, the size of the catchment area and the quality and duration of the hydrometric data. On the lower and middle Mississippi, flood peaks of 10 to 20 m can be forecast to within an accuracy of about 10 cm several weeks ahead, whereas in the case of flash floods in desert areas it may be difficult to forecast even the timing, still less the height, of the flood peak one hour in advance. Following the WMO *Guide to Hydrometeorological Practices* it seems reasonable to recognise short-term flood forecasts as covering a period of up to 15 days and long-term forecasts as covering a period of more than 15 days. In practice the former are the more common and relate largely to rainfall floods, while long-term forecasts are associated with snowmelt or ice-break-up events and are of greatest significance in medium and high latitudes where spring runoff accounts for up to 90 per cent of the annual streamflow (Miljukov, 1972). In this chapter we will concentrate largely on short-term forecasts of rainfall floods and to a lesser extent on the long-term forecasting of snowmelt floods. In addition, brief consideration will also be given to floods resulting from ice break-up and to the forecasting of coastal and estuarine floods.

RAINFALL FLOODS

Although the process linking rainfall and streamflow is a deterministic one in that it is governed by known physical laws, it has so far not proved practicable to forecast river flow simply by applying these laws to the measured rainfall and boundary conditions within a catchment area, largely because of the complexity of the boundary conditions (Nash and Sutcliffe, 1970). Since there seems little point in applying exact physical laws to approximate boundary conditions, a traditional approach to flood forecasting has developed which is largely empirical or analytical. The basic stages in this approach are:

(1) the calculation of areal precipitation over the catchment in question

(2) the calculation of the amount of direct runoff or quickflow resulting from that precipitation

(3) the conversion of the direct runoff volume into a time-distributed hydrograph

(4) the use, where appropriate, of flood routing procedures to estimate the change in shape of the hydrograph as it moves to a selected downstream location.

Brief comments on the first three stages will be made here while the fourth stage, flood routing, which is equally applicable to all river flood hydrographs whether derived from rainfall or any other cause, will be discussed separately later in the chapter.

Calculation of areal precipitation

The procedures for calculating the precipitation input to a catchment area are well known and discussed in detail in most of the standard hydrological texts (for example, Ward, 1975). Most of the problems arise from the need to average point rainfall values from a number of raingauges distributed throughout the catchment, in particular the weaknesses of averaging techniques and the relative representativeness of the raingauge network. As a result, more attention is now paid to methods which yield a direct integration of precipitation over an entire catchment. Of these, the use of radar measurements (Battan, 1973; Harrold and Nicholass, 1972) and satellite data (Barrett, 1973; Woodley and Sancho, 1971) seem the most promising, although both are still in early stages of development.

The timing of a flood forecast in relation to the collection of precipitation data will vary depending on a number of factors such as the quality of the data, the duration of the storm and the size of the catchment area. The three main possibilities are that the flood forecast may be: (1) delayed until the storm has ended, (2) made during the storm but before its completion, or (3) made before the storm occurs, and thus on the basis of a rainfall forecast. Clearly, the advance warning time to floodplain occupants and the margin of error of the forecast are likely to increase from the first through the last type. In a large catchment area, downstream locations will probably receive an adequate warning time even with a type 1 forecast; but in smaller catchments there may be the need for as much advance warning as possible, outweighing the potential inaccuracies of the type 2 or 3 forecasts. A type 2 forecast may be made on the basis of the maximum historical rainfall, or on the basis of either the deterministic rainfall forecast or a probability forecast, based on past experience (for example, that there is a 90 per cent chance that a further 25 mm of rain will fall). Type 3 forecasts, although rarely used at the present time, will almost certainly be deterministic and, because of the high standard of reliability required in flood forecasting, are likely to be based on satellite data (Barrett, 1973).

Calculation of direct runoff

In chapter 2, discussion of rainfall floods indicated that, during and after a storm, water reaches stream channels by a variety of routes and at varying speeds and that it is the quickflow or direct runoff which is largely responsible for the flood hydrograph. However, such is the complexity of the runoff process, it is not possible to relate the speed of arrival of water in the channel to the route taken by that water. As a result, traditional techniques of hydrograph analysis, intended to separate direct runoff from base runoff, have been discredited. Furthermore, the persistence of runoff for a long period after a storm event implies a very slow recession of runoff making it difficult to define even the gross runoff volume associated with each storm event. The need to calculate the quickflow resulting from a rainstorm seems, therefore, to represent a fundamental weakness in the analytical approach to flood forecasting and will undoubtedly lead to its eventual demise.

Until this happens, however, the volume of direct runoff will continue to be estimated by such traditional and well-tried techniques as hydrograph analysis, discussed in detail by Ward (1975); the infiltration approach of Horton (1933), which has been shown to be generally incorrect in the light of modern concepts of the runoff process; and the use of rainfall–runoff relationships for the catchment area, which usually incorporate an index of initial soil moisture conditions, either as an antecedent precipitation index (API) or a soil moisture deficit (SMD). If it is assumed that the infiltration characteristics of the catchment are related to its initial wetness, then the 'losses' from rainfall will decrease with increasing API or with decreasing SMD. One of the earliest and probably best-known attempts to forecast direct runoff volumes from rainfall was the coaxial graphical correlation method developed by Linsley *et al.* (1949). This method uses an API combined with time of year to give an integrated index of catchment wetness at the beginning of rainfall. The index is corrected for storm duration and is then used with storm precipitation to calculate direct runoff, as shown in figure 7.1a. The use of an API in estimating direct runoff can probably be justified less satisfactorily in simple infiltration terms, as has previously been the case, than in terms of the fact that conditions favouring a high API will also favour source area expansion.

The direct calculation of SMD by means of a water-balance accounting procedure, whereby the difference between potential evapotranspiration and rainfall is accumulated progressively, was initially suggested by Thornthwaite and Mather (1955). Grindley (1967) described the method used by the Meteorological Office to produce maps of SMD and effective precipitation for use by Regional Water Authorities in flood forecasting in Britain. Goodhew (1970), referring to British conditions, concluded that API is a better indicator of potential flood risk during winter when low evapotranspiration rates mean that the SMD is always close to zero, and SMD is more useful in summer for approximating the proportion of rainfall which will runoff from a particular storm, provided the rainfall intensity is not greatly in excess of the infiltration capacity of the catchment.

Conversion of direct runoff volume into a time-distributed hydrograph

A valuable, succinct review of traditional methods for calculating flood hydrographs – for example the isochrone method, the unit hydrograph and linear reservoir transformation – was presented by Popov (1964). The theoretical basis of these methods is the principle of linear superposition which can be expressed mathematically by the Duhamel integral

$$Q(t) = \int_0^t q(t - \tau)\,\mu(\tau)\,d\tau \tag{7.1}$$

where Q is flood discharge, $q(t - \tau)$ is the effective rainfall or inflow of water, $\mu(\tau)$ is the runoff distribution function, variously referred to in the literature as the travel time curve and the instantaneous unit hydrograph, and t and τ are time. The main difference between the various methods lies in the practical determination of the distribution function $\mu(\tau)$. The basic premise of the isochrone method is that, for any given graph of effective rainfall, flood discharge is proportional to the areas from which the water simultaneously reaches the outlet of the catchment. The unit hydrograph method has been discussed at great length in the hydrological literature and has been briefly described in chapter 6 (p. 91). This is undoubtedly the most popular method for deriving the flood hydrograph from a given volume of direct runoff. The conversion of rainfall excess to runoff in a catchment area is, to some extent, analogous to the transformation of a flood wave by a series of linear reservoirs. This approach has been used by a number of authors – Nash (1958); Dooge (1959) – to derive a first approxi-

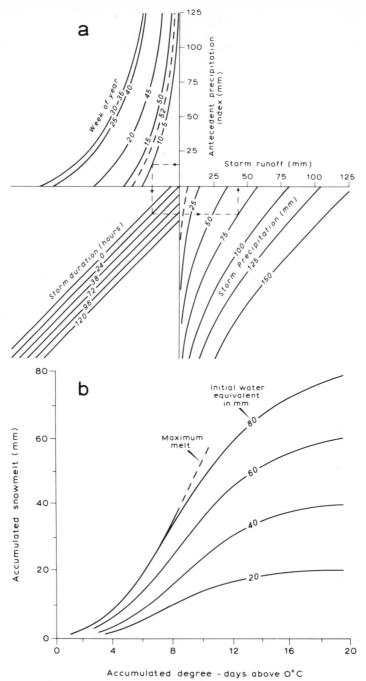

Figure 7.1   Estimations of direct runoff and snowmelt: *a*, Coaxial diagram for estimating direct (storm) runoff; *b*, Relationship between accumulated degree-days, initial water equivalent and accumulated snowmelt
Source: *a*, Kohler and Linsley (1951); *b*, Richards (1964).

mation for the analytical expression of the unit hydrograph. Other methods have been suggested, and recently increased attention has been devoted to the problem of flood forecasting in ungauged catchments. Eagleson's proposed use of kinematic wave equations to study the generation of streamflow hydrographs from rainfall and catchment characteristics (Eagleson, 1970; 1972) have already been noted in chapter 6 (p. 92).

SNOWMELT FLOODS

Some of the most consistently reliable flood forecasting relates to periods of high discharge resulting from snowmelt (Alekhin, 1964). Here the flood-producing mechanism is directly related to the energy balance and to air temperature in particular, where changes are comparatively easier to forecast than are aspects of rainfall occurrence such as timing, duration and intensity. In addition, there is normally a substantial interval between the occurrence of snow and its subsequent melting which allows time to assess the accumulation of snowfall. On the other hand, environmental conditions in winter snowfall areas, particularly in mountains, are such that the distribution, frequency and often accuracy of measurements may be far from satisfactory. The main stages in snowmelt-flood forecasting are: first, the calculation of accumulated snowfall and its water equivalent; second, the calculation of melt rates and the resulting hydrograph; and third, where appropriate, the routing of the snowmelt hydrograph to a selected downstream location. Since flood routing procedures will be discussed later in the chapter, only the first two stages will be commented on here.

Calculation of snowfall and its water equivalent

In terms of flood forecasting it is not the depth of snow but the water equivalent of the snowpack – the equivalent water depth of the melted snow – which is important. Water equivalent may be measured directly in a number of ways, most of which involve weighing or the use of radioactive isotopes. The traditional weighing precipitation gauge has been superseded in recent years by the much larger snow pillow, which registers the accumulated weight of snow as a pressure change, and by various radioactive probes (Warnick and Penton, 1971). The cost of such instruments is high and yet, because of the normally uneven accumulation of snow, the need for replication of measurements is great. Supplementary measurements, therefore, are normally made along predetermined snow courses which are selected as representative of conditions over a wide area. These may measure either the depth of snow or the weight of sample cores using a snow sampler which extends through the snowpack (Church, 1942; Garstka, 1964). Aerial surveys and other remote sensing techniques make it possible to obtain information on the distribution of snow in remote areas where direct measurement is difficult.

In some situations the amount of precipitation, often rainfall, at low altitudes may be used as an index of snow accumulation in adjacent mountain catchments or to supplement information on snowpack water equivalents in the higher areas of a catchment (Linsley, 1967).

Calculation of melt rates and the resulting hydrograph

The shape of the snowmelt flood hydrograph reflects, in large measure, the rate of melt, which in turn depends ultimately on the radiation balance of the snow cover. The components of this radiation balance are numerous, their interrelations are complex, and their accurate measurement poses considerable problems. Heat is gained by direct radiation from the sun and sky, and sensible heat (particularly in turbulent conditions) from the overlying air. Heat is also gained in smaller quantities by conduction from the underlying ground surface, from falling rain and by condensation on the snow surface. In order to simplify snowmelt forecasting procedures, correlations are frequently made between aspects of air temperature, for example, accumulated degree-days above melting point, and snowmelt. This simplified approach has some justification in that the transfer of sensible heat is one of the more important factors involved in the melting process and that air temperature largely reflects the integration of the radiation balance of the overlying air (Collins, 1934; Østrem, 1964; U.S. Army Corps of Engineers, 1956). A widely used approach is to multiply the average of the degree-days above melting point for the catchment by a factor which usually varies from 1 to 4 mm, with 2 mm the most common value (Richards, 1964). This factor is then correlated with time of year or with accumulated degree-days (illustrated in figure 7.1b), to determine the total amount of melt. Other approaches, described in detail by Davar (1970) and U.S. Army Corps of Engineers (1960), include the incorporation of recession analysis with the degree-day method and the use of generalised snowmelt equations.

Derivation of the flood hydrograph for a given volume of melt is usually difficult. Unit hydrograph procedures are frequently discounted because of the problem of determining the appropriate unit duration. Trial and error curve-fitting procedures based on previous floods, for example the Phase Routing method, which were inordinately time-consuming before the advent of computers, are now much more acceptable (Davar, 1970).

ICE FORECASTS

It was shown in chapter 3 that in areas where rivers freeze over in the winter months, during the spring thaw and break-up severe flooding may result from ice-jam effects. The ability to forecast accurately the date of ice break-up is, therefore, of considerable importance in areas such as Canada, Scandinavia and the USSR. As might be expected, forecasting procedures are far advanced in these countries. According to Miljukov (1972), methods for predicting ice break-up are based on estimates of the amount of icemelt produced by heat at its upper and lower boundaries. In the latter case, air temperature and the temperature and rate of waterflow under the ice cover are taken into account.

FLOOD ROUTING

The final stage of flood forecasting in all but small catchments involves the technique of flood routing, which is the process of determining progressively the timing and shape of the flood wave at successive points along a river, and calculating the floodwater depth at any specified location. Flood routing may be necessary for a number of reasons. For example, unit hydrograph and similar procedures for deriving the shape of the flood hydrograph are normally most suited to comparatively small catchments, so that, in order to forecast the flood hydrograph at the outlet of a major river catchment, it is necessary to route the individual hydrographs for each of the constituent sub-catchments. Again, flood routing procedures are required when a flood-producing storm covers only part of the catchment lying above the area in question. Flood routing is also used extensively for design purposes to evaluate the probable effects of channel modifications and control structures. Routing is not confined to river channels but can be applied as well to reservoirs, lakes and swamps and indeed, with the help of computers, to the entire catchment area (see next section). Nor is routing always carried out in a downstream direction since the process can be reversed for upstream routing (the determination of upstream hydrographs from downstream measurements), although this is unlikely to be relevant to the problem of flood forecasting.

The movement of a flood wave in a stream channel is a highly complex phenomenon of non-steady and usually non-uniform flow. Not only does flow vary with time as the wave progresses downstream, but channel properties and the amounts of lateral inflow and outflow may also vary (Gray and Wigham, 1970). If we consider the simple case of a channel reach with no entering tributaries, where there is no gain of water from rainfall and no loss by evaporation, the effects of storage both within the channel and in and on the adjacent floodplain will be sufficient to dampen the floodwave as it travels down the reach, thereby attenuating the peak and extending the time base. A simple system of this type is illustrated in figure 7.2a (inset) while the main diagram shows a typical example of attenuation, in this case of a flood wave moving down the Savannah River in Georgia. At first, water enters the channel reach faster than it exits at the downstream end, the excess water being retained in channel and floodplain storages thereby raising water levels within the reach. Later, the inflow into the reach drops below the rate of flow at the downstream end and the excess water stored between the two gauging stations comes out of storage.

There are essentially two approaches to flood routing, the one complex and theoretical and the other simplified and empirical. The theoretical approach involves either convection/diffusion equations or, more usually, the St Venant equations to model the one-dimensional bulk flow of water in a river channel. The St Venant equations are two partial differential equations of motion and continuity

$$\text{motion} \qquad \frac{Q^2}{K^2} + \frac{l\partial v}{g\partial t} + \frac{v\partial v}{g\partial x} + \frac{lqv}{gA} = \frac{\partial H}{\partial x} \qquad\qquad (7.2)$$

$$\text{continuity} \qquad \frac{\partial Q}{\partial x} + \frac{\partial A}{\partial t} = q(x,t)$$

where H, v, A, Q and K are respectively the water level and mean velocity, and cross-sectional area, discharge and conveyance of flow at point x and time t, while q is inflow into the channel per unit reach in unit time, and g is the acceleration due to gravity. These equations can only be solved by simplification and numerical integration with small steps of Δx and Δt. Because of the large amount of computation required, such integration was not feasible before the introduction of large fast computers, but now that these are available the integration of the St Venant equations presents no mathematical difficulties. The problems lie, according to Miljukov (1972), in determining the coefficients of the differential equations and in establishing the initial and

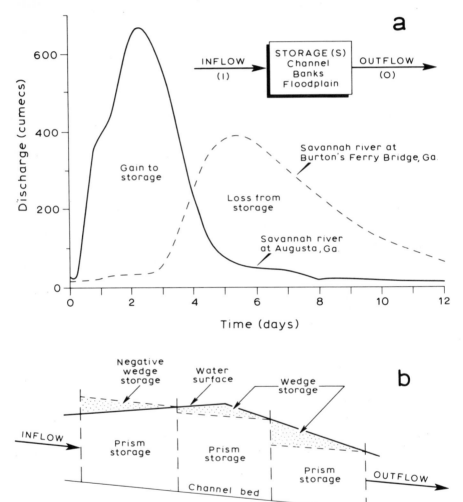

Figure 7.2 Aspects of flood routing; *a*, Attenuation of a flood wave between two gauging stations on the Savannah River in Georgia. *Inset* simplified systems diagram of a channel reach; *b*, Flood wave profile illustrating wedge and prism storage
Source: *a*, Fox (1965).

boundary conditions, and it is largely because of these that simplified flood routing methods are normally used.

The most common of the simplified flood routing methods are those based only on the continuity (storage) equation, using the principle that for any channel reach the difference between inflow and outflow is equal to the stored or depleted water in a given time interval. Although, in the simple example of a reservoir, outflow may be a function of storage represented by water elevation, this is not the case for a floodwave passing through a channel reach because of the changes in slope of the water surface. In figure 7.2b, outflow indicates only that storage beneath a line parallel to the stream bed, the prism storage. Between this parallel line and the water profile is the wedge storage, which represents the excess of inflow over outflow during the advance of the flood wave. Similarly, the excess of outflow over inflow during the recession is represented by negative wedge storage.

In the Muskingum flood routing method, which has probably become as well known and widely used as any in this category, McCarthy (1938) proposed that storage should be expressed as a function of both inflow and outflow

$$S = K[xI + (1 - x)O] \qquad (7.3)$$

where x is a dimensionless constant for a given channel reach and K is a storage constant with dimension of time which is derived from observed hydrographs of I and O at each end of the reach. Outflow from the reach can be obtained by solving simultaneously equation 7.3 and the water balance equation for the reach (equation 7.4)

$$\Delta S = I - O \qquad (7.4)$$

for a discrete time interval

$$O_2 = c_0 I_1 + c_1 I_2 + c_2 O_1 \qquad (7.5)$$

in which O_1 and O_2 and I_1 and I_2 are respectively the outflow and inflow at the beginning and end of the routing period, and where the values of the coefficients c_0, c_1, and c_2 are found from the empirically determined values of x and K, and the value of the calculated time interval Δt. The necessary empirical determinations are adequately described in the literature (Gray and Wigham, 1970; Lawler, 1964; Wilson, 1969, Yevjevich, 1964).

Various other simplified approaches to flood routing, based principally on the continuity equation, have been proposed, and include time-lag routing using the method of characteristics. In addition, there are various graphical, mechanical and analogue methods, although these have been largely superseded in recent years by the use of digital computers. Some of these methods and the related literature were reviewed in detail by Yevjevich and Barnes (1970).

As an alternative to the normal flood routing approach described above, in which the channel reach system is represented by a set of equations which convert inflow to outflow, Lane *et al.* (1971) regarded the channel reach as a system defined in terms of its effect on certain parameters of the inflow and outflow hydrographs, for example the attenuation of the peak, the change in time to peak and the time of travel of the wave front. A three-parameter gamma distribution function was used to represent the inflow and outflow hydrographs and regression equations developed to relate the parameters of the outflow distribution to the parameters of the inflow distribution graph.

COMPUTER SIMULATION

During the past few decades the enormous increase in the world-wide availability of computer time to virtually all flood forecasting organisations has largely made obsolete the step-by-step approach to flood forecasting described in the preceding sections. Modern high-speed, large-capacity computers make it feasible to model the entire flood-producing process in one operation. This approach has been encouraged not only by developments in computer technology and the complexity of flood-routing calculations, but also by advances in our hydrological understanding of the runoff process and in particular by many hydrologists' increasing rejection of the arbitrary separation of the quickflow and baseflow components of total runoff. As Nash and Sutcliffe (1970) observed, if arbitrary hydrograph separation is rejected, the steps by which rainfall is converted to effective rainfall and effective rainfall to runoff can no longer be handled separately but must be treated simultaneously, and thus a model of the conversion of rainfall into runoff must be assumed.

The complexity of natural catchments and of the flood-producing process itself inevitably mean that even the most rigorous model must involve considerable simplification and approximation. The model's parameters may be determined from field measurement of hydrological data or by successive optimisation procedures continued until model behaviour approximates most closely to catchment behaviour, although the quest for 'curve-fitting' must not produce a model with no inherent physical validity.

Among the plethora of computer models of hydrologic systems which have been developed, relatively few are generally applicable. Here we will select only a few of those computer simulations which are particularly suitable for flood forecasting.

The Hydrocomp Simulation Program (HSP) is a direct development from the Stanford Watershed Model (Crawford and Linsley, 1966), one of the earliest of the modern continuous simulation computer models. *HSP/Floods* (Hydrocomp, 1970) is identical to the general HSP program except for certain modifications to the input and output specifications. HSP/Floods includes special programming for data management in a module called 'Library'; a module 'Lands', which computes runoff to the channel system; and a module 'Channel', which routes the flow through the channel system and can calculate values of stage and discharge at intervals of fifteen minutes or more at any number of points within the channel system (Linsley and Crawford, 1974). Input consists of either measured or forecast hydrological and meteorological data, with simulated or forecast data being replaced by measured data as the latter become available. When a storm occurs, hydrological data are fed in and the simulation of the flow magnitudes is produced as the storm builds up to flood-producing proportions. Forecast meteorological data or assumed rainfall rates can be used to estimate potential flood flows, as shown in figure 7.3.

The *Streamflow Synthesis and Reservoir Regulation (SSARR)* model (Scher-

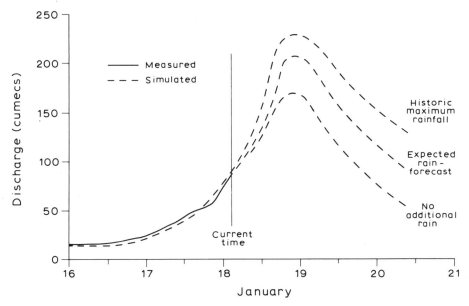

Figure 7.3   HSP/Floods simulation of potential flood flows
Source: Hydrocomp (1970).

merhorn and Kuehl, 1969) is a flexible general model, designed originally to per-
form streamflow synthesis for planning and daily operational forecasting during
the snowmelt flood period on the Columbia River in the Pacific North-west of
the United States. The present version is a third generation development of the
model originally proposed by Rockwood (1958) and has been applied successfully to the Mekong River (Rockwood, 1969). The program can be used for any
study involving computation of streamflows resulting from snowmelt and/or
rainfall. Complex drainage basins are separated into relatively homogeneous
hydrologic units, channel storage specified for channel reaches to represent the
natural delay to runoff encountered in a complex river system, and the storage
effects of lakes and man-made reservoirs incorporated. Flood flows can thus be
developed for all key locations on the river system.

The U.S. Army Corps of Engineers Hydrologic Engineering Center has developed the *Flood Hydrograph Package (HEC-1)*. This is a comprehensive program
which performs virtually all types of flood hydrograph study needed in a flood
forecasting and control situation (Beard, 1969; 1971). Thus HEC-1 enables the
flood forecaster solve automatically for runoff characteristics, such as unit
hydrographs, loss relationships and routing coefficients, from observed point
data on precipitation, snowpack characteristics, temperature and runoff. It can

be used for simple tasks, such as flood routing through a reservoir, or more elaborately for the simultaneous computation of 40 or 50 different floods at each location in a stream system, thereby reproducing the flood range that could occur with various projected development or improvement plans. At the same time, flood damages for each of the computed floods is evaluated.

A program designed specifically to forecast snowmelt runoff was described by Erickson and McCorquodale (1967) and valuable work on the development of flow-forecasting models has been done at the U.K. Institute of Hydrology (Mandeville *et al.*, 1970; Nash and Sutcliffe, 1970; O'Connell *et al.*, 1970).

As Schermerhorn and Kuehl (1969) observed, time is an essential factor in all flood forecasting, the value of even a perfect forecast decreasing with time as the event approaches, reaching zero at its advent. Understandably, the reduction of the preparation time of flood forecasts is continually being investigated. It is unlikely that further computer development will significantly reduce the time taken to analyse the input data and produce the forecast, but there is considerable scope for reducing the programming of the basic hydrological and meteorological data. One possibility under current investigation and development is the direct linking of computers with weather radar (Sugawara, 1969) or the use of weather satellite data (Barrett, 1973; Jensen, 1974; NOAA, 1973*a*). More widespread is the use of automatic transmitting raingauges and water-level recorders and these now form a standard part of most flood warning systems.

FLOOD WARNING SYSTEMS

Preparing an accurate forecast well in advance of a flood event represents only one, albeit vitally important, aspect of the flood forecasting problem. An equally essential feature is the rapid dissemination of the flood forecast to the floodplain occupants at risk. The procedures, whether rudimentary or highly sophisticated, represent a vital stage in the complete flood warning system and frequently involve a high degree of local community participation and organisation.

Miljukov (1972) referred to two contrasting approaches to the improvement of flood warning systems. First is the possibility of establishing global or semi-global systems of hydrological and meteorological forecasting linked to the WMO World Weather Watch. Second, there is the individual catchment approach involving local automatic systems for the observation, transmission and processing of hydrometeorological data. As Miljukov observed, centralisation of hydrological forecasting does not always prove the most economic solution. When the catchments are comparatively small, it is more expedient to create local automatic systems. Moreover, it is not likely that a global system could operate at the level of detail required for a small catchment warning system, and a small-scale approach will always be a necessary part of the total system.

Undoubtedly, the world's most advanced and comprehensively organised national flood warning system is in the United States. This system is a reflection of the high level of technological development in the U.S.A., the hydrometeorological severity of the flood risk and the magnitude of the socio-economic problems which result from large-scale settlement of flood-prone areas. In an average year between 80 and 90 people are killed, 75 000 driven from their homes and more than \$260 million of damage is caused by floods. The United States flood warning system is operated through the National Weather Service of the National Oceanic and Atmospheric Administration (NOAA). Its essential features are illustrated in figure 7.4a,b. Twelve Weather Service River Forecast Centers monitor meteorological and hydrological conditions and provide water level predictions for more than 2500 points on the river network. Flood forecasts require continuous information on present and expected atmospheric conditions. Part of this information is supplied to the River Forecast Centers, through special communication links, by the National Meteorological Center in Washington D.C., where current forecasts are prepared using satellite and radar observations, computer models of the atmosphere and data from the numerous conventional weather stations. The area served by a River Forecast Center is divided into a number of river districts in each of which one weather service station is designated as a River District Office. This office maintains a network of observation stations that report river stage and precipitation data which are collected and relayed from the district office to the River Forecast Center. Finally, the flood forecast prepared by the Center is transmitted to the River District Offices for dissemination to the agencies responsible for flood protection and to the public by radio, television and newspapers. There are major plans to improve the effectiveness of the flood warning system within the Automation of Field Operations and Services (AFOS) programme which is in the early stages of implementation (Jensen, 1974).

The above procedures usually work well in large catchment areas when there is sufficient time between the precipitation or melt event and the ensuing flood peak to effect evacuation and other reactive measures. In small tributary areas, however, particularly those with steep slopes or considerable urban development, the time lag may be so short that, while swift action will save lives, it is seldom possible to protect or remove property. To deal with the potentially very dangerous flash-flood situation, the NOAA National Weather Service has developed three basic methods to be used individually, or in combination. First, they established about 100 community self-help systems, a rainfall and river data network of volunteers who report directly to their local flood warning coordinator who can prepare a flood forecast and spread a warning within minutes. The successful operation of this embryonic flash-flood warning system requires active community participation (on the lines shown in figure 7.4c), but very little financial outlay. Second, it may be feasible to install a flash-flood alarm system in which sensors at an upstream river station detect critical water levels. Water level information is transmitted continuously to an alarm station within the community, for example to the fire or police station, and when the critical level is reached at the river station, the alarm is activated. It is then the responsibility of the community to disseminate the warning through its own communications system (NOAA, 1973b). A similar system, activating flashing traffic lights, has been proposed for bridgeless road crossings of flood-prone channels in desert areas (Porath and Schick, 1974). Third, if neither of the first two methods is feasible, more generalised warnings are used. In such cases, the National Weather Service issues either flash-flood watches or flash-flood warnings. If there is the

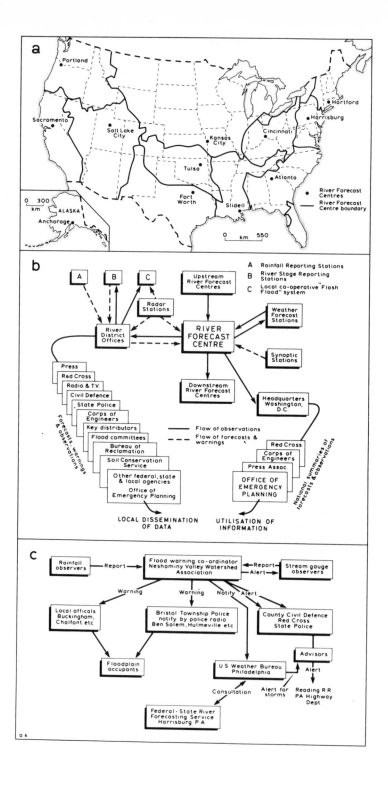

a

Portland

Sacramento

Salt Lake City

Kansas City

Tulsa

Fort Worth

Slidell

Atlanta

Cincinnati

Harrisburg

Hartford

● River Forecast Centres

— River Forecast Centre boundary

0   300
km

ALASKA

Anchorage

0   km   550

b

A   B   C

A Rainfall Reporting Stations
B River Stage Reporting Stations
C Local co-operative "Flash Flood" system

Radar Stations

Upstream River Forecast Centres

River District Offices

RIVER FORECAST CENTRE

Weather Forecast Stations

Synoptic Stations

Downstream River Forecast Centres

Headquarters Washington, D.C.

Press
Red Cross
Radio & T.V.
Civil Defence
State Police
Corps of Engineers
Key distributors
Flood committees
Bureau of Reclamation
Soil Conservation Service
Other federal, state & local agencies
Office of Emergency Planning

Forecasts, warnings & observations

——— Flow of observations
– – – Flow of forecasts & warnings

Red Cross
Corps of Engineers
Press Assoc.
OFFICE OF EMERGENCY PLANNING

National summaries of forecasts & observations

LOCAL DISSEMINATION OF DATA

UTILISATION OF INFORMATION

c

Rainfall observers →Report→ Flood warning co-ordinator Neshaminy Valley Watershed Association ←Report← ←Alert→ Stream gauge observers

Warning   Warning   Notify Alert

Local officals Buckingham, Chalfont etc

Bristol Township Police notify by police radio Ben Salem, Hulmeville etc

County Civil Defence Red Cross State Police

Floodplain occupants

U S Weather Bureau Philadelphia

Advisors

Alert

Reading R R. PA Highway Dept

Consultation   Alert for storms

Federal-State River Forecasting Service Harrisburg P.A.

o k

threat of heavy, intense rainfall, a *flood watch* is issued; if heavy rainfall is actually observed, or an ice-jam begins to break up or a levee fail, a *flood warning* is issued.

Similar, although perhaps less comprehensive, arrangements exist in many other countries. In the United Kingdom, for example, the main responsibility for river flood warnings lies with the Regional Water Authorities, with cooperation from the Meteorological Office which supplies rainfall and soil moisture deficit data (Grindley and Singleton, 1969). Although there have been notable exceptions, some of which were referred to in chapter 2, the danger of flash-floods is far less severe in the United Kingdom than in the United States. For many downstream situations and large catchment areas, flood forecasts and warnings are based on the routing of measured flows. Where particular problem areas exist, however, the warning systems are similar to those described for the United States involving the monitoring and collection of precipitation and river-level data, its transmission to a central assembly point, its interpretation and its dissemination to the public, generally through the agency of the police (Hall and White, 1976). In the past the City of Bath in the Bristol Avon catchment area has been subjected to serious flooding with comparatively little advance warning. The Wessex Water Authority recently installed a flood warning system in which hydrometeorological information will be fed at one-minute intervals into a central computer when flood conditions are imminent, thereby providing an extra two hours' warning before flooding occurs. Thirty-two outlying hydrometeorological stations are linked to the Bath Control Centre where high priority alarms are automatically telephoned to the duty officer in the event of high water levels or excessive rainfall (Bond, 1974). Another problem town is Shrewsbury. Harding and Parker (1972) described the system of danger warnings and alerts operated there by the Severn Water Authority. Warnings are sent to local government officials and to the Chief Constable and flags are displayed on bridges – yellow for an alert and red for a confirmed warning. In addition, road diversions are signposted by the motoring organisations and residential and business occupants contacted by flood wardens and the police.

FORECASTING COASTAL AND ESTUARINE FLOODS

In the sense that coastal floods often result from events hundreds or even thousands of kilometres from the flooded area, their forecasting should be relatively easier than that of river floods in a small catchment. For a long time, however, accurate forecasting of coastal floods was prevented by a combination of inadequate understanding of the flood-producing processes, whether surges or tsunamis, and by inadequate data from the oceans before the growth of aviation and particularly before the advent of weather satellites. In recent years, even with ad-

---

Figure 7.4   United States river and flood forecasting service: *a*, Location map; *b*, Organisational flow chart; *c*, Community-based flash flood warning system – Neshaminy Valley Watershed Association, Pennsylvania organisational flow chart
Source: *a* and *b*, NOAA (1973*a*); *c*, Day, Bugliarello and Houghton (1969) pp. 937–46.

equate oceanographic and hydrometeorological data, satisfactory forecasting was hampered by inadequate data-processing facilities, overcome only in the mid-1970s by the development of larger, faster computers. As a result, long after reasonable forecasting of river floods was possible and indeed, long after integrated flood warning systems were established in countries like the United States, there was scarcely any provision for coastal floods forecasting, nor were there many properly established flood warning systems.

This was illustrated dramatically during the 1953 east coast flooding of England, detailed in chapter 4. Despite the fact that floods in the Thames estuary had been forecast for a quarter of a century, there were no warnings elsewhere on the east coast. Indeed, according to Grieve (1959), at the coroner's inquest on one group of flood victims, the jury added a rider which reflected public opinion: 'We feel strongly that the consequences of this disaster might have been avoided if warning had been sent down the east coast.' Belatedly, the Government recognised the deficiency. The Waverley Committee, set up as a result of the flooding, recommended the establishment of a Storm Tide Warning Service (STWS). This came into service on 15 September 1953 and each year operates for a period covering the large equinoctial spring tides of late August or early September until 30 April. The STWS is based on a comparison between predicted and observed tide levels at a network of tide gauges, although subsequent experience suggested that a location some 30 km east of Aberdeen was the best place for an early warning station for flooding along the whole of the east coast and the Thames estuary (NERC, 1972). Eventually, a network of automatic data-gathering stations will be operated jointly with Germany, the Netherlands and Belgium. Twelve hours before high tide, preliminary flood 'alerts', based mainly on meteorological analyses by the Meteorological Office, are sent to Water Authorities through the police. Tidal data transmitted from various points along the coastline are then analysed by hydrographers and may substantiate or negate the meteorologically-based alert. In the case of a substantiated alert, a further message is sent four hours before high tide. This 'danger warning' states by how much the tide is expected to exceed predictions and also indicates whether the danger level is likely to occur before the predicted time of high tide. Where an alert is not substantiated a 'cancellation' message is sent four hours before high tide. A third type of four-hour message, an 'alert confirmed', designed to avoid a large number of false alarms, is sent if it is thought that the tide will be within plus or minus 15 cm of danger level. Obviously the number of warnings issued by the STWS varies from season to season. According to Townsend (1975), however, approximate seasonal averages are 100 alerts, of which 75 are subsequently cancelled, 20 continue as 'alert confirmed' messages and five become 'danger warnings'.

This type of warning system works well in situations where the storm surge moves progressively along the coast, as it tends to in the North Sea. Where the surge takes the form of an oscillating seiche, however, it is normally necessary to model the boundary and meteorological conditions and attempt a forward extrapolation on the basis of tide-gauge information for the section of coastline at risk. Such an approach was reported by Robinson *et al.* (1973) for Adriatic surges at Venice and by Labzovskii (1966) for surges in the Leningrad region of the Gulf of Finland.

It was seen in chapter 4 that along many coasts, storm surges result from the effects of hurricanes, typhoons and other similar tropical storms. To a large extent, then, the adequacy of a coastal flood forecasting and warning system is dependent upon the accuracy with which the path of such storms can be forecast. Until recently this has been limited, partly by computer capacity and speed. Official warnings of hurricanes in the United States, for example, are normally issued only 12 to 18 hours in advance, when it is at last possible to tell fairly precisely where they will strike. Improved computers have recently facilitated the construction of much more detailed models which promise to extend considerably the warning period (Anon, 1973).

Other improvements in coastal flood forecasting are being brought about by more sophisticated data-collection techniques. For many years, radar detection of echo lines associated with wind shifts in coastal areas threatened by heavy flooding has been used to improve forecast lead-times. For example, Johnson (1967) showed how the careful analysis of the radar presentation in the early morning hours of 10 November 1962 permitted a four-hour advance notice of the flooding at Atlantic City, New Jersey. In the United States the basic weather radar network is supplemented by Defence Department aerial reconnaissance of

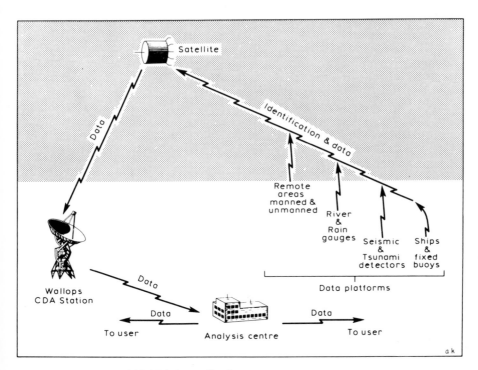

Figure 7.5   The SMS/GOES data collection system
Source: Jensen (1974).

tropical storms in the eastern Pacific, Atlantic ocean, Caribbean sea and Gulf of Mexico in accordance with the provisions of the 'National Hurricane Operations Plan'. In addition, extratropical winter storm reconnaissance is flown in the western Atlantic in compliance with the 'National East Coast Winter Storms Operations Plan'. Hurricane and winter storm forecasts are further aided by the operation of the Ocean Weather Station 'Hotel' off the east coast (Jensen, 1974). Finally, weather satellite data provide an increasingly effective complement to other forms of flood forecasting data. In the United States major improvements in short-range forecasting are expected as a result of the recent launching of the Synchronous Meteorological Satellites (SMS), prototypes of the Geostationary Operational Environmental Satellite (GOES) system. The SMS/GOES system will provide almost continuous surveillance of the development and movement of destructive weather systems, such as tropical storms and hurricanes and major mid-latitude storms. It includes a highly developed data collection system (see figure 7.5) for obtaining environmental information observed at remote locations and relaying it to a central location for further distribution (Jensen, 1974).

The first effective tsunami warning system was developed after the 1946 tsunami disaster in Hawaii. This system, initially known as the Seismic Sea-Wave Warning System (SSWWS), consists of a network of 50 tidal and 31 seismographic stations centred on Honolulu but scattered from Alaska to the southern tip of South America and west to Hong Kong and was fully described by U.S. Coast and Geodetic Survey (1965). The tidal instruments disregard water movements resulting from normal wind and tides, but when waves with a critical period are formed a warning is automatically triggered and transmitted to Honolulu. At the same time the seismographic information permits preliminary determination of the epicentre and the two sets of information can be combined with information on wave-travel times and ocean depths to enable forecasts of the speed of travel and probable time of arrival of the tsunami at selected locations. The system has been operated by the U.S. National Oceanic and Atmospheric Administration since 1973.

8 Human Response to the Flood Hazard: I Introduction and Possible Adjustments

INTRODUCTION

In most parts of the world floodplains and coasts have attracted economic development and settlements. In arid areas floodplains were moist oases of agricultural development and in rugged areas they often represented the only extensive tracts of flat land for easy cultivation and communication. The proximity to water, which first proved an agricultural attraction, later became an industrial one in some areas, and on both floodplains and coasts there developed the use of water for transportation and as a trade link.

The economic advantages of floodplains and coasts did not, however, automatically lead to permanent floodplain settlements. In Britain, for example, the early settlers of pre-Roman times preferred the high, drier land and shunned the damp and marshy lowlands. Later settlement came down into the valleys but rarely into the valley-bottoms, concentrating instead on relatively safer minor eminences and river terraces. It was not, in fact, until the Industrial Revolution that indiscriminate floodplain development took place (Nixon, 1963).

Many of the initial attractions of the floodplains have by now diminished. Today water transport is comparatively unimportant except for bulk products; water supplies are usually piped from the relatively unpolluted upland areas of river catchments; the water-wheel has largely gone out of use; modern techniques of highway engineering enable roads to be built across rugged terrain instead of being forced to follow congested valley routes; and many of the settlements that have developed in floodplain locations are often too congested for modern traffic and industrial development. Despite all this, the encroachment of settlement on to floodplains continues to increase partly because of the geographical inertia whereby existing settlements continue to grow through peripheral accretion. Sometimes this encroachment takes place in ignorance of the flood hazard. Often, however, the encroacher is fully cognisant of the flood hazard but goes ahead in the belief or hope that society will come to his aid either in the form of improved flood protection or, after the event, with financial assistance from governmental or other organisations. By the same process of geographical inertia existing settlements have continued to develop on lowland coasts even more markedly than on floodplains, with an accelerating growth in recent years of recreational and resort settlement in the form of summer cabins, caravans and second homes, etc.

Clearly, man's affinity for floodplains and coasts exposes him to the risk of flooding which would, in any case, have taken place. This re-emphasises a theme

113

which has been implicit in earlier discussions in this book: that floods only become a hazard when they impinge unfavourably upon human activity, and that the flood hazard must therefore be considered not simply as a physical but also as a socio-economic phenomenon. Although this seemingly obvious truth has long been recognised by some workers (for example White, 1939), its implications appear to have been grasped only recently by planners, legislators and engineers concerned with ameliorating the flood hazard. Many, if not the majority of, floods go unremarked either because they occur in uninhabited areas or because they inconvenience only a handful of people. Some floods are favourably received, as when the flood deposits improve soil fertility or when the flood waters recharge depleted groundwater supplies. However, this chapter and the subsequent two are concerned with flooding as a hazard and with man's response to that hazard.

The flood hazard comprises many aspects including, according to Hewitt and Burton (1971), structural and erosional damage, loss of life and property, contamination of food, water and other materials, disruption of socio-economic activity including transport and communications, and the spoiling of agricultural land. The principal relationships between flood hazard and response were formalised by Kates (1971), some of whose ideas are incorporated into figure 8.1 which shows schematically the main facets of man's response to the flood hazard. According to Kates, human response is determined partly by the nature of the hazard which, as we have seen, is the result of the joint interaction between physical and socio-economic processes, and partly by the characteristics of the decision-maker, whether he is an individual floodplain occupant or farmer, government official, industrial production manager, etc. In particular, the characteristics of the individual decision-maker and of the flood hazard itself combine to influence perception of the flood hazard, which may be sharp, blurred or non-existent. This helps to explain why response is often not well matched to either the probability or the observed distribution of flooding. Figure 8.1 illustrates that, in systems terminology, there is positive feedback in the sense that response to the flood hazard may modify the three inputs to the 'system' – the physical and socio-economic processes and the characteristics of the decision-maker.

The extreme responses to the flood hazard are, on the one hand, indiscriminate development of floodplains and flood-prone coastal areas, thereby inviting considerable damage, suffering and loss of life, and, on the other hand, the complete abandonment of these areas, which would clearly represent gross waste of a valuable resource (Bue, 1967). In reality an intermediate view normally prevails in which response is strongly related to perception of the hazard which, in turn, is very much dependent upon experience. Kates (1962) found that past knowledge and experience of floods is related, although not in a particularly simple manner, to the perceived probability distribution of floods, but memory is short and all too often the next flood again catches an area unprepared. Perception is also obscured by the irregularity of flooding in many floodplain and virtually all coastal areas. Thus, Harding and Parker (1972) interviewed a sample of occupants of those parts of the Severn floodplain near Shrewsbury which were inundated by the worst recorded flood, in 1947, and found that only 45 per cent of them felt there was a flood problem in the area and only 27 per cent thought there would be another flood in the future! Finally, the perception of flood

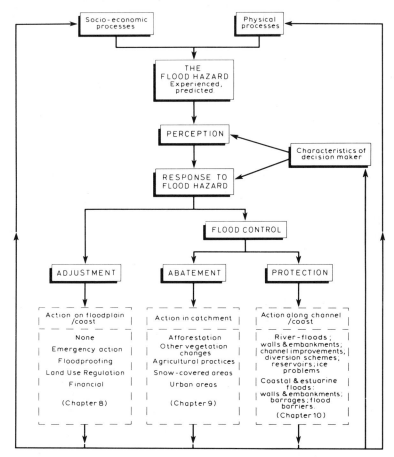

Figure 8.1   The main elements of man's response to the flood hazard

hazard is moderated by one's concept of floods and of flood causality. This was clearly illustrated by a survey reported by Gately (1973), which showed that floodplain occupants on the lower Severn believed there were at least six main 'causes' of flooding, the primary one being that the lower Severn is tidal and the second interference with the river course by engineers. One explanation, advanced by three of the 42 interviewees, was related to the biblical account in Genesis. As Gately explained: 'If the water enters the house, that is an act of Nature; if one is driven upstairs or onto the roof, that is an act of God; but if one should have so incurred His displeasure that one is swept away, then *that* is a flood.'

The main types of response to the preceived flood hazard are detailed in figure

8.1. Basically, the choice lies between moderating human activities in flood-prone areas and moderating the floods themselves, either by action taken in the catchment area of a river or by action taken along the channel or coast. In other words, the choice is between *adjustment, abatement* or *protection* which form, respectively, the subject matters of chapters 8, 9 and 10. For a number of reasons the most frequent choice until comparatively recently was that of protection by means of the physical 'control' of the river or sea. Gradually, as general awareness of the socio-economic aspects of flooding heightened, particularly through the work of Gilbert F. White in the Department of Geography at Chicago University, adjustment became a more widely canvassed and more imaginative alternative to the engineering approach. A third possibility, long applied in the field of erosion control, is that of abatement by means of improved catchment management techniques. The continuing development of our understanding of flood-producing processes has opened up the possibility of replacing the previous *ad hoc* attempts at catchment manipulation by a scientifically based approach to flood abatement.

Often rapid scientific and applied development is accompanied by a duplication, confusion and imprecision of terminology. Thus, 'flood control' has been used to refer not only to the broad field of response to the flood hazard – that is adjustment, abatement and protection – but also specifically to protective works. Similarly, 'adjustment' has sometimes been taken to include protection and abatement. Goddard (1969) preferred 'floodplain management' as a comprehensive term including flood control and all other possible responses. Unfortunately, the terms seems, by definition, to exclude abatement procedures carried out beyond the floodplain in the remainder of the catchment area. In this book, therefore, no attempt is made to adopt or adapt a comprehensive term other than 'response to the flood hazard'. Instead, the threefold terminology of adjustment, abatement and protection is pursued with the understanding that adjustment implies 'man control' and abatement and protection together imply 'flood control'. The change of emphasis away from the naive approach of the engineer has now received wide acceptance; and, significantly, a report by the Task Force on Federal flood control policy in the United States (Task Force, 1966) opens with these words: 'The Nation needs a broader and more unified national program for managing flood losses. Flood protection has been immensely helpful in many parts of the country – and must be continued. Beyond this, additional tools and integrated policies are required to promote sound and economic development of the flood plains.'

Some of these 'additional tools' are discussed in the following section, and subsequently in the context of 'Flood Abatement' (chapter 9), before consideration of the traditional approach of 'Flood Protection' in chapter 10.

POSSIBLE ADJUSTMENTS

There can be no doubt that in the discussion of human adjustment to the flood hazard the work of Gilbert F. White played a dominant pioneering and developmental role. It was White who first showed clearly what now seems self-evident, that human beings adjust in a number of ways to the flood hazard and that their

Plate 1   Front of advancing floodwave in Mexican Springs wash on 23 July 1941. Depth of flow approximately 60 cm. (With acknowledgement to the USDA Agricultural Research Service)

Plate 2   An ice jam on the Ottawa River, Ohio. (Redrawn from an original photograph by R. E. Laudick, Jr., published in USGS Circular 418, by permission of the photographer)

Plate 3 Coastal flooding and flood damage at Jaywick Sands on the east coast of England, February 1953. (© Aerofilms Ltd)

Plate 4 Remains of the failed Malpasset dam near Fréjus, France in December 1959. (With acknowledgement to Associated Newspapers Ltd)

Plate 5 Coarse deposition on the upper fringes of a floodplain after the passage of a flood-wave. Note abrasion of trunks by debris. The perched boulder is 1m. in diameter. (This photograph appeared as Fig. 10 in USGS Professional Paper 422-M. With acknowledgement to the U.S. Geological Survey)

Plate 6   Flooding of Lothair (bottom) and of Hazard, Kentucky by the North Fork of the Kentucky River during March 1963 clearly illustrates the dangers of indiscriminate floodplain development. (Photograph by Billy Davis, courtesy of *The Louisville Courier-Journal and Times*)

Plate 7   Aerial view of experimental forest cutting to reduce flood discharges and improve the timing of water yields at Fool Creek, Fraser Experimental Forest, Colorado. (U.S Forest Service photograph)

Plate 8 Three stages in the reversion of the widened River Tame near Birmingham, England; 1932, 1937 and 1958. (With acknowledgement to the Severn–Trent Water Authority)

Plate 9   Channel improvement on Pymmes Brook, Edmonton, London. (With acknowledgement to the Lea Division of the Thames Water Authority)

Plate 10   Aerial view of the downstream end of the Coronation relief channel, Spalding, England. The relief channel is the wide channel at the top. (© Aerofilms Ltd)

Plate 11 Views from Lookout Mountain, Tennessee, showing the record flooding at Chattanooga in March 1867 and the improved channel of the Tennessee River in 1967. (With acknowledgement to the Tennessee Valley Authority)

adjustments may represent a viable complement to, and in some cases substitute for, the control of water in river channels or the wholesale removal of intensive land-use from flood-prone areas. As Miller (1966) observed, White considered that changes in land-use could be made selectively and in effective combination with emergency action, structural changes and other measures that imply accepting a degree of coexistence of man and water on the same land. Some of the possibilities that White and his fellow workers canvassed, not all of them feasible in a particular flood hazard area, will now be briefly considered.

No adjustment

The most common adjustment to the flood hazard in both floodplains and coastal areas is simply to suffer and bear the losses when they occur. This is certainly the response in countries where the people are too poor to do anything else or where there is ignorance either of the flood hazard or of any alternative response. Even in advanced areas, however, individual householders or business firms may choose to bear the occasional loss whether or not they have deliberately set aside reserves against this contingency. As White (1964) pointed out, some large firms make specific provision for such reserves while others regard flood loss as an unpredictable event to be covered by a general contingency account, and still others make no provision whatever against the flood hazard.

The growing emphasis on assessing all types of response to the flood hazard in benefit–cost terms (see chapter 11) implies that in many cases bearing the loss may be the cheapest of the range of possible adjustments, certainly as far as the expenditure of public monies is concerned. In most developed countries, however, the experience of being flooded usually results in some conscious adjustment intended to offset future losses.

Emergency action

A widely adopted adjustment involves emergency action following the receipt of a flood warning. By implication, emergency action constitutes a more or less unpremeditated response to a flood warning and involves varying degrees of prior preparation by private individuals, but often a high degree of prior organisation by the responsible public services. Emergency action usually encompasses the removal of persons and property from the flood hazard area, the protection of immovable property and the rescheduling of certain operations. The success of such measures will depend largely on the amount of advance warning that can be given (which varies widely in both coastal and valley-bottom situations, as discussed in chapter 7) and in part on the type of evacuation, protection and rescheduling which has to be carried out.

Although the costs of emergency action are often high, this approach may still represent one of the most economical adjustments to the flood hazard, and many authorities regard it as one of the most important adjustments. In addition, field surveys indicate that the occupants of flood-prone areas feel strongly about the need for emergency action programmes and are keenly aware of the real or apparent deficiences. (Penning-Rowsell, 1972).

White (1939) described the three main types of emergency adjustment. First, even with a very short warning time, it is usually possible to *remove* people and certain livestock, goods and possessions, provided suitable transportation is available. As far as people and livestock are concerned, this normally means evacuation by vehicle or on foot; but, in the case of goods and possessions, it may simply be a question of taking them upstairs. Both types of action may meet with problems. Large-scale evacuation may cause congestion and ultimately the breakdown of transport facilities. In terms of removal of goods upstairs, as Hoyt and Langbein (1955) observed, 'The factory-owner has a hoist or lift, but a homeowner cannot hope to carry his piano upstairs'. Secondly, it may be possible to *protect* immovable goods and possessions by making them less susceptible to damage by water, silt and floating debris. Protection might involve packing heavy machinery with grease to keep out silt, sandbagging or 'battening down', simply tying up a boat or mooring down structures which could become buoyant and thereby constitute floating hazards. Finally, it is possible to *reschedule* certain operations, although in most cases a lengthy warning time would be required. Thus crops may be harvested early or planted late, traffic rerouted, manufacturing operations rearranged, and supplies accumulated for homes and factories which will be isolated by floodwaters.

Clearly, these actions will be more effective in reducing damage and loss of life in some circumstances than in others. On the whole, removal is highly successful where it is possible – as with the contents of a house, store or garage; but it is virtually impossible to remove the buildings themselves. The success of emergency protection is often high but, despite the precautions taken, some damage usually does occur, particularly to machinery and mechanical equipment. Similarly, the success of rescheduling is highly variable so that, while the rerouting of goods in transit may be successful, premature harvesting will almost certainly result in reduction of yields and quality of crops, and delayed planting in total crop failure. Tables prepared by J. R. Sheaffer (in White *et al.*, 1958; White, 1964) show in detail the relative effectiveness of the various types of emergency action in a variety of rural and urban situations.

It has already been observed that emergency action often constitutes an unprepared response on the part of the individual occupier of flood hazard areas, despite the fact that in those same areas the responsible public authorities are well organised and prepared. In the United States, for example, the Army Corps of Engineers (1959) recommended a four-stage plan for flood emergencies. At the *alert* stage key personnel are alerted through the warning system and equipment and supplies are checked; at the *activation* stage personnel are called to duty and equipment and supplies dispatched to duty locations; at the *operation* stage the various emergency procedures are carried out; and at the *deactivation and reporting* stage procedures are reviewed, necessary revisions made and the mopping-up operation begun. Since, ultimately, the success of emergency actions will depend very largely on the degree of community preparedness and alertness, a continuing programme of public education is desirable. Again using the United States as an example, the National Oceanic and Atmospheric Administration publishes and circulates widely its flood safety rules which are reproduced in table 8.1. Attempts to increase the alertness of the community must, however, guard against the 'cry wolf' syndrome. A continued

TABLE 8.1
FLOOD SAFETY RULES

Before the flood

1 Keep on hand materials like sandbags, plywood, plastic sheeting and lumber.
2 Install check valves in building sewer traps, to prevent flood water from backing up in sewer drains.
3 Arrange for auxiliary electrical supplies for hospitals and other operations which are critically affected by power failure.
4 Keep first aid supplies at hand.
5 Keep your automobile fueled; if electric power is cut off, filling stations may not be able to operate pumps for several days.
6 Keep a stock of food which requires little cooking and no refrigeration; electric power may be interrupted.
7 Keep a portable radio, emergency cooking equipment, lights and flashlights in working order.

When you receive a flood warning

8 Store drinking water in clean bathtubs, and in various containers. Water service may be interrupted.
9 If forced to leave your home and time permits, move essential items to safe ground; fill tanks to keep them from floating away; grease immovable machinery.
10 Move to a safe area before access is cut off by flood water.

During the flood

11 Avoid areas subject to sudden flooding.
12 Do not attempt to cross a flowing stream where water is above your knees.
13 Do not attempt to drive over a flooded road – you can be stranded, and trapped.

After the flood

14 Do not use fresh food that has come in contact with flood waters.
15 Test drinking water for potability: wells should be pumped out and the water tested before drinking.
16 Seek necessary medical care at nearest hospital. Food, clothing, shelter and first aid are available at Red Cross shelters.
17 Do not visit disaster area; your presence might hamper rescue and other emergency operations.
18 Do not handle live electrical equipment in wet areas; electrical equipment should be checked and dried before returning to service.
19 Use flashlights, not lanterns or torches, to examine buildings; flammables may be inside.
20 Report broken utility lines to appropriate authorities.

FLASH FLOODS

Flash flood waves, moving at incredible speeds, can roll boulders, tear out trees, destroy buildings and bridges, and scour out new channels. Killing walls of water can reach 10 to 20 feet. You won't always have warning that these deadly, sudden floods are coming.

WHEN A FLASH FLOOD WARNING IS ISSUED FOR YOUR AREA OR THE MOMENT YOU FIRST REALISE THAT A FLASH FLOOD IS IMMINENT, ACT QUICKLY TO SAVE YOURSELF. YOU MAY HAVE ONLY SECONDS.

Get out of areas subject to flooding. Avoid already flooded areas. Do not attempt to cross a flowing stream on foot where water is above your knees. If driving, know the depth of water in a dip before crossing. The road may not be intact under the water. If the vehicle stalls, abandon it immediately and seek higher ground – rapidly rising water may engulf the vehicle and its occupants and sweep them away. Be especially cautious at night when it is harder to recognise flood dangers.

DURING ANY FLOOD EMERGENCY, STAY TUNED TO YOUR RADIO OR TELEVISION STATION
INFORMATION FROM NOAA AND CIVIL EMERGENCY FORCES MAY SAVE YOUR LIFE

state of alertness through a long floodless period, particularly if there have been one or more false alarms, is difficult to maintain and may indeed give way to a sense of complacency which will inevitably exacerbate the next major flood disaster.

As expected, emergency action is a more effective adjustment to flood hazard in those areas where the frequency of flooding is high. This point was made by Sewell (1969) who observed that the effectiveness of emergency action would also increase with an increase in the flood-to-peak interval and a decrease in both flood duration and the velocity of the floodwaters.

Floodproofing

It has long been realised that there are a number of ways in which a combination of emergency action with structural changes or the adoption of appropriate structural design standards can be used to reduce the vulnerability of individual buildings and units to the flood hazard. Hoyt and Langbein (1955) outlined some of the possible courses of action, such as the installation of submersible electrical circuits, the anchorage of 'floatable' buildings, proper bridge and culvert design to avoid damage by floodwaters, the bulkheading of buildings, the sealing of non-essential openings in buildings below flood level, and so on. Later Sheaffer (1960) coined the term 'floodproofing' to designate this particular adjustment to the flood hazard and suggested that it would be most appropriate in the following situations: where moderate flooding with low stage, low velocity and short duration is experienced; where the traditional type of flood protection is not feasible; where individuals desire to solve their flood problems without collective action or where collective action is not possible; where cultural groups shun government aid and subsidy but wish to moderate their vulnerability to the flood hazard; where activities which demand coastal or riverine locations in order to function need some degree of protection; and where a particular resource manager wants a higher degree of protection than that provided by an existing or proposed flood control project.

Floodproofing measures range widely from temporary emergency action taken upon receipt of a flood warning, for example sandbagging doorways and other openings, to permanent, long-term building – and site – design features. Accordingly, Sheaffer (1960) classified floodproofing measures as 'permanent', 'contingent' or 'emergency' and in a much reproduced table (see table 8.2) set out some of the relationships between the type of measure, the material protected and the prerequisites to its effective operation. The main components of a floodproofing programme are likely to involve structural *design changes*, the adoption and implementation of suitable *design standards* and *land filling*.

Structural design changes are of four main types. First, there are anchorage devices designed to prevent structures being washed away. In Britain most houses are of such substantial construction that there is no possibility of their floating, but in much of the world the timber-clad frame-house typical of North America is common. These are likely to become buoyant in substantial depths of water and may be anchored down by steel cables, as are similar buildings in areas affected by hurricanes. In most countries considerable dangers are posed by large chemical and oil storage containers which are buoyant, particularly when only part-full, thereby suffering pipeline rupture and spillage. Hoyt and Langbein (1955) referred to the disaster at Titusville and Oil City in Pennsylvania on 4 June 1892 when oil on the floodwaters ignited causing such terrific heat that every house in the flooded area was burned to the water level and more than 130 lives were lost. Secondly, buildings and other structures can be modified to keep water out. Such modifications may consist of sandbagging doorways, temporary or permanent bulkheading, the bricking up of unnecessary windows and other openings in walls, the installation of valves and cutoffs on drains and sewers to prevent backing-up, and the waterproofing of underground telephone cables and electrical circuits. A third type of structural design change is frequently used where the original design (of a wooden building, for instance) makes it virtually impossible to keep flood water out. In such cases alterations can facilitate the throughflow of water, thereby reducing buoyancy

TABLE 8.2

STRUCTURAL ADJUSTMENTS AS
FLOODPROOFING MEASURES

Measure	Material protected	Class of measure	Prerequisites Structural	Hydrological
Seepage control	St–Co	P–C	Well constructed	None
Sewer adjustment	St–Co	P–C	None	H–W
Permanent closure	St–Co	P	Impervious walls	H–S
Openings protected	St–Co	C–E	Impervious walls	H–S–W
Interiors protected	St	P–C	None	S–W
Protective coverings	St–Co	P–C–E	None	H–W–F
Fire protection	St–Co	P	None	None
Appliance protection	Co	E	None	W
Utilities service	Co	P–C–E	None	S–W–V
Roadbed protection	St	P–E	Sound structure	H–W–V–D
Elevation	St–Co	P–C–E	Sound structure	S–W–V–F
Temporary removal	Co	E	None	W–F
Rescheduling	Co	E	Alternatives	W
Proper salvage	Co		None	None
Watertight caps	Co	P–C	None	W
Proper anchorage	St–Co	P–C	Sound structure	S–W–V–D
Underpinning	St	P	Sound structure	V
Timber treatment	St	P	None	None
Deliberate flooding	St–Co	E	None	None
Structural design	St–Co	P	Design	H–S
Reorganised use	Co	P	Alternatives	None

St = structure   P = permanent   H = hydrostatic pressure   F = flood-to-peak interval
Co = content   C = contingent   S = stage of flood   V = velocity of flow
   E = emergency   W = warning   D = duration of flood

(After Sheaffer (1960))

or hydrostatic pressures. Finally, some structures (including some types of house) may be either temporarily or permanently raised above the most frequent flood levels.

Most of such preventative measures are normally more easily and economically provided for at the time of construction. Hence the stronger stress now being laid in flood hazard areas on the adoption and implementation of suitable design standards, through building codes and planning regulations, to ensure the integrity of structures during flooding. Design standards may involve consideration of the strength and susceptibility to deterioration of basic materials under flood conditions, or the building of lower stories without windows and with some means of watertight sealing of doors so that, even if the building is surrounded by water, its contents can be kept dry and its activities continue to function normally. This approach has been used successfully with such buildings as telephone exchanges (Linsley and Franzini, 1972), in which the operation is either automatic or requires minimum attendance of personnel. Alternatively, floodproofed designs may involve elevating buildings and using the ground level inter-pile area as a car park which can be quickly evacuated at short notice. This approach has even been adopted in some tent and caravan sites in Europe. Piling can also give additional stability to buildings in flood-prone areas, notably where rapid erosion by floodwaters is likely. Particular attention has also been paid to the design of culverts and bridges. Thus, in parts of the North American prairies, bridges designed against the 100-year flood which were destroyed almost immediately have been replaced by bridges designed against the 5-year flood but installed on hinges so that they can be moved rapidly out of the way of the floodwaters (Newson, 1975).

The elevation of the ground surface through the use of landfill may greatly reduce the impact of flooding. Depending on its height, landfill may or may not be associated with individually flood-proofed buildings. As Sewell (1969) observed, this approach is normally only feasible when it is undertaken prior to construction in an urban or industrial area and becomes prohibitively expensive once such development has taken place. Unless carefully controlled, landfill may encroach into the floodway thereby exacerbating the flood problem (see next section).

Land-use regulation

The purpose of land-use regulation is to obtain the beneficial use of floodplains and flood-prone coastal areas with a minimum of flood damage and a minimum expenditure on flood protection. In other words, it is to promote such land usage that the benefits derived from using the land exceed the flood damage plus the cost of providing a specified degree of protection (Bue, 1967). Some of the many adverse implications of human occupancy of floodplains and coastal areas have been repeatedly emphasised, as has the impracticability, in most cases, of abandoning such areas altogether. Land-use regulation aims, therefore, at a policy which combines the abandonment of limited parts of the flood-prone areas with the careful regulation of land-use in the remainder of such areas. In the floodplain situation, Murphy (1958) distinguished between the *floodway* – the channel and those adjacent parts of the floodplain necessary for the conveyance of a selected flood discharge, for example the 100-year flood – and the remainder of the floodplain, sometimes referred to as the *floodway fringe*. He suggested that the aims of land-use regulation are to prevent encroachment on the floodway cross section, to prevent carelessness in the maintenance of channels, to prevent the installation of structures which, if they became buoyant in flood conditions, could cause damage to bridges and other property, to restrict uses which would constitute hazards to health and welfare, to protect land owners from being victimised and to restrict uses which could result in undue claims upon the public purse. In general terms, then, the purpose of land-use regulation is to maintain an adequate floodway and to regulate land-use development alongside it. Similar concepts can be applied in coastal areas.

The need for land-use regulation has increased, partly because previously unused flood-prone areas are gradually being brought into use, but mainly because of the increasing intensity of land-use in those flood-prone areas utilised for decades or even centuries for flood-tolerant agricultural purposes, but which are now subjected to the increasing pressures of urbanisation, industrialisation and the improvement of transportation routes. In Britain, Nottingham and Gloucester are two of the most frequently quoted examples of urban encroachment into the floodway (see figure 8.2). Although numerous additional examples could also be quoted, the situation is considerably less serious than in many other countries. For example Burton (1961) concluded that Britain has, for the most part, avoided some of the costly urban floodplain development which has taken place in the United States and which is exemplified in plate 6. Particularly severe encroachments on floodways have resulted where landfill is used to facilitate the construction of buildings or roads. Regulation also becomes a political pressure-point when governments are repeatedly called upon to provide financial assistance to flood-stricken areas. Thus in the United States the Task Force on federal flood control policy (Task Force, 1966) recommended that '. . . provision should be made for State regulation of floodplain encroachment and, where appropriate, for local land-use regulation as conditions for the construction of Federal and federally assisted projects'. In some areas, of course, the need for regulation has long been understood. For example, in Britain, the Netherlands and some other countries in Europe washlands or 'winter beds' have been effectively established for centuries. These are normally maintained as pasture land and kept free from urban encroachments and other obstructions. This tradition has been preserved in recent new-town development in Britain where temporary controlled flood-storage has been provided on recreation land.

The method of land-use regulation which is adopted will depend upon the immediate objectives of that regulation. One possibility is the type of transhumance which has been practised for centuries in the lower Nile valley, whereby the floodplain farmers leave their land as the flood waters rise and return to cultivate it as the floods recede. Such mobile adaptability is probably only feasible in the context of a regular, annual flood cycle. Normally there are two objectives of land-use regulation: one is the *maintenance of 'status quo'* where there is already a low intensity of land-use, in which case the methods adopted might be

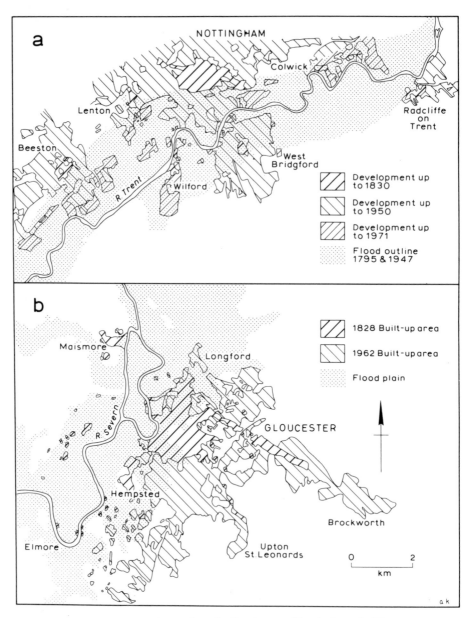

a

NOTTINGHAM

Colwick

Lenton

Radcliffe
on
Trent

Beeston

West
Bridgford

R Trent

Wilford

	Development up to 1830
	Development up to 1950
	Development up to 1971
	Flood outline 1795 & 1947

b

Maismore

Longford

R. Severn

GLOUCESTER

Hempsted

Brockworth

Elmore

Upton
St.Leonards

	1828 Built-up area
	1962 Built-up area
	Flood plain

0   2
km

Figure 8.2   Urban encroachment into the floodway: *a*, Nottingham; *b*, Gloucester
Source: *a*, Severn–Trent Water Authority; *b*, Penning-Rowsell and Parker (1973).

the prevention of subdivision and further building development on agricultural land; or second, the reduction in intensity of land-use, especially in urban and industrial areas, where the objective is a *change of land-use*. Changing land-use in urban or or other intensively developed areas is normally both so difficult and so expensive that the inconvenience of being flooded from time to time is preferred. This is particularly true where, as in the western United States, urban areas grew rapidly and were often well established before the full magnitude of the flood hazard was apparent. Changes have been effected in some urban areas, however, and would be positively desirable in many more. In some cases dramatic changes in urban land-use have been achieved as a direct result of a particularly severe flood. In the United Kingdom, for example, many of the houses and other buildings in Lynmouth which were demolished by the August 1952 flood (see pp. 19–21) were not rebuilt but were instead replaced by an improved river channel, public parks and gardens and car parks. Burton *et al.* (1969) referred to similar instances in some of the eastern coastal areas of the United States, observing that 'Nature herself may be an instrument of land-use change. . .'. For the most part, however, dramatic reductions in the intensity of urban land use in flood-prone areas are possible only where the land concerned is purchased by a State or local government agency. Some of the most frequently adopted methods of land-use regulation, particularly in Britain and the United States, will now be briefly discussed.

The outright *purchase of land* by government agencies, through a form of compulsory purchase order, solely to reduce flood damages is still comparatively rare, although it has increased greatly in the United States in recent years. The method is often used more obliquely, however, in two types of situation. First, land may be purchased for public uses, often recreational, which are flood tolerant and effectively inhibit further intensification of land-use. The development, through the National Park Service, of the Assateague National Seashore is a major example of this approach in the eastern United States. Secondly, where the older sections of urban areas are located in flood-prone areas programmes of 'urban renewal' may be implemented which not only remove buildings from floodable areas but also create more public open space and more parking space, thereby adding to the attractiveness and the accessibility of the central business district.

Another method of land-use regulation frequently applied in the United States is the establishment of lines or limits on the floodplain beyond which further encroachment may not take place. In some cases channel *encroachment limits* are defined separately from floodway encroachment limits but in all cases the primary objective is to ensure an unobstructed floodway capable of accommodating the passage of a designated frequency flood. The basic concepts are illustrated in figure 8.3. A narrower floodway than that required for the transmission of the unconfined flood may be acceptable provided that the resulting increase in water surface elevation (ΔH) does not exceed 30 cm. In such cases developments in the floodway fringe area will need to be raised on fill or protected to the appropriate level by other floodproofing measures. Land-use in the floodway should be severely restricted to, for example, agriculture, recreation, car parks or the construction of improvements not subject to damage by inundation. In the United States the criteria for setting encroachment limits varies from one state or local government to another and may range from the annual flood to seven times the mean annual flood, or in a few local instances, to floods with estimated frequencies of as little as once in 100 years (White, 1964).

Implicit in the distinction between floodway and floodway fringe, and in the

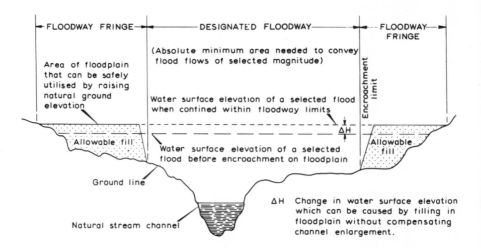

Figure 8.3   Floodplain cross-section showing the concept of encroachment limits
Source: U.S. Army Corps of Engineers (1973).

establishment of encroachment lines, is the concept of land-use *zoning* whereby, through an ordinance or by-law, increasingly severe restrictions are placed on land-use as one approaches the river or sea. According to U.S. Army Corps of Engineers (1973), '. . . selective zoning ensures the most beneficial use of flood-plain lands while safeguarding the safety, health and welfare of the total com-munity'. The floodway thus constitutes a prohibitive zone in which land-use is confined to the categories referred to in the preceding paragraph. The floodway fringe is also a restrictive zone in which land-use is limited by the detailed zoning criteria for a particular area and by an accepted degree of flood risk, usually related directly to the frequency of flooding and requiring the avail-ability of a substantial amount of data on flood magnitudes and frequencies. Land-use zoning is equally applicable in coastal areas and was briefly discussed by Burton *et al*. (1969) in the context of the Atlantic coast of the United States.

Floodplain zoning makes sense only within the context of more general plan-ning regulations. In the United States this is achieved through the medium of zoning ordinances and regulations analagous to other types of zoning law. In other countries the procedure may differ greatly, as exemplified by the situation in the United Kingdom. Here most action on floodplain regulation is taken within the context of the Town and Country Planning Acts. The procedure appears to be an effective one which works, for the most part, in a negative way in that the various Town and Country Planning Acts do not specify the types of development which are permitted, but instead, by requiring planning permission for new development, have laid down in a piecemeal way what is not permitted. Under the terms of the now famous 'Medway Letter', rightly described by Burton (1961) as a 'major document' in the annals of flood control, the Ministry of Agriculture and Fisheries limited the areas to be included in drainage districts to those that will 'derive benefit or avoid danger' – land 2.4m (8 feet) or less above known flood levels in inland areas, 1.5m (5 feet) or less in coastal areas and no higher than flood level in urban areas. Applications to a Planning Authority for permission to build or rebuild in drainage districts are referred to the appropriate Water Authority which normally recommends against granting permission if the site is in a flood hazard area. Refusal of permission by the Planning Authority may then be the subject of appeal to the Department of the Environment.

The early history of planning developments affecting floodplain regulation in the United Kingdom were well reviewed by Burton (1961). Subsequently the Town Planning Acts of 1947, 1951, 1953, 1954 and 1959 were repealed and the whole of their provisions subsumed in the Town and Country Planning Act of 1962 which has itself been amended on a number of occasions. Under the terms of this Act compensation may be payable if planning permission is refused or is granted subject to conditions. However, there is no compensation on a refusal of planning permission to develop land liable to flooding (Heap, 1969). Regulation of the use of drainage districts for building and other development has been achieved not only through the medium of the Town and Country Planning Acts but also by the passing of local government by-laws which may, for example, require that new buildings in flood-prone areas are raised on landfill. Obviously, compliance with such regulations can prove so costly that, in effect, the by-law acts as an encroachment line (Burton, 1961).

Although the United Kingdom situation generally works well, some authorities feel that in the areas worst affected by flooding there is need for further control, possibly in the form of 'statutorily designated areas'. Penning-Rowsell and Parker (1973) observed that this is a planning provision which has been used effectively during the past thirty years to control development in particular problem areas. Thus areas have been designated as National Parks, Areas of Outstanding Natural Beauty, Green Belts, Conservation Areas and General Improvement Areas. In each case the aim of statutory designation has been to assist planning authorities in areas where repeated cases must be presented against requests for permission to develop. Penning-Rowsell and Parker (1973) suggest that the designation of Flood Risk Areas might similarly assist Water Authorities and other organisations involved in resisting or regulating development.

Although land-use regulation is one of the main adjustments to the flood hazard, its potential role as the most important adjustment is only just being realised. This is not due to failure to recognise its advantages, which are clear and relate primarily to a balance between land-use and the estimated flood risk so that optimum floodplain occupancy is achieved. Rather, the further development of floodplain regulation must await the solution of a number of problems associated with this particular adjustment. The main problems relate to the fact that it can normally operate only very slowly in an already developed area unless large-scale compulsory purchase and redevelopment are carried out. Also, in a free society, land-use regulation is inextricably linked with the politically biased process of planning and by definition, therefore, impinges upon individual liberty and freedom of choice. This means that regulations which impose restrictions on choice must be seen to be fair and soundly based if they are to stand up in court. Accordingly, where an attempt is made to relate land-use to flood risk, the necessary regulations must rest upon sound estimates of flood magnitude and frequency (see chapter 6) and on a satisfactory delimitation of the floodplain or other flood-prone areas. In the latter context there is often the additional problem, pointed out by Kates and White (1961), that a line drawn on a map to mark a floodplain boundary or floodplain zone may encourage a false sense of security and therefore additional development in the immediately adjacent upslope area. The line will eventually fail, unless it is drawn at the level of the maximum possible flood, and when flooding does occur damage beyond the line may be more pronounced than if it had never existed. This is a problem common to several types of flood adjustment and flood protection and will be further discussed in later chapters. Another major difficulty is that land-use regulation normally represents an effective adjustment to the flood hazard only where there is firm control by the central government. As Sewell (1969) observed, although some local authorities have enacted appropriate regulations, most fear that by doing so they will lose to more lenient authorities profitable activities which might otherwise have located in their own area. In such situations direction by the central government, or co-operation between the local authorities concerned, seems the only way for land-use regulation to succeed. In the context of the United States, Task Force (1966) discussed the respective roles of federal, state and local government.

Financial

There are a number of financial procedures which may be used to modify human response to the flood hazard. Some, like certain other types of adjustment and control, in the long term often exacerbate the flood problem rather than alleviate it. Two examples are: the governmental and private 'hat-passing' in the form of the *disaster fund appeals* which inevitably accompany any large flood disaster; and governmental charity dispensed in the form of *special assistance*, particularly to industry and commerce, through the medium of low-interest loans and tax relief. Those affected by 'natural' disasters now seem to expect such help as a matter of right and urgency. While one would not wish to see well-intentioned and charitable assistance refused to those in need, it is pertinent to observe that, of all 'natural' disasters, flooding is the most obviously self-inflicted; hence, in effect, disaster fund appeals and special assistance represent a levy imposed by an improvident minority upon the majority. It is important to recognise that such assistance does nothing to reduce the flood hazard; indeed, by encouraging rebuilding and modernisation of damaged property, it may substantially increase the potential flood damage. Moreover, the expectation that financial help will be available in any emergency may encourage new development in flood-prone areas, further adding to the problem.

It is clearly desirable to recognise that those who knowingly expose themselves to the greatest risks should assume the greatest financial burden. Schemes of *flood insurance*, with premiums adjusted to the degree of risk, seem to offer the best solution. Flood insurance may not reduce the occupancy of flood-prone areas, and may even increase it, but at least – as Krutilla (1966) observed – only those who can afford the premiums will continue occupancy. A system of flood insurance based on this premise could achieve the following long-term results (Task Force, 1966): (a) the decision to locate in a flood-prone area would be seen by society to be the responsibility of the individual occupant; (b) new development in flood-prone areas would be precluded unless the expected advantages exceeded or at least equalled the total public and private cost; (c) there would be an incentive to undertake measures of adjustment, abatement and control where the costs of these were less than the consequent reduction in potential flood damage; (d) there would be stronger public support for appropriate land-use regulation in order to reduce the costs of occupancy in flood-prone areas.

The underlying principle of insurance – that the small premiums of the many cover the large losses of the few – requires that the risks be calculable and randomly distributed. Particular problems for flood insurance have in the past resulted not only from the inability to predict flood magnitudes and frequencies with sufficient accuracy (see chapter 6), but also from the fact that, whereas in most forms of property insurance few of the insured become claimants, in the case of flood insurance (presumably undertaken only by those in flood-prone areas) nearly all those insured would become claimants. Furthermore, even though flood frequencies can now be estimated with reasonable accuracy, major floods may occur in successive years. In other words, the underlying principle of insurance needs to be modified in the case of floods, so that small premiums paid over many years cover the large losses of a few years. Additional problems arise from the presumed difficulty and expense of calculating premiums that relate to flood risk for individual structures, since two adjacent structures at the same elevation may sustain very different flood damage. Methods of calculating flood insurance premiums have been reviewed by Kunreuther and Sheaffer (1970).

Until quite recently the private insurance industry showed great reluctance to enter the field of flood insurance. In part, this lack of enthusiasm was a reflection of early failures, like that of the company formed to sell flood insurance after the Mississippi floods of 1895 and 1896 which was destroyed financially by the flood of 1899 (Hoyt and Langbein, 1955). Most of the difficulties, however, relate to the calculation of premiums and the extent to which premiums should be averaged between flood-prone and immediately adjacent areas. If uniform averaged premiums were charged companies would be loaded with an adverse selection of risks since only those in the most flood-prone areas are likely to buy insurance (Sewell, 1969). In any case, below-cost premiums in high-risk areas would promote rather than discourage occupancy (Task Force, 1966). On the other hand, premiums directly related to risk are certain to be very expensive. Another major deterrent to the private insurance industry has been the possibility that major floods in successive years could lead to bankruptcies unless there was some form of insurance-industry/governmental underwriting of flood insurance schemes.

Because of such problems flood insurance has been slow to develop, even in such insurance-conscious countries as the United States. Despite the passing of the Federal Flood Insurance Act of 1956, flood insurance was not generally available during the succeeding decade except where there was clear evidence of the physical characteristics of the flood hazard and where the insured carried out floodproofing to minimise losses from the more frequent floods (White, 1964). To encourage optimal future use of floodplain and other flood-prone land, in 1968 the United States Congress passed the National Flood Insurance Act establishing the National Flood Insurance Program which became effective on 28 January 1969. According to Kunreuther and Sheaffer (1970), it was this act which really set the stage for the inclusion of flood insurance as a viable floodplain management alternative. The major objectives of the National Flood Insurance Program, under which existing occupants pay a chargeable or subsidised premium whereas future developers would pay the full actuarial premium, were defined by Congress and summarised by Loughlin (1971) as: (a) the distribution of burdens equitably among the insured and the general public; (b) the encouragement of state and local governments to control land-use in flood-prone areas; (c) the deflection of future construction, where practicable, away from flood hazard locations; and (d) the assurance that any federal assistance provided under the programme would be related closely to all flood related programmes and activities of the federal government. Insurance cover was restricted initially to residential property, with the expectation that it would become available at a later date for small businesses and other classes of property, exclusive of federal properties. Flood insurance was available only to those states and administrative areas expressing a positive interest and giving assurances that permanent land-use controls would be adopted by 31 December 1971.

In the first five years of the programme some 3000 communities throughout the country became participants of the programme (Gillett, 1974), controlling land-use through subdivision reviews, building permits and in some cases zoning ordinances. Even so, the programme's growth was only modestly successful and various efforts were made to improve participation, such as a 40 per cent reduction in subsidised premiums for the Pennsylvania–Maryland area in the wake of damage caused by tropical storm Agnes in 1972. It became clear, however, that more general incentives were needed to speed up the development of the programme and that a very large and rapidly increasing federal financial interest in the acquisition and development of flood-prone areas should be compulsorily covered by insurance. Accordingly, the Flood Disaster Protection Act of 1973, which was signed into Public Law 93–234 on 31 December 1973, made major changes to the National Flood Insurance Program which were reviewed by Gillett (1974). Specifically, the Act: (a) substantially increased the available insurance coverage; (b) provided for the expeditious identification of and dissemination of information concerning flood-prone areas; (c) required participation in the program as a condition of future federal financial assistance to states or local communities; and (d) required the purchase of flood insurance by property owners in flood-prone areas who are receiving federal assistance towards the acquisition or improvement of their property. The 1973 Act deferred the application of actuarial premium rates until 31 December 1974, or until the official publication date of the initial Flood Insurance Rate Map and elevation data for the area, whichever was later, and until such time made subsidised insurance coverage available.

The United States provides what is undoubtedly one of the best examples of the development of an effective flood insurance programme. In most other countries flood insurance is either non-existent or else in an early stage of development. In Britain, for example, flood insurance is entirely in the hands of the private insurance companies; some insurance policies include flood coverage, others do not. Faced with A$100 million reconstruction bill after the 1974 floods, the Australian government is now looking at the possibility of a national flood insurance scheme (Douglas and Hobbs, 1974).

In summary, then, it is clear that a well-developed national flood insurance programme can serve as an alternative adjustment to the flood hazard and, in particular, as a complement to some of the other adjustments which have been discussed. It is equally clear that the availability of flood insurance will have no effect on adjustment to the flood hazard if no-one buys it. The incentives to purchase insurance cover must be sufficiently strong and may range from compulsory insurance at one extreme to attractive, uneconomic premiums at the other. Alternatively, the occupants of flood-prone areas may be 'persuaded' to purchase by making planning approval or financial assistance conditional upon satisfactory insurance cover. On the other hand, the availability of flood insurance may be made conditional upon the introduction of land-use controls or the floodproofing of individual structures.

> Objectives of any degree of flood insurance should be to achieve flood damage abatement, an efficient use of the floodplain, and to provide financial relief at times of flooding. Achieving a sensible use of floodplain lands would be equally or more important than the indemnification of loss. High among the considerations of any insurance scheme should be assessment of its effect upon the national effort to abate damages, and upon State and local governments' efforts to achieve good planning in the use of floodplain lands.
>
> (Task Force, 1966)

Choice of adjustment

In conclusion it must be stressed that, although each of the adjustments which have been discussed here may be theoretically available to a given individual, company or administration, it may not in practice represent a realistic choice. For example, insurance will have little effect unless there are strong incentives to purchase it. Again certain solutions may be politically unacceptable and others ruled out by physical conditions, as in those desert and other areas where the flashiness of flooding makes emergency evacuation almost impossible. It is equally important to reiterate that these possible adjustments are by no means mutually exclusive; indeed, a combination of alternatives will often provide the most economically attractive solution. Similar arguments apply to the range of possibilities canvassed under the headings of flood abatement and flood protection which will be discussed in the next two chapters.

9 Human Response to the Flood Hazard: II Flood Abatement

INTRODUCTION

In the preceding chapter the discussions of possible adjustments to the flood hazard considered some of the principal ways in which man's behaviour may be 'controlled' in order to ameliorate the effects of flooding. The present and succeeding chapters complete the picture by considering how the floods themselves may be 'controlled'. In neither case is the idea of control used in an absolute sense. It has already been seen, for example, that absolute 'man control' in flood-prone areas is impossible, except presumably in a totalitarian society, because of the numerous, often conflicting, political, social and economic pressures to develop such areas. 'Flood control', in the physical sense, is equally impossible. There is no way in which man can control the very rare, high-magnitude flood event except by designing everything against the correctly estimated maximum possible flood. There are, however, two ways in which flood events of lesser magnitude and greater frequency can be partially controlled so that flood damage is mitigated. One approach involves *flood protection* – physical controls constructed in the river channel or, where appropriate, along the coast to reduce either the peak discharge, the area of inundation or the depth of floodwaters. The other approach, applicable only to river floods, involves *flood abatement* – land-use modification or some other action taken within the catchment area upstream of a given flood hazard location to reduce the severity of flood discharges.

Flood abatement, sometimes referred to as watershed (or catchment) management, constitutes an initially attractive scientific procedure in which the flood problem is approached from first principles and action is taken at the point upstream where the flood is generated rather than waiting to take action downstream at locations where that flood would represent a potential threat. Flood abatement thus subscribes to the basic maxim that 'prevention is better than cure'. Arguments over the relative merits of the upstream and downstream methods of flood control have occupied hydrologists and engineers for many years and are the subject of a book by Leopold and Maddock (1954). It would, of course, be ideal if, through the proper management of catchment areas, floods could be avoided. It will be seen, however, that this is not always possible and that, even where it is, the flood abatement approach is often hampered by a number of problems.

A major problem in the past has been a lack of understanding of the physical processes involved in flooding. From the discussion of flood-producing

132

processes in chapters 2 and 3 it is clear that much more is now known, although it is still doubtful whether we have a sufficiently detailed under- standing of these processes to manage catchments so that flood production can be controlled. A related problem is that much that has been achieved so far in this field is of a piecemeal and empirical nature. Outside of experimental and re- search programmes, there has been very little organised catchment treatment of flood control. The situation is more positive in some countries, such as the United States, where there is a legislative framework for watershed treatment and a fairly substantial annual expenditure, commonly amounting to about 10 per cent of the total expenditure on flood control.

Because of the sparsity of land-treatment programmes for flood control, to- gether with the large number of watershed experiments aiming at increased water yields from river catchment areas, much of the evidence concerning the ef- fects of upstream land-use manipulation is of a negative kind in regard to flood prevention. For example, the effects of deforestation in increasing streamflow are well-documented, but comparatively few experiments have investigated the effects of afforestation in decreasing streamflow. In some cases, however, this negative evidence may be reversible, and will be referred to later in this chapter.

PHYSICAL CONSIDERATIONS

In chapters 2 and 3 it was emphasised that climatologically produced floods con- sist almost entirely of quickflow which reaches the stream channels rapidly during and immediately after precipitation or snowmelt. This quickflow is com- posed largely of the surface flow from variable source areas and to a lesser extent of direct interflow and Hortonian overland flow resulting when rainfall intensity exceeds the infiltration capacity of the soil. Clearly, those factors which reduce the growth of variable source areas within a catchment will thereby also reduce flood magnitudes. Such factors include the introduction of vegetation covers having either higher interception capacities, which reduce the amount of precipi- tation entering the soil moisture store, or higher evapotranspiration rates, which increase the available water storage capacity in the soil profile. Also, agricultural and other practices can improve the water holding capacity of the soil and/or its infiltration capacity.

These factors can only operate effectively, however, in rather limited circum- stances. For example, if the catchment is already thoroughly wetted, then differ- ences in interception or soil moisture storage capacities have no effect on flood response; and similarly, during a prolonged storm in initially dry conditions, the storages will become filled and the source areas gradually envelop the entire catchment. Where watershed management techniques *are* able to abate floods, therefore, they are likely to be most effective for small floods. In such cases there may be some possibility of reducing flood volumes and delaying flood response. Even in very wet, prolonged-storm conditions there may be advantage in en- couraging water to move through the soil and subsoil, rather than flow over the surface, if this slows down the movement of water, thereby reducing the peak discharge and extending the time base of the flood hydrograph. However, this type of flood amelioration will be effective only in small catchment areas where the time taken for precipitated water to reach the stream channels is considerable compared with the time taken for the flood peak to move down-channel to the catchment outlet. In a large catchment area the in-channel travel time of the flood peaks is so extended that the effects of catchment management in delaying the arrival of water at the stream channels is virtually insignificant.

In summary, physical considerations suggest that the effects of catchment management on flood abatement are likely to be most significant with small floods on small streams and demonstrate the fallibility of early soil-conservationist views that, if one could 'stop the raindrop where it falls', flood abatement could be achieved. Such over-optimism was quickly countered by a physically-based pessimism which Linsley *et al.* (1949) expressed: 'It does not appear . . . that the present-day engineer can consider any effective flood reduction by means of land-management practices.' Recent re-evaluation of the runoff process, together with more rigorous experimental work on the hydrological effects of land-management techniques, have begun to revive a cautious optimism. Thus Hewlett and Helvey (1970) found that the felling of forest stands and the consequent reduction in evapotranspiration alone can significantly increase flood volumes, and concluded that 'Forest vegetation plays a definite role as a practical factor in downstream flooding even where cutting does not disturb the soil's infiltration capacity'.

The hydrological effects of some of the main types of land-use manipulation will now be briefly considered.

AFFORESTATION

One of the most striking manipulations of land-use is that involved in afforestation or deforestation, the hydrological effects of which continue to engender considerable controversy. Methodical investigations of these effects in small experimental watersheds began in Europe and North America in the early years of this century. Since then numerous experiments, reviewed by Hibbert (1967) and Ward (1971), have demonstrated that the volume and timing of runoff may be substantially modified by forest cutting and removal practices, such as clear cutting, block or strip cutting, and selective thinning. Work done to date has emphasised the clear relationship between forest cutting and increased runoff, and the possibility of developing sound forest management practice which is also sound hydrological practice. Other possibilities include the replacement of one type of forest cover by another or the replacement of forest by grassland or other agricultural crops. In general, runoff is reduced when deciduous trees are replaced by conifers, and increased when forest is replaced by lower growing vegetation such as grass or crops.

Partly because of a world-wide concern with problems of water shortage and the possibilities of increasing streamflow, and partly because it is experimentally easier and quicker to start with a forested area and chop it down than with a non-forested area and grow a uniform canopy-cover forest on it most of the available experimental evidence is of the negative type already mentioned. Frequently even this negative evidence does not relate specifically to the effects of forest cutting or removal on the timing, duration and magnitude of flood peaks. Despite, or perhaps because of, the lack of hard data there have long been fervent advocates of the effectiveness of afforestation in flood control. Thus, recurring floods on the Arno in north–central Italy led Gianbattista Vico del Çilento in 1334 to recommend a government-sponsored reforestation programme. This was never carried out and Florence continues to suffer major flood catastrophes, such as that of 1966. In France, an engineer, Fabre, concluded in 1797 that lowland flooding by Alpine torrents was a direct result of deforestation in the mountains. A century later in 1890, the French Government undertook the job of reforestation in the Hautes-Alpes and it was reported that, as reforestation continued, floods decreased in number and severity (Klein, 1969). Similarly, early settlers in North America noted an apparent relationship between forest clearance, particularly by burning, and the severity of flooding, and pressed for reforestation programmes (Nelson and Byrne, 1966), while the implantation of western agriculture methods into the tropical rainforest environment of South–east Asia led initially to major soil erosion and flood problems. In this area it was not until the early predilection for clean weeding between long standing crops, such as rubber, was overcome that the damage began to be restored. The rubber plantations were transformed into enormous man-made forests in which sound conservation procedures were practised (Douglas, 1972).

Clear, unambiguous, positive experimental evidence on the role of afforestation and reforestation in flood abatement is still comparatively sparse. Much of the recent controversy in this field was sparked off by Law (1956) who showed that afforestation in British upland catchments – a standard water engineering practice at the time – substantially reduced streamflow amounts. A valuable review of some of the experimental work carried out in the United States on reforestation is provided by Lull and Reinhart (1967) who drew examples from Ohio and New York State. Black (1968) and Schneider (1969) described changes in streamflow as more than 137 000 ha (340 000 acres) of farmland abandoned in the early 1930s in New York State gradually reverted, through brush and scrub forest, to mature forest. In one small experimental watershed reforestation of 58 per cent of the area reduced winter and spring flood peaks by amounts ranging from 66 per cent in November to 16 per cent in April. No significant change in flood peaks was observed after 1958 when canopy coverage had attained 90 per cent (Schneider, 1969). Particularly in the southern states, reforestation has been carried out in an attempt to combat and restore the ravages of erosion caused by earlier inferior agricultural methods. In these areas, therefore, attention has concentrated on the flood hydrographs and sediment yields. Sodemann and Tysinger (1965) found that afforestation on a small degraded agricultural watershed in a limestone area of eastern Tennessee resulted in a reduction of summer flood flows, a change in the time distribution of surface runoff and a reduction in total sediment yields. No appreciable change appeared to have taken place in total water yield, however, or in the volume of either surface or subsurface runoff. Similarly, Ursic (1968) suggested that reforestation in another severely eroded watershed in the eastern United States had reduced sedimentation and restored the infiltration and storage characteristics of the permeable areas, thereby reducing the flood potential.

Apparently conflicting evidence was presented by Howe *et al*. (1967) in a long-term study of flooding on the Severn in Britain. They argued that there is an early phase, after the initial plough-ditching for afforestation and before complete crown cover is achieved, during which flood potential is actually increased by afforestation (see figure 9.1). This results from the improved drainage created by the furrows opened up at intervals of 1 to 1.5 m between the mounds on which the saplings are planted. Were these furrows to be cut along the natural contours, they would have a ponding effect and act as infiltration basins, but because of the danger of ploughing across steep hillsides many of the furrows follow the slope of the ground.

From these brief comments on afforestation it will be clear that such experimental evidence as does exist is somewhat conflicting and largely restricted to floodflows from comparatively small catchments. In this confused situation the most effective summary is probably one based on physical reasoning rather than on empirical results. Hewlett and Nutter (1969) suggested that a forest cover plays three main roles in flood hydrology. First, it stabilises soils, minimising erosion and the downstream sedimentation associated with increased flood stages; second, it provides additional water storage through the effects of interception storage and through evapotranspiration in drying out the underlying soil; and third, it maintains high infiltration rates, although so far '. . . there is little convincing evidence that the mere presence or absence of forest cover affects infiltration to such an extent that either the prevention or cause of major floods can be related directly to it'. Finally, there are some conditions, such as swamplands or areas of high precipitation on steep slopes and shallow soils, where flood-producing quickflow will be generated whether or not a forest cover exists.

OTHER VEGETATION CHANGES

Recognition that different plant communities may each have different hydrological roles forms the basis of research into the possibilities of flood abatement by catchment management in non-forested areas. As with investigations into the effects of afforestation, some of the most rigorous and best-known work in this field has been achieved in the United States – for example by the USDA-ARS Watershed Technology Research Branch at the Cochocton research station in Ohio and by the Tennessee Valley Authority. Harrold *et al*. (1962), in a major publication, discussed the influence of land-use and treatment on the hydrology of small watersheds at Cochocton between 1938 and 1957. Other aspects of the Cochocton work have figured in numerous reports (e.g., Harrold, 1962; McGuinness *et al*., 1958).

In Wisconsin, Minshall (1961) found that changes in the cultivated area of a watershed had a considerable influence on the flood discharge from moderately permeable soils but only a minor effect on claypan soils. Again, it is estimated that over 400 000 ha (1 000 000 acres) of marginal cropland in the Great Plains of the United States have been converted to permanent grassland as a result of federal conservation programmes, and conversion is proposed for a further considerable area. The effects of this change in land-use were examined in Nebraska by Dragoun (1969). He found that surface runoff was significantly reduced two years after conversion and was representative of runoff from native meadow after the third year, whereas runoff increased considerably in the first year after

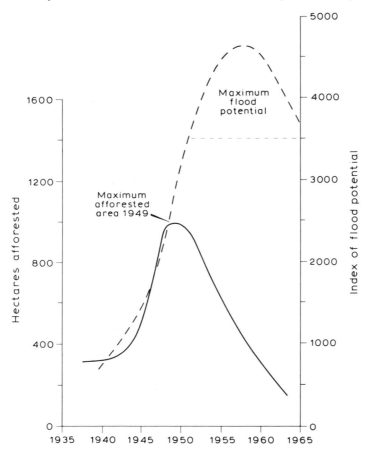

Figure 9.1   Apparent increase in flood potential associated with early stages of afforestation
Source: Howe *et al.* (1967).

native meadow was placed under cultivation.

Elsewhere, other aspects of the moderating role of grassland in reducing flood flows and erosion were reported by Dunin and Downes (1962) who noted that changes in land-use to obtain greater production often create problems which must be solved if increased production is to be maintained. Thus the widespread replacement of perennial grasses by improved annual species in Victoria, Australia has had the desirable effect of increasing infiltration and reducing the flood and erosion hazard, but the undesirable effect of decreasing water yields in an area where water is already in short supply.

Wildfire is a major cause of vegetation change in many parts of the world and usually results in a dramatically increased severity of flooding until the damage is repaired, either naturally or more rapidly through human intervention. In Arizona, Pase and Ingebo (1965) compared runoff and sediment yields from catchments seeded with grass after wildfire destruction with those from other catchments which had been allowed to revert naturally after the fire to a cover of chaparral scrub. After a few years it was found that not only were water yields higher from the grassland but that flood discharges and sediment yields were lower. Other assessments of the hydrological effects of vegetation rehabilitation after wildfire are provided by Krammes and Rice (1963) and Corbett and Green (1965) for California, and by Brown (1972) for New South Wales.

As with afforestation, it is difficult from the available evidence to generalise about the flood abatement potential of various types of non-forest vegetation change, except to repeat the physically reasoned conclusion to the preceding section – that vegetation cover which promotes soil stability, high interception and evapotranspiration losses, and high infiltration rates tends to reduce the flood potential, at least for small floods in comparatively small catchments. In this respect, grasses and shrubs are often just as effective as forest cover, whereas crops which do not create a complete canopy cover for much of the time, or require frequent cultivation or grazing, are likely to be substantially less effective.

AGRICULTURAL PRACTICES

Numerous agricultural practices have been developed over the years to combat man-induced erosion, particularly in newly-developed agricultural areas. As soil (and water) conservation measures these practices, operating either by protecting the soil surface from raindrop compaction or encouraging higher rates of infiltration, have been highly successful. Contour ploughing and contour terracing, for example, promote infiltration and reduce overland flow by impeding the downslope movement of water. Similarly, basin listing, which refers to a variety of methods used to score the land surface along the contour, increases depression storage and infiltration and reduces overland flow. Sometimes basin listing takes the form of contour ditches with cross walls at intervals to prevent water from moving along the ditch (Hewlett and Nutter, 1969). Strip cropping takes advantage of contour cultivation by using alternate strips of contrasting vegetation to break up the water flow path and to provide some areas of high infiltration throughout the year. Deep subsoiling is used to break up hard pans and thereby promote more rapid percolation and infiltration. Most conservation programmes also include minor supplementary structures to retain water on the surface. These may take the form of farm ponds or small check dams built across incipient or developing gullies.

It has frequently been suggested that these same methods could be used as flood abatement procedures, although evidence of their effectiveness is inconclusive. According to Hewlett and Nutter (1969), their role in flood abatement is largely restricted to controlling on-site damage to fields and crops, and to the secondary effect of reducing the sediment loads carried by streams. Bedell *et al.* (1946) reported on early work in Indiana to study the effect of contouring on runoff and erosion, while the effect of land-forming measures, including terracing and basin listing, in various parts of the United States were discussed by Bailey and Copeland (1960), Hopkins *et al.* (1961) and Smith and Henderson (1961). The control of grazing and/or burning to increase the density of protective vegetal cover as a flood-abatement procedure was described by Costin (1952) in relation to the Upper Snowy basin in Australia, and by Keppel (1961) and Sharp *et al.* (1964) for the arid and semi-arid United States.

New agricultural practices are developed from time to time. At the Coshocton research station in Ohio, for example, a number of tests have been made of the hydrological effects of no-tillage corn production (Harrold, 1962; Harrold *et al.*, 1962; Harrold, Triplett and Youker, 1967) in which, instead of ploughing, herbicides were used to kill weeds and grass, and the corn seed dropped into a slot opened up by a disc planter. Early results were encouraging for both erosion and flood control.

Some agricultural practices tend to increase rather than abate the flood potential. Land drainage, particularly under-drainage by tiling and moling, has frequently been regarded in this light.

In most cases, however, whether one is considering a flood-abating or flood-intensifying agricultural practice, the treated area will normally represent only a small proportion of the entire drainage basin and will, like afforestation and other vegetation changes, operate most effectively on small floods from small streams.

SNOW-COVERED AREAS

In many areas of winter snow accumulation and subsequent spring or early summer snowmelt the desirability of flood abatement is substantially increased by the need for water conservation. The pattern in such areas (see chapter 3) is for severe damaging spring floods, which may account for 80 per cent or more of the annual runoff, to be followed almost immediately by severe water shortages in both the agricultural and public water supply sectors. A major requirement, therefore, is the development of catchment management procedures which so modify patterns of snow accumulation and melt (for example, by encouraging maximum snow accumulation in those areas where subsequent melting will take place most slowly) that the period of melting is prolonged and the intensity of runoff thereby reduced.

In *forested areas* these problems are often further complicated by the requirements of forest management and timber harvesting procedures. Ideally, management practices would aim to achieve the highest timber yields, using economically viable harvesting methods, consistent with the highest water yields distributed as uniformly as possible in time so as to minimise flood damage and water wastage. Such optimisation, which is discussed in more detail in Ward

(1975), is not possible without a detailed understanding of the energy balance and water balance relationships of snowmelt and the way in which the energy and water balances are affected by changing geographical conditions, including factors of climate, vegetation, soils, topography and hydrology. Numerous investigations of the effects of various patterns of forest cutting on snow accumulation and snowmelt have confirmed the long-held conclusion (Costin *et al.*, 1961) that a forest honeycombed with numerous small openings or cleared strips is the most efficient in accumulating and conserving snow (see plate 7).

Afforestation, therefore, may not always have the flood-abating effect in snow-covered areas which is generally attributed to it elsewhere (see earlier section on Afforestation). Thus, Satterlund and Eschner (1965), on the northern Allegheny Plateau in New York state, found that, because the period of melt became more concentrated, snowmelt flood potential increased as the reforestation of formerly open, agricultural land proceeded. They concluded that a combination of open and reforested areas would yield a more uniform streamflow regime during the winter–spring period.

Catchment management procedures have also been used in *non-forested areas* to improve the temporal pattern of snowmelt runoff and thus reduce the flood potential. Again, the basic aim has been to manipulate the patterns of snow accumulation and melt so as to extend melting over as long a period as possible. Snow management experiments involving the erection of a series of snow fences on mountain grassland catchments in Wyoming were described by Berndt (1964). The results showed that on flat upland areas, during winters with average snowfall, 100 m was the most effective snow fence spacing. Similar experiments in the alpine zones of the Fraser River headwaters in Colorado were described by Martinelli (1964). Here tests were started in 1958–9 to see if normal slatted snow fencing, placed at the upwind edge of natural catchments, would increase the depth of snow accumulation. In four years appreciable increases were found in three out of four sites.

The effects of ploughing on flood formation have been investigated in a variety of climatic conditions. In snow-free areas it has normally been found that ploughing is associated with increased flood peaks but in snow-covered areas the reverse is often true. Thus, Ayers (1965) reported that well-managed ploughed soils in southern Ontario yielded much less runoff during the winter months than sod-covered areas, and attributed the differences largely to the fact that in the ploughed areas the rough condition of the soil surface, and the relatively shallow depths of accumulated snow, result in extensive narrow ridges of black soil being exposed to solar energy. Heat is absorbed and transmitted by these patches to melt the soil. In addition, a large potential for depression storage occurs on the ploughed land. Ayers was able to quote supporting evidence from other cold-winter areas – for example Wisconsin and the Transvolga region of Russia, where similar relations seem to hold.

URBAN AREAS

It is generally accepted that urbanisation, particularly when this encroaches on areas which were once farmland or forest, is a flood-intensifying land-use change. The replacement of permeable by impervious surfaces, the improved hydraulic character of the artificial drainage network, and the intense utilisation and resulting compaction of the remaining non-paved surfaces, all contribute to an increase in the volume of quickflow and a more rapid movement of runoff in an urbanised area. Anderson (1968) found that these two factors combined to increase flood peaks in northern Virginia by between two and nearly eight times while, in Texas, Espey *et al.* (1966) found that urban development resulted in peak discharges which were from 100 to 300 per cent greater than those from undeveloped areas. Again the scale at which urban development is taking place adds to the severity of the flood problem. Ackermann *et al.* (1966) noted that by 1990 an estimated 80 per cent of the population of the United States will be concentrated in urban areas, and that this increased concentration will necessitate the creation of 78 000 km² (30 000 square miles) of new urban development.

Most work in urban hydrology has concentrated on characterising the changed hydrological response of the urban areas and surprisingly few investigations have considered the possibilities of flood abatement. Among the exceptions of a study (Felton and Lull, 1963) of suburban Philadelphia where in a period of nine years the developed area more than doubled, largely at the expense of open fields. The authors demonstrated drastic and damaging reductions of infiltration and suggested that the flood hazard could be abated by devoting less space to low-infiltration surfaces such as lawns, and more to high-infiltration surfaces using shrubberies and small patches of trees. More recently AWRA (1972) described investigations of ways in which rates of runoff in urban areas might be controlled. One method involves placing a series of 10 cm high barriers of 6 mm gravel on flat roofs. In one experiment the barriers reduced flood peaks by about 50 per cent and doubled the duration of the runoff period. Extensive installation of such barriers on flat roofs in an urban catchment could be expected to delay runoff in a similar manner, thereby giving storm sewers more time to evacuate flood runoff.

In America many states require that all newly developed urban areas incorporate some means, for example small detention basins, of on-site detention or storage of storm waters to moderate flood discharges. Unfortunately, as McCuen (1974) observed, existing laws tend to use an 'individual-site' rather than the more efficient regional approach to storm water management, and in some cases the individual-site approach may actually increase the potential for localised flooding. Similar flood storage areas have been constructed in numerous locations throughout the United Kingdom to serve as temporary storage reservoirs for the control of flood flows. These have proved particularly necessary in the flatter, lowland areas of eastern England where the intensified quickflow from additional impervious areas would rapidly overtax the pre-existing low-gradient drainage networks, as in the new urban development at Bransholme on the northern outskirts of Hull, North Humberside and at Basildon, Essex (Bunyan, 1975).

FLOOD ABATEMENT IN THE UNITED STATES

It has been emphasised in this chapter that catchment management procedures are likely to have only a limited effect in terms of flood abatement. Initial high expectations of this approach, developed before the flood generating processes were fully understood, proved premature and, as is often the case, the eventual realisation of this led to the wholesale rejection of flood-abatement procedures by many authorities. Even limited abatement, however, is better than no abatement at all, especially where flood-abatement procedures result in other, related benefits, such as erosion control, improved agricultural output, improved landscape quality and additional recreational facilities. In most cases, encouragement of even limited flood abatement has been minimal. Very few countries have had a prolonged, government-backed programme of flood abatement. In this respect, as in many others, the United States represents a well-documented exception and a valuable example.

In the United States recognition of the value of flood abatement has been apparent in a long sequence of Federal legislation, dating back to the late nineteenth century and continuing through to the Watershed Protection and Flood Prevention Act, Public Law No. 566, and its subsequent amendments. Early interpretation of the Constitution seemed to exclude flood control as a Federal Government activity, although in fact some work was authorised under the guise of 'navigation improvements' which were considered a Federal province. Increasing flood damages, however, culminating in the California and lower Mississippi floods of 1916, led to a broadening of constitutional interpretation and to the authorisation of the first Federal flood control projects (Ciriacy-Wantrup, 1964). Subsequently, Congress responded to other major floods with the Flood Control Acts of 1928, 1936 and 1944 and the Watershed Protection and Flood Prevention Act of 1954.

It was in the 1936 Act that Congress first recognised specifically the role of catchment management in flood control by authorising the Department of Agriculture to consider water and related land resources problems on a catchment or watershed basis. At this stage the basic framework of responsibility, which still exists, was first established. The U.S. Army Corps of Engineers was designated the principal agency responsible for preparing and carrying out flood control schemes on the major rivers, while the scope of the Department of Agriculture was limited to retarding water flow and preventing soil erosion in the upper reaches of streams by land-treatment measures (Ciriacy-Wantrup, 1964). The fundamental contradistinction between the 'upstream' and 'downstream' approaches to flood control, to which reference has already been made, was thus embodied at an early stage in the flood control legislation of the United States. Gradually, however, there has been a blending of the upstream and downstream approaches. As Hewlett and Nutter (1969) observed, the Corps of Engineers, the main agency responsible for downstream flood control, is moving further upstream to build smaller reservoirs and is at the same time devoting more attention to the role of land management, while the Soil Conservation Service of the Department of Agriculture, responsible for upstream flood control, is moving downstream to build larger dams and other structures to supplement land treatment measures. The greatest single impetus to this merging of approaches was given by Public Law No. 566 which authorised the Department of Agriculture to construct engineering works for controlling floods on catchments of less than

100 000 ha (250 000 acres). P.L. 566 projects are, however, uniquely circum-scribed in a number of respects, as Burdick (1966) pointed out. For example, every project is multi-purpose in that it must include land treatment in addition to structural measures for at least flood prevention or agricultural water man-agement. Although recreation, municipal and industrial water supply, and fish and wildlife benefits may be included in P.L. 566 projects, the projects must be justified for watershed protection and flood prevention or agricultural water management before these other purposes can be added. In addition, each struc-ture in the project must make a significant contribution to flood prevention or agricultural water management.

P.L. 566 was a major turning-point in the history of flood control for two main reasons. First, its terms of reference covered some 8300 small watersheds, comprising half the land area of the United States, which are in need of flood protection and related land and water resources development (Hickok, 1963). Despite a comparatively slow start (eight years after its approval only about 8 per cent of the needed watershed improvement had been carried out or author-ised (Hicock, 1963)), considerable improvements in flood control are now taking place. Second, P.L. 566 was the culmination of a sequence of flood control legis-lation which demonstrated the emerging recognition that catchment manage-ment procedures cannot reasonably stand alone but must be developed in connection with structural measures for flood protection. This second point leads us felicitously to the subject matter of the next chapter.

10 Human Response to the Flood Hazard: III Flood Protection

As emphasised in chapters 8 and 9, the structural engineering measures which singly or in combination comprise flood protection represent the obvious, traditional and publicly acceptable response to the flood hazard. The construction of protection works is recorded in the histories of most early civilisations and, as Kuiper (1965) observed, the method of building large mounds to act as refuges is thousands of years old and still applied. It is known that the Chinese built flood-banks on the Hwang Ho 2500 years ago and that the Babylonians diverted the floodwaters of the Euphrates into natural depressions to protect the city of Babylon, but the first flood protection works were probably those of the Egyptian king Amenenhat, who constructed floodbanks on both sides of the Nile and diverted floodwaters into Lake Moeris (Nixon, 1963). Much later, in Britain, the Romans pioneered the use of floodbanks to limit flooding from the sea, while in more recently developed countries such as the United States the engineer's response to the flood hazard was dominant from the start and became even more strongly established with the development of improved technology during the present century.

The terms 'flood protection' and 'flood control' are misleading, at least as far as the general public is concerned. Such is the nature of extreme events that protection against, or control of, the really severe flood is never complete but is always partial. As Hoyt and Langbein (1955) wrote: 'Every dike or flood wall, every reservoir, has a limit to its effectiveness. The limit may be high or it may be low, depending on how much protection one wants to buy, but that there is a limit should not be forgotten or overlooked.'

This limit naturally varies with national and local government policy and according to the prevailing geographical conditions at the given location but it is commonly quite large. In the United States, for example, reservoirs are normally constructed to contain the 65 to 100-year flood and to remain undamaged even when overtopped by substantially larger floods. But if the limit is not explicitly stated and repeatedly re-emphasised the population resident behind the protective works may be lulled into a false sense of security and not evacuate in time when a large flood threatens. In such a situation loss of life and property can actually be greater than if no protective works had existed. Engineers, extremely conscious of this paradox, realise they must clearly explain to the public the degree of protection afforded by each structure (Linsley and Franzini, 1972).

Flood protection, therefore, refers to attempts to minimise or mitigate flood damages by means of structural measures in a way which is economically feasible. It is in this sense that the term is used in the present chapter. Protection against river floods is discussed first; then follows a consideration of protection against coastal and estuarine floods.

RIVER FLOODS

Over the centuries, and indeed millennia, a variety of structures have been evolved to mitigate the flood hazard. Their aim was to achieve at least one of the following objectives: a reduction in the area flooded, a reduction in the depth of floodwaters or a reduction in flood discharge. Specifically, the four main approaches (see figure 8.1) involve:

(1) The construction of embankments (sometimes referred to as dikes or levees) and floodwalls to confine the floodwaters.

(2) The improvement of river channels to enlarge their discharge capacity, for example, by straightening, widening or deepening.

(3) The construction of bypass and diversion channels to carry some of the excess floodwater away from the area to be protected.

(4) The construction of reservoirs for the temporary storage of floodwaters.

In most circumstances a combination of two or more of these approaches is used to develop an optimum solution to the flood problem. Since, however, even within one region no two rivers have an identical regime, and even a single river rarely has two floods with the same characteristics, methods of flood protection vary from place to place and it is difficult to assess whether a method which has been successful at one location will be equally so at another (United Nations, 1951). In any case, to a large extent the method of flood protection used shows a fairly close relationship with the progress of economic development. It is not so much the lack of technical skill in under-developed countries, but the absence of financial and economic justification that prevents the employment of more advanced and usually more expensive methods (United Nations, 1951). Thus the use of concrete blocks and crib works to protect flood embankments in a highly developed country like Japan would be uneconomic on similar rivers in, say, Bangladesh where the normal response to bank erosion is to sacrifice land currently protected by embankments and construct a new embankment further away from the river.

Each of the four approaches listed above has its merits and demerits; some of them, in fact, exacerbate the flood problem upstream and/or downstream of the area being protected. It is appropriate, therefore to consider each individually before discussing examples of their combined use in particular situations.

Embankments and floodwalls

The construction of embankments and floodwalls along rivers of comparatively gentle gradient represents one of the oldest, most common and often the most economical method of flood protection in virtually every country of the world. Techniques and materials have changed little through the centuries as far as embankments, dikes and levees are concerned, and it is interesting that early developments in China, India and along the Nile were almost exactly mirrored more than two thousand years later by the levee system in the Mississippi valley.

Originally, flood embankments were built up by individuals or small groups of agriculturalists seeking to protect their lands against the fairly common, high-frequency flood events. The subsequent occurrence of rarer, larger floods led to the strengthening, raising and elaboration of the embankments and to the amal-gamation of neighbouring systems. It has been suggested (United Nations, 1951) that only when this type of spontaneous system had become sufficiently exten-sive and continuous did local, regional and ultimately national governments take over their control, maintenance, reinforcement and expansion. Seldom did such governments create original, new systems, as was the case on the Irrawaddy in Burma.

In Britain, flood embankments have been used extensively to protect the rich agricultural land of eastern England, particularly in the Fens, but such schemes are minuscule in comparison with the great embankment systems running more than 1000 km alongside the Nile, 700 km along the Hwang Ho, 1400 km by the Red River in North Vietnam (figure 10.1a) and over 4500 km in the Mississippi valley (figure 10.1b). Sometimes flood protection structures are a major land-scape feature, as in the 324 000 km² of the North China plain which is 'domin-ated' by the levees of the Hwang Ho and the Yungting Ho (Beckinsale, 1969).

Flood embankments are normally built of alluvial material excavated *in situ* from borrow pits. Their cross-section is therefore dependent on the material available, the need to keep the seepage gradient inside the body of the embank-ment with a minimum cover of at least one metre, and on other site conditions. A comparison of dikes on various rivers (United Nations, 1951) revealed that they vary little from country to country; fairly typical dimensions are shown in figure 10.1c. The top width ranges from 3 to 10 m, largely depending on its future use – although some of the Hwang Ho dikes have a top width of up to 30 m (United Nations, 1951). The bank slopes are very gentle partly because of the relative un-suitability of the constructional material and partly for aesthetic reasons, in that gentle slopes are visually less intrusive. Because of their shape even moderately high embankments occupy a very large basal area and, in terms of land value alone, can be prohibitively expensive in densely settled urban and industrial areas. In such cases floodwalls, normally built of reinforced concrete, masonry or sheet piling, and therefore very much narrower than earth em-bankments, may be a more acceptable solution. Floodwalls are designed to withstand the hydrostatic pressure of the design flood from one side and if backed by an earth fill they must also act as retaining walls against earth pressures when river levels are low (Linsley and Franzini, 1972). Some typi-cal floodwall cross-sections are shown in figure 10.1d.

During exceptionally severe flood events, embankments may be gradually increased in height, for instance by sandbagging, to prevent them from being overtopped and thus either destroyed or severely damaged. Pardé (1964) reported that during one of the major floods on the Yangtse-Kiang, as many as 280 000 workers at a time laboured for weeks to progressively raise the height of the embankments over a distance of some 135 km, thereby saving the three large towns of Hankow, Wuchang and Hanyang from inundation.

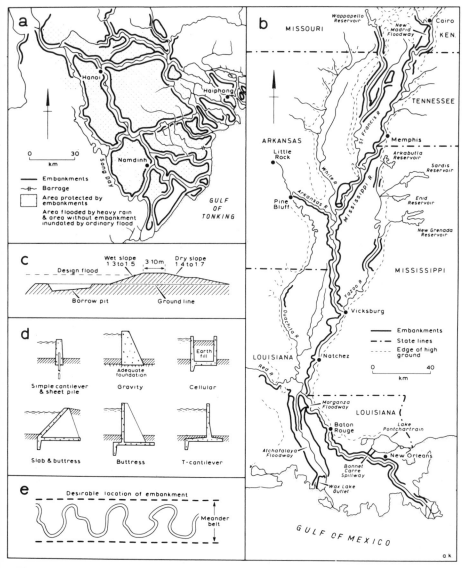

Figure 10.1   Flood embankment systems: *a*, System on the Red River delta, North Vietnam; *b*, Major embankments in the lower Mississippi valley; *c*, Cross-section of a typical flood embankment; *d*, Typical floodwall cross-sections; *e*, Preferred location of embankments along a meandering channel
Source: *a*, United Nations (1966); *b* and *d*, Linsley and Franzini (1972).

For a number of historical, and in urban areas economic, reasons embankments and floodwalls have often been constructed close to the river and parallel to its course. In such situations not only is the discharge capacity of the floodway between the embankments much reduced, but in the case of meandering, alluvial rivers the embankments themselves are continuously threatened by erosion. Where possible, therefore, embankments should be located well away from the river channels (see figure 10.1e). In agricultural areas this poses no great problems since the land between the embankments may be used for pasture. In urban areas, however, the loss of potentially valuable land arising from setting back the embankments in this way would be very serious. On the other hand, floodwalls built close to the channel are less susceptible to erosion than are earth embankments, although the latter can be suitably armoured if the economic returns are sufficiently great.

Despite their long history and widespread use, embankments and floodwalls suffer from a number of major disadvantages. Not the least of these is their reducing natural storage for floodwaters both by preventing water from spilling on to much of the floodplain, and by stopping bank storage in cases where impermeable floodwalls are used. The effect of this reduced storage depends very much on the physical characteristics of the situation, but usually means a general increase in flood stages both upstream and downstream of the embanked section, unless reservoirs or extensive channel improvements are also provided (Linsley and Franzini, 1972).

A second disadvantage is that embankments and floodwalls provide full protection up to a certain stage but no protection at all once that stage is exceeded. As a result, a long succession of moderate flood events will create a strong sense of security in the protected areas so that, when a really severe flood does occur, the dangers of overtopping may not be recognised until it is too late to evacuate. Throughout the ages numerous catastrophes have borne witness to the complacency engendered by systems of flood embankments.

A third disadvantage relates to the fact that embankments and floodwalls along a river must, inevitably, cross the tributary channels of that river. In such cases the main alternatives are either to embank the tributary streams to the same level as the main river and to tie the embankments in to high ground at some appropriate point, or to block the tributary channels. This latter method creates an internal drainage problem behind the main channel embankments; the problem can be treated, according to the regime and size of the tributary channels, by sluices, flaps, pumping, diversion or the provision of adequate flood storage reservoirs.

A fourth disadvantage (already remarked on) is that the best materials for the construction of embankments are not always available *in situ*. This often results in excessive seepage into the embankment, particularly during periods of prolonged high water, which may lead to the wetting of the dry slope (the landward side of the embankment), thereby causing instability. In severe cases piping may occur near the toe of the embankment, and if this goes unchecked it can result in embankment collapse even without the occurrence of overtopping. Such is the usual nature of the constructional materials that overtopping is likely to erode the dry slope and lead to eventual collapse unless some form of surface armouring is applied. Moreover, embankments are particularly subject to damage by burrowing and grazing animals, so that there is need for continuous inspection, maintenance and repair, albeit by comparatively unskilled labour.

A further disadvantage of embankments is that, when breaching or even severe overtopping occurs, there is a sudden and considerable inflow of water in the 'protected' area. One breach alone could render the entire system useless. The embankments may, indeed, exacerbate the flood problem by preventing floodwaters downstream of the breach from draining back into the channel once the peak has passed.

Finally, embankments prevent or greatly reduce the raising and fertilisation of floodplain lands which would have occurred naturally as a result of inundation.

Channel improvements

Any increase in the cross-sectional area of a river channel and/or in the rate of flow of water through the channel will, for a given discharge, result in a lowering of the water surface and a corresponding reduction of the flood hazard. This method of flood protection is normally achieved through one of three main approaches. First, the roughness of the channel may be decreased by clearing the banks and bed of vegetation and other obstacles, or even by lining the channel with an hydraulically smooth surface such as concrete; second, the channel may be widened and/or deepened by dredging; and third, the channel may be shortened (for example, by straightening bends and cutting off meander loops) and its gradient, therefore, steepened in order to increase water velocity. A fourth approach, less frequently used, is to reduce the solids load or increase the load-carrying capacity of the channel, on the assumption that the channel section is normally in equilibrium with the combined water and solids load being carried and will, therefore, adjust its channel, albeit slowly, to any artificially induced load change.

Although initially attractive and indeed extensively used, channel improvement suffers from a number of disadvantages. The most important of these relates to the equilibrium between channel form and discharge just mentioned. Clearly, if a channel presently in equilibrium or quasi-equilibrium is suddenly enlarged, straightened or steepened, natural fluvial processes will immediately tend to reduce the cross-sectional area and/or the gradient by means of deposition. In addition, the shallow water depth in over-large channels during low-flow periods greatly increases weed growth, with consequent increase in channel roughness; and this, in turn, encourages further deposition. The rate at which channels will revert to their pre-improvement condition will depend on a large number of variables, within and outside the channel itself, but is often quite rapid. Nixon (1963) referred to the River Tame, enlarged in 1930 as part of a Birmingham flood protection project, which had reverted to near its original size by 1959 (see plate 8). This means that there is always the need for costly maintenance, like dredging and weed control, entailing expenditure which is roughly proportional to the amount of channel improvement, at least in unlined channels. Maintenance costs alone usually set a comparatively low limit to the level of protection afforded by channel improvement schemes in agricultural areas. In the United States, for example, protection rarely extends beyond the 10-year flood (Ogrosky and Mockus, 1964) while in Britain, Nixon (1963) recommended that channel improvement should aim only to reduce the frequency of overspill to two or three days in the year.

Channel-lining with durable materials, such as concrete, although usually too expensive for the protection of agricultural land, prevents channel reversion and substantially reduces maintenance costs over long periods. It is widely used in urban and other high land-value areas throughout the world. In such situations the original stream channel may become a completely artificial concrete trough (see plate 9), often of a composite nature so that low flows can be accommodated in a small secondary channel set into the otherwise dry bed of the larger channel. Small streams may be entirely enclosed in conduits.

Another major disadvantage of channel improvement is that the more rapid movement of water through the hydraulically improved channel section can aggravate flood peaks further downstream and cause excessive channel erosion both upstream and downstream of the improved reach. Again, the lowering of water levels in the improved reach may cause overdrainage of adjacent agricultural land so that sluices must be constructed in the channel to maintain water levels during periods of low flow and to conserve water for riparian use (Nixon, 1963). In other circumstances, of course, the improved drainage of riparian lands may be welcomed and, by improving the subsurface water storage capacity, may substantially reduce flood-producing quickflow.

Lined channels, particularly in urban areas, suffer from a number of additional disadvantages. The lining may obstruct interflow and shallow groundwater flow and so cause surface saturation. Again, in populous areas a lined channel with vertical sidewalls is a continual danger because a person falling into the channel when it is dry may be seriously injured, and when it contains water will have no means of escape (Linsley and Franzini, 1972). Lined channels are not particularly aesthetic; they are, furthermore, regarded by some conservationists as 'biological deserts' because channel improvement can affect the aquatic community catastrophically by increased water velocity, reduction of sheltered areas, increased temperature range and greatly reduced nutrient input due to destruction of riparian vegetation and disruption of the food chain Mrowka, 1974).

In summary, channel improvement has a limited effectiveness and should not be over used. Even so, the extent of channel improvement is considerable on rivers like the Mississippi. On the lower Mississippi, south of Cairo, channel straightening has effected a reduction in river length of more than 150 km.

Diversion schemes

One of the most direct and effective ways of achieving flood protection is to divert water away from the channel reach where flood conditions threaten. Not surprisingly, this method has been in use for a considerable time. Hoyt and Langbein (1955) referred to Marco Polo's discovery of diversion schemes in thirteenth century China but presumed that the technique was older still. There are two types of flood diversion scheme, one involving *temporary diversion* in which the normal channel is supplemented or duplicated by a flood relief channel, by-

pass channel or floodway which is brought into operatic
period of time. The other uses *permanent diversion* in which a
cepting or cut-off channel is built to replace the existing cha.
technique was certainly used by the early land drainage enginee
was well known to the Romans (Nixon, 1963). The two approacι
discussed in greater detail.

Floodwaters may be temporarily diverted through relief channels.
be broad 'floodways', like those in the Mississippi valley, constructeυ
ing a pair of embankments or levees across the natural floodplain, or,   .ιcu-
larly in urban and high land-value areas, excavated channels lying within, in
some cases outside, the floodplain. The floodway type of diversion channel has
the advantage that it provides storage capacity as well as discharge capacity for
the floodwaters, but the disadvantage that comparatively large areas of floodplain are involved. Although the land within the diversion channel might have a
limited agricultural use for much of the year, the increasing population pressure
on floodplains has meant that many floodway-type diversion channels have
been replaced by excavated diversion channels where discharge capacity is the
main function and any storage effect incidental (Kuiper, 1965).

Clearly some means must be provided for diverting water from the normal
channel into the relief channel when a predetermined danger level has been
reached. A primitive approach, now used mainly in emergencies, is to breach a
flood embankment by mechanical means or with explosives. Alternatively, a
'fuseplug' section may be incorporated into a levee or embankment, a weaker
section which will collapse and wash out when the water level in the main channel reaches a given height. In both cases embankments must be reconstructed
after the floodwaters subside. If a relief channel is to be used frequently it is customary to incorporate a more permanent means of diverting water into it – for
example, a fixed-crest spillway or a system of sluices. Depending on channel gradients and other hydrological and topographical considerations it may also be
necessary to provide some means of closing off the relief channel at its downstream end – obviously essential in tidal rivers.

As Nixon (1963) pointed out, the advantage of temporary diversions over
channel improvement schemes is that the normal channels remain untouched
and continue to carry the non-flood flows for all but a few days in the year. It is
therefore especially appropriate in highly developed areas where it may be virtually impossible to increase the size of the existing channels without large-scale
demolition of property. Of course, any improvement which can be effected in the
normal channel will reduce the required size, and therefore the cost, of the relief
channel. Temporary diversions are most effective in reducing flood levels when
the diverted water is removed completely from the normal channel and not
returned to it further downstream. It may, for example, be possible to lead the
diverted water into the sea, into another river system or, as in the case of the diversion of the Assiniboine River to protect Winnipeg, into a freshwater lake.
More frequently, however, it is necessary to return the diverted water to a downstream point in the same channel. In this situation the diversion channel must be
of sufficient length to minimise backwater effects in the reach which is being protected.

The system of massive floodway relief channels constructed in the lower Mississippi valley is shown in figure 10.1b. During critical flood conditions diversions can be made through the New Madrid floodway south of Cairo, Illinois, through the Boeuf floodway between the Arkansas and Ouachita rivers (not shown), through the Morganza and Atchafalaya floodways directly to the Gulf, and through the Bonnet Carré spillway to Lake Pontchartrain. These floodways play an important role in the protection of major towns such as Cairo, Baton Rouge and New Orleans. In Britain, a very good example of a relief channel is the Coronation Channel which diverts part of the flow of the River Welland past the town of Spalding. This channel has a bed width of 27 m and is more than 4.5 km in length (Nixon, 1963). It has sluices at both ends and is crossed by seven road bridges, one railway bridge and a drainage syphon (see plate 10).

While temporary diversion schemes duplicate existing river channels, permanent diversions using intercepting or cut-off channels involve a replacement channel whose object is to divert either all or a substantial part of the flow away from the flood-prone reach, making provision down the existing channel only for essential riparian use. Permanent diversion schemes are normally used to protect intensively developed areas, although the largest of these schemes in Britain was designed to protect some of the country's richest farmland in the Great Ouse valley (see figure 10.2). Rivers crossing the low-lying Fens are embanked to heights of 4 to 5.5 m and receive water pumped from the adjacent lowlands and drainage by gravity from the surrounding highlands. Tidal interruptions of drainage through the Denver Sluice outlet, coupled with continuing subsidence of the flood embankments, led to widespread overtopping and breaching of the embankments during major floods. A cut-off channel, 43 km long and with a bed width of 60 m, was constructed from Mildenhall to Denver Sluice to intercept the upland drainage of the rivers Lark, Little Ouse and Wissey. This cut-off channel discharges into a relief channel, 17 km in length, which in turn discharges into the tidal river at Tail Sluice, just upstream of King's Lynn (Nixon, 1963).

Massive permanent river diversions are embodied in schemes like NAWAPA (North American Water and Power Alliance) and would, if implemented, undoubtedly make a major, albeit incidental, contribution towards flood protection, particularly on the Canadian prairies. Other large-scale river diversions have been proposed more recently, specifically to alleviate flood problems in the Russian north. Here, as pointed out in chapter 3, the frequent catastrophic flooding on long northward-flowing rivers results partly from the fact that meltwaters are produced between late April and mid-May in the middle and upper reaches while the lower reaches may remain frozen until early June. Proposals for the southward diversion of some of the major rivers in western Siberia are now being seriously considered, although the potential environmental consequences are severe. Aagaard and Coachman (1975) showed that the combined flow of the rivers Ob and Yenisei alone represents about half the total river discharge into the Arctic Ocean and if this flow were diverted elsewhere, the resulting salinity and circulation changes could have major effects upon the heat balance of the ocean. They concluded that, in the absence of possible feedback

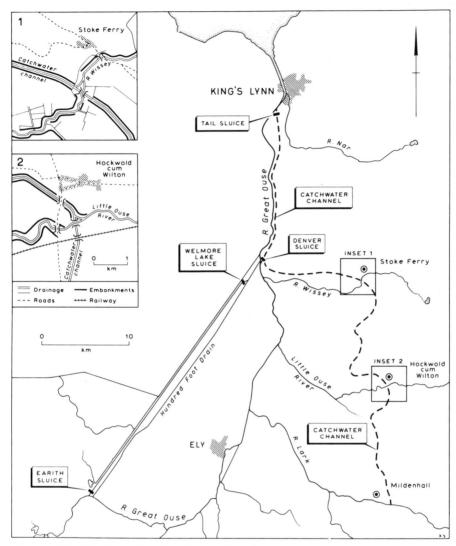

Figure 10.2   The Great Ouse flood protection scheme
Source: Ordnance Survey map.

mechanisms, two of the likely consequences would be the rapid development of prolonged ice-free conditions in the Arctic Ocean because of deep-reaching free convection in the ocean, and the release of large amounts of heat to the atmosphere from warm water masses during the cold months.

Reservoirs

Of the specified four main approaches to flood protection, the construction of reservoirs for the temporary storage of floodwaters probably appeals most to the general public. It has the value of conserving waste-water which could have caused damage and of utilising that water at a later date when it is most needed. However, although offering an obvious and direct solution to many flood problems, reservoirs are frequently uneconomic and though widely used in some countries, as in the United States, they have been almost entirely discounted or ignored in others, as in Britain until quite recently.

In fact, flood mitigation by reservoirs is achieved naturally or incidentally in every part of the world. On many rivers, the lakes and swamps store floodwaters temporarily and release them gradually, thereby effecting naturally a certain regulation of discharge, which can often be greatly enhanced by the construction of comparatively small dams near the natural outlets. Again, natural reservoir storage is afforded beneath the ground surface in the soil and subsoil layers. Some of the ways in which shallow subsurface storage can be better utilised were discussed under the heading of 'flood abatement' in chapter 9. Deeper groundwater storage of floodwaters occurs naturally when floodplains are inundated, especially in arid and semi-arid conditions where the initial water table is at some considerable distance beneath the ground surface. Groundwater storage can be induced artificially through the use of water-spreading in shallow basins and by means of injection wells, although at present the use of these techniques is directed more towards water conservation than flood mitigation. Again, some flood protection may be achieved incidentally through the operation of reservoirs constructed for other purposes. The majority of reservoirs in Britain were made solely for water supply purposes but clearly, unless they are already full before the onset of snowmelt or a flood-producing storm, their spare storage capacity will exert some flood-mitigating effect.

However, our exclusive concern in the remainder of this section will be with surface reservoirs which have been specifically constructed to achieve a measure of flood protection. These are of many types (Rutter and Engstrom, 1964), but for our present purpose they can be broadly categorised as flood-mitigation reservoirs, of the uncontrolled or controlled type, and multi-purpose regulating reservoirs.

Although single-purpose *flood-mitigation reservoirs* were frequently built in the past, such large expenditures on flood control alone can rarely be justified at the present time. Since the sole use of this type of reservoir is to store water during peak flow periods and to release it later, through either an uncontrolled or controlled outlet so that downstream channel capacities are not overtaxed, they remain empty except during floods. The simplest form of flood-mitigation reservoir is the *uncontrolled*, self-regulating detention basin from which the outflow passes through a fixed conduit or orifice, or a series of orifices at different elevations. Outflow is, therefore, a direct function of the volume of water stored behind the dam and the flood peak at the dam is always reduced. This peak reduction is proportionately better with small floods than large because during large floods much of the reservoir storage capacity is already taken up before the peak arrives. The detention basin empties automatically after each flood and since it will be inundated only occasionally, the land below maximum water level can be used for low-intensity agricultural purposes most of the time. An outstanding example of this type of system in the United States is the five detention basins of the Miami Conservancy District in Ohio (see figure 10.3a). These were designed to provide protection to settlements on the Miami River against floods up to 40 per cent greater than the disastrous one of 1913 (Rutter and Engstrom, 1964). The effect of the Germanstown basin on a flood like that of 1913 is shown in figure 10.3b, while the combined effect of the other four detention basins on flows at Dayton for the next highest flood, which occurred in 1937, is shown in figure 10.3c.

Controlled-outlet flood-mitigating reservoirs, although performing essentially the same function as detention basins, have the advantage that they permit the immediate evacuation of the early, non-damaging part of the rising hydrograph, thereby increasing the storage available for subsequent higher flows which can then be discharged either at a selected constant or variable rate, depending on flow conditions downstream. Controlled reservoirs can be used most efficiently when an accurate forecast of incoming streamflow is available. The ideal flood control operation in such cases was described by Linsley, Kohler and Paulhus (1949) and is illustrated in figure 10.4a. The location of point A on the rising limb of the hydrograph is such that the remaining forecast floodwater volume, in excess of current discharge through the dam, exactly equals the remaining available storage capacity of the reservoir. Up to point A, therefore, all inflow is discharged and after point A discharge is held at a constant rate and all excess inflow is stored in the reservoir. Clearly, the reservoir will become full at that point on the falling hydrograph when the inflow rate equals the discharge rate and the flood peak at the dam will have been reduced by the amount BC. Thereafter, depending on downstream flow conditions, the constant discharge rate may be maintained or reduced. Normally, of course, such an accurate forecast of floodflows is not available. In that case all inflow to the reservoir during the early part of the flood hydrograph is discharged until the outflow through the dam equals the safe capacity of the downstream channel, after which excess inflow is stored until the inflow rate once again drops below the safe channel capacity.

Figure 10.4a illustrates that the controlled outflow hydrograph at the dam will change considerably in shape as it moves downstream (see also the discussion of Flood Routing, pp. 100–104). Therefore, unless the area to be protected is immediately adjacent to the dam, the controlled outflow must be determined by the storage effects on the hydrograph of the downstream channel and also by the actual or forecast of local inflow into the channel below the reservoir. This will produce the greatest flood peak reduction at the protected area rather than at the dam. Linsley and Franzini (1972) noted that in the normal case, where local inflow reaches a peak sooner than the inflow from further upstream, the operation of an upstream flood-mitigation reservoir usually involves small releases early in the flood, with relatively larger releases timed to arrive after the local inflow peak has passed the protected area. The success of such operations depends greatly on the accuracy of forecasts of reservoir and local channel inflow, and even comparatively small mistimings in the release of outflow from the reservoir can lead to an exacerbation rather than an amelioration of flood conditions.

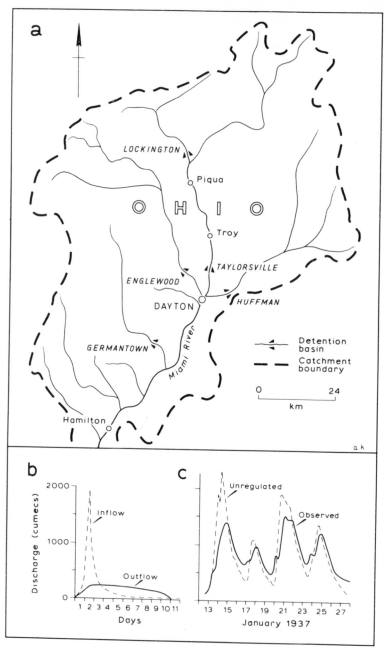

Figure 10.3   Detention basin systems: *a*, Miami Conservancy District detention basins above Hamilton, Ohio; *b*, Flood regulating effect of the Germanstown detention basin; *c*, Regulating effect of the four upstream detention basins on river discharge at Dayton, Ohio

Source: *b* and *c*, Rutter and Engstrom (1964).

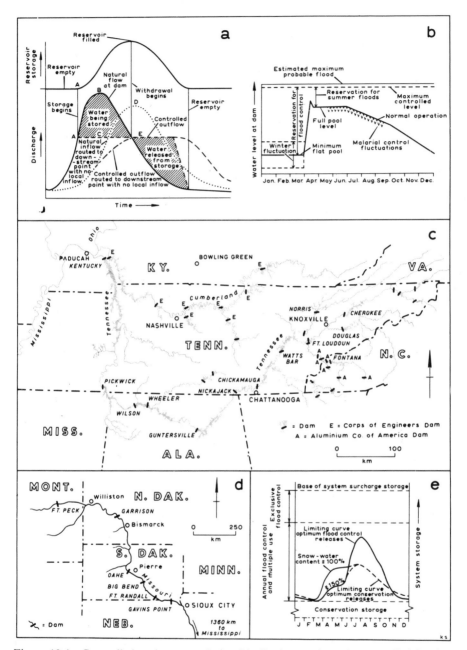

Figure 10.4   Controlled-outlet reservoirs: *a*, Idealised operation of a controlled flood mitigation reservoir; *b*, Annual operational plan of the multi-purpose Chickamauga reservoir; *c*, The TVA reservoir system; *d*, The Missouri River Main Stem system; *e*, Preliminary operating curves for the Missouri River system reservoirs
Source: *a*, Linsley, Kohler and Paulhus (1949); *b*, *d* and *e*, Rutter and Engstrom (1964); *c*, TVA (1967).

Like the detention basin, the controlled flood-mitigation reservoir affords the greatest potential flood protection when it is empty. If, therefore, another flood-producing event occurs before a reservoir is emptied of all the water retained during a previous event, the effectiveness of the reservoir will be greatly reduced. Indeed, because of the greater speed of a floodwave in deep water, the down-stream effects of a second flood occurring while a reservoir is still full may well be intensified. In most cases, therefore, the effectiveness of flood-mitigating reservoirs is considerably lower than their maximum potential under ideal conditions, except for small floods which require only a small portion of the reservoir capacity for adequate control (Linsley and Franzini, 1972).

Because of the high cost of reservoir construction, flood protection is normally only one of the functions of a reservoir in addition to others such as irrigation, sanitation and water supply, navigation improvement, recreation and power development. These *multi-purpose river-regulating reservoirs* are now the most important part of the total reservoir population and have been incorporated into massive, complex schemes on some of the world's major rivers in Asia, the Far East and North America. For example, the six major reservoirs on the middle Missouri have a gross storage capacity of 93 480 million m^3 equivalent to three years of the river's average flow, and on the Tennessee River there are 31 major reservoirs, 19 of them multi-purpose projects (Rutter and Engstrom, 1964).

Clearly, the different functions of a multi-purpose reservoir are frequently in conflict. Maximum flood protection demands an empty reservoir, maximum power development demands a full one; irrigation normally involves maximum releases during the summer while many recreational pursuits require a full reservoir in summer. Multiple use of reservoirs therefore implies a compromise which inevitably results in less than the maximum possible benefits for any one use but which should realise the maximum benefit from the project as a whole, provided that accurate flow forecasts are available well in advance (Linsley, Kohler and Paulhus, 1949). It will be clear from the discussions in chapter 7 that limitations on the effectiveness of multi-purpose reservoir operation are still imposed by the inadequacy of river forecasts. Such limitations are often manifested most clearly in the failure of the flood protection role.

As would be expected, the compromises inherent in multi-purpose projects vary from reservoir to reservoir, depending on the conflicts to be resolved, and also vary within a reservoir from year to year and from season to season. It is virtually impossible, therefore, to select examples to illustrate typical or ideal multi-purpose reservoir operations. Those which follow illustrate some of the conditions involved in the two major North American projects which have already been mentioned.

A simplified map of the TVA reservoir system is shown in figure 10.4c. The nine multi-purpose reservoirs on the main stream are used principally to maintain a 1000 km navigation channel from Knoxville to the Ohio River, to reduce flood damages both within the valley (the greatest flood damage potential being at Chattanooga) and along the lower Ohio–Mississippi system, and finally to generate hydroelectric power on a largely seasonal basis after the flood season is over. A typical plan of operation at the Chickamauga reservoir is shown in figure 10.4b. During the main flood season water levels are maintained at a minimum consistent with an adequate navigation depth. After 31 March, when the danger of major flooding is past, the reservoir is filled and maintained at near full-pool through much of the summer. Regular 30 cm fluctuations are used to strand floating debris, thereby controlling the mosquito population and reducing malaria. Drawdown for power and navigation then brings the water level to within the winter fluctuating range by 1 December.

The six multi-purpose reservoirs comprising the Missouri River Main Stem Reservoir System are shown in figure 10.4d. These reservoirs were constructed for flood control and for a number of conservation uses including irrigation, water supply and effluent disposal, navigation and hydroelectric power. Preliminary operating plans for the reservoirs are shown in figure 10.4e and were described by Rutter and Engstrom (1964). During the main meltwater flood season the amount of early filling is adjusted to the upstream snow–water content. If storage exceeds the level indicated by the optimum flood control release curve, then water must be discharged at the maximum rate determined by downstream channel capacity in order to evacuate the flood control space as rapidly as possible. Additional operating curves have also been developed to guide the use of the exclusive flood control space. At the other extreme, when storage is below the level of the optimum conservation release curve, restrictions on conservation use may be necessary to prevent excessive drawdown into the carryover storage space.

There has been a long and comparatively sterile argument, forming part of the more general upstream/downstream controversy previously mentioned, about the relative merits of a greater number of small headwater reservoirs and a smaller number of large mainstream reservoirs. It was emphasised earlier that the degree of flood protection afforded by a reservoir diminishes with distance downstream, or strictly speaking, with the percentage of the total catchment area which is reservoired. Linsley and Franzini (1972) suggested that, in general, at least one-third of the total catchment area should be under reservoir control for effective flood protection. It is also obvious that a large reservoir will store more floodwater than a small one. Clearly, then, if the aim is to protect a low-land city site, a large reservoir situated at a downstream point on the main stem immediately above the city seems the obvious choice. Such a reservoir would guard against a prolonged, large-area flood-producing event. If, however, the primary objective is to protect upstream rural areas and, in addition, provide some measure of erosion control, then a number of small headwater reservoirs are called for, although each of these can only give protection against a comparatively short-duration and small-area storm.

Although the hydrological arguments are quite clear, the socio-economic and political considerations may be much more confused. In terms of the latter, one can point, for example, at the flood protection role of the U.S. Department of Agriculture under Public Law 566 where the structural emphasis is specifically on small dams and reservoirs (see pp. 142–143). Also, as Linsley and Franzini (1972) pointed out, economic analyses and other factors may favour upstream sites despite the inferior flood protection which they afford. For example, the use of several small reservoirs, instead of a single large one, offers the possibility of initially developing only those units of the system which yield the highest economic return and constructing the additional units as development of the area increases their potential benefits. Again, in developing urban areas the incremental provision of adequate flood storage may be desirable or mandatory and will normally be met by the construction of small reservoirs (see p. 141).

In this section the value of reservoirs as a means of flood protection has been both assumed and demonstrated by example. Their disadvantages, which are many, have not always been referred to explicitly and it is appropriate, therefore, to list them now by way of conclusion. First, dam failure can be catastrophic and even substantial overtopping disastrous (see chapter 4), partly because of the enormous amount of water suddenly released and partly because of the inevitably intensified land-use downstream of the dam reflecting the reactive sense of security afforded by flood protection schemes. Second, depending on the type of reservoir, some land must be temporarily or permanently submerged in order to protect other land. Hewlett and Nutter (1969) referred to an estimate that 2 million hectares in the United States are flooded by existing reservoirs to protect 5.2 million hectares downstream. Because the best sites have already been utilised, the ratio of flooded area to protected area will deteriorate in future. In densely populated agricultural land of, say, South–east Asia the problem is particularly severe and in this situation it would be absurd to submerge 10 000 ha of arable land in order to protect an area of 50 000 ha against the risk of being flooded once in five years (United Nations, 1951). Third, in many areas suitable new reservoir sites are increasingly difficult to find; in other areas, for example in Britain, such sites may be virtually non-existent from the outset. Fourth, because the effectiveness of reservoirs diminishes downstream they must be located close to the protected area. Fifth, flood protection reservoirs of the controlled type can only be operated efficiently if accurate flow forecasts are available. Sixth, unless special provision is made during construction, reservoirs trap much of the suspended load carried by the inflowing rivers and therefore act as large sediment traps. This factor is allowed for in the design of most major reservoirs but many smaller ones have silted up within a few decades and even before this stage has been reached their effective flood storage capacity will have progressively diminished. A concomitant of silting in the reservoir is a reduced suspended load in the downstream channel which may so affect the quasi-equilibrium between the discharge of water and solids load on the one hand and the form of the channel on the other, that marked channel erosion is initiated. This has already occurred to a serious extent in the Nile below the Aswan dam (Dorozynski, 1975). Finally, by modifying water quality, not only in terms of suspended solids, but also in terms of temperature and chemical content, reservoirs may have a disturbing ecological impact on the downstream reaches of the river channel, while the barrier of the dam itself can seriously affect the populations of migrating species.

For all these reasons reservoirs can only form one part of the total flood protection programme in a given area, although they are likely to be more important in some locations than in others if conditions particularly favour their construction.

A combined approach

The response to virtually all major flood problems, and indeed to many minor ones, involves some combination of the four main approaches individually discussed in the preceding pages. In some cases the adoption of a combined approach is simply a reflection of constructional techniques. For example, the spoil created by channel enlargement can be most conveniently deposited as flood embankments alongside the improved channel. In other cases combination may reflect particular hydrological circumstances. Thus, whatever other flood protection measures have been adopted, on rivers prone to ice-jam formation and the resulting water level rise upstream of the jam, a system of embankments along the vulnerable reaches is virtually essential, as along the Bow River at Calgary (Burton, 1969). In yet other cases the considerations are almost entirely economic, so that it may be cheaper to build a smaller reservoir and embank and/or improve particularly flood-prone sections of the downstream channel. Or, again, it will almost certainly be cheaper to reduce the design size of a diversion channel by improving the existing river channel as much as possible.

Many of the really large combined flood protection schemes are well known and reference has already been made to them in earlier discussions. One of the most successful of the major flood protection projects, for example, is the combination of reservoirs, channel improvement, flood embankments and flood abatement developed by the Tennessee Valley Authority. Plate 11a shows a view over Chattanooga in March 1867 during the greatest flood ever recorded in the Tennessee valley. Plate 11b was taken from the same point and shows Chattanooga one hundred years later by which time the combined flood protection scheme of the TVA had averted damage of more than $326 million, chiefly in this one city (TVA, 1967). Two less ambitious and less well-known schemes within the United Kingdom will now be briefly described in order to give a different perspective on the combined approach to flood protection.

The River Lee, draining an area of some 1400 km², flows southward into the heart of the London urban area (figure 10.5a). Flood problems were intensified, partly by the large area of impervious surface of London itself in the south, the older but growing settlements of Luton, Hertford and Bishop's Stortford, and the 'new towns' of Harlow, Stevenage, Hatfield and Welwyn Garden City, and partly by the way in which the upper tributaries converge on the main trunk system near Hertford. Accordingly, the main river south of Hertford was characterised by frequent, damaging floods. The range of feasible flood protection measures was limited to some extent by the intensity of land-use and urban development, and by the topography of the lower catchment.

Medrington (1969) described a major, integrated flood protection scheme which began before the Second World War, with improvements to the tidal channels and embankments in the densely developed low-lying areas of West Ham and Stratford, and which has continued progressively upstream since then. The main components of the scheme, illustrated in figure 10.5b, are the widening and improvement of the Lee in order to approximately double its discharge capacity; the construction of an entirely new channel, 33 m wide and 1.2 km in length, between Enfield lock and Waltham Abbey; the construction of a new, concrete-lined relief channel, 16.7 m wide, 2.7 m deep and 5.5 km

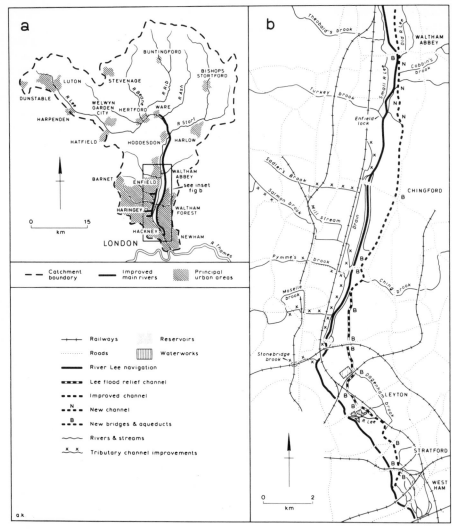

Figure 10.5   The Lee flood protection scheme: *a*, The catchment area of the River Lee; *b*, Flood protection measures in the middle and lower Lee valley
Source: Medrington (1969).

long, from Leyton to Chingford; the provision of automatic lifting sluices to divert floodflows into the appropriate channel; the construction of new bridges and aqueducts to minimise obstructions in the waterways; and finally, the extensive improvement, usually through the construction of a concrete-lined channel, of the main tributary streams (see plate 9). Medrington (1969) estimated that to provide equivalent flood protection using only reservoirs or detention basins in the main valley an area of approximately the same size as that at risk, 18 km², would have been required, while if the reservoirs were located in tributary valleys more than 50 km² would have been taken.

The city of Bath is another urban centre where the intensity of land-use and the local topography imposed constraints on the range of feasible flood protection measures. It was noted in chapter 7 (p. 109) that the city has been subjected in the past to frequent serious flooding from the River Avon which drains a catchment area of some 1665 km² above Bath. Newson (1975) described the comprehensive flood protection programme introduced by the then Bristol Avon River Authority between 1964 and 1973 and illustrated in figure 10.6. A flood relief channel would have involved tunnelling into surrounding hills, embankments would have caused internal drainage problems and land-fill would have adversely affected historical properties in this important tourist centre. The scheme which was eventually adopted for a 13 km reach of the Avon between Bathampton and Saltford (figure 10.6a) involved new bridges, the grading and straightening of the channel downstream of Twerton, extensive bank protection, new sluices at Twerton and Pulteney, new flood walls through the city, dredging to a new river grade (figure 10.6b) and sewer reconstruction to meet the new river level. Vertical channel banks were used to obtain maximum channel capacity without the requisition of property, various parts of the scheme were presented for initial approval to the Royal Fine Arts Commission to safeguard the river scenery and a number of aesthetically pleasing features were built into the final design.

COASTAL AND ESTUARINE FLOODS

Somewhat different problems are encountered when attempts are made to protect against coastal and estuarine flooding, not the least being the sheer magnitude of the forces involved as high tides and large waves pound the coast. Except on a local scale man can do very little to prevent the advance of the sea on an eroding coastline. In severe circumstances, as along the North Humberside coast of England, coastal retreat will continue on either side of the protected area and may indeed be intensified by the localised presence of protective works, so that the protected area becomes more and more exposed until it eventually succumbs. As emphasised in chapter 4, coastal flooding is of importance only on naturally low-lying coasts and along coasts backed by land reclaimed from the sea which lies below the level of high tides. On normal low-lying coasts the best protection against flooding is often afforded by natural defences, such as a belt of dunes and a high beach. Along reclaimed coasts embankments and floodwalls are essential, and may also be used to reinforce natural defences elsewhere.

Apart from *embankments and floodwalls,* however, the choice of flood protection measures along coasts is much more restricted than in the case of river floods. It really extends only to the possibility of constructing coastal (usually estuarine) *barrages* in the comparatively few locations where conditions are favourable or to the use, again in estuaries, of *flood barriers* to protect high-value urban areas. Each of these measures will now be discussed separately.

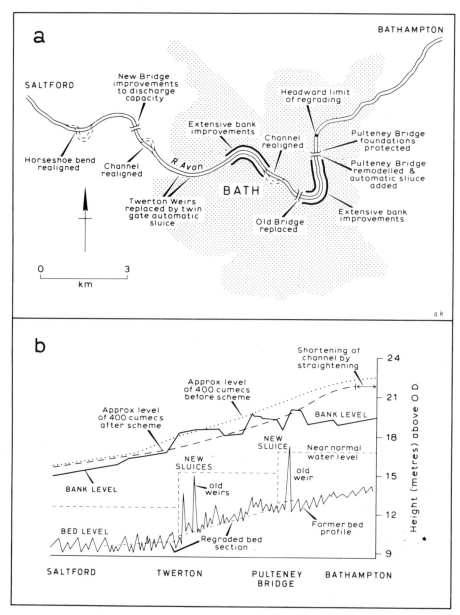

Figure 10.6   The Avon flood protection scheme: *a*, Flood protection measures at Bath; *b*, Long profiles of the bed, bank and water level before and after channel improvement
Source: Newson (1975).

Embankments and floodwalls

Sand dunes and high beaches form natural flood protecting embankments which are usually far more effective than man-made substitutes. These natural defences can be maintained or strengthened artificially in a number of ways, although it must be emphasised that such interference with natural coastal processes may create problems equal to or greater than those they were intended to solve (Burton, Kates and Snead, 1969). Thus groynes and jetties, constructed to retain beach material by interfering with littoral drift, may starve areas farther along the coast of mobile sand and shingle, thereby causing beach degradation. This problem intensifies as the use of groynes and jetties increases and on many coasts beaches are now nourished artificially with sand and shingle pumped from nearby lagoons, hauled by road or dredged from the offshore sea bed. Similarly, sand dunes may be built up by sand tipping and bulldozing or by encouraging accretion through the construction of permeable screens of brushwood or basketwork, and they may be stabilised by planting marram grass or buckthorn (Thorn, 1960). Attempts to protect dune belts by constructing concrete or other impermeable revetments are doomed to failure. The concrete tends to transfer wave energy to adjacent unprotected areas, which are then attacked on the flank, and the revetments hinder or prevent natural dune growth behind them, thereby condemning the dunes to botanical degeneration and eventual erosion by the wind (Barnes and King, 1953).

Along many coasts and estuaries the absence of adequate natural defences has necessitated the construction of embankments and floodwalls. Embankments may be built of silt and sand, as in Sweden and Holland, or of clay, as is normally the case in Britain, except where good supplies of clay are difficult to obtain. In that case the seaward portion of the embankment is made of clay and the landward side of more easily obtainable material such as chalk, clinker, etc. (Thorn, 1960). Like river flood embankments, coastal embankments are normally constructed from on-site materials taken from borrow pits so that the suitability of constructional materials inevitably varies from place to place. Earth embankments are susceptible to direct erosion by wave action, scour on the landward face due to overtopping and to seepage and slip failures. In addition, when dry the upper part of clay embankments suffer from fissuring which, in turn, can lead to excessive seepage and slumping unless the embankment is raised to at least one metre above the highest tide (Thorn, 1960). Embankments are extensively used to protect coastal, and particularly estuarine, areas around the North Sea. Unfortunately, the North Sea basin is prone to quite severe subsidence. In the region of the Thames estuary, the subsidence is about 10 to 20 cm each century, and at the head of the Humber estuary has amounted to some 12 cm since the first Ordnance Survey map of the area was produced (Radley and Simms, 1971). As a result, tidal influence gradually reaches farther upstream and estuarine and coastal areas are exposed to increasing flood risk. The Thames, for example, is now tidal to Teddington, whereas in Roman times tidal influence probably reached only as far upstream as London Bridge (Steers, 1953). In order to protect against this escalating risk, flood embankment height has been gradually increased over the years (considerably after the 1953 flooding, see p. 46) until many embankments have now reached their practical limit in terms of either the stability of constructional materials used or the strength of the subsoil foundations on which they rest. Any further increase in height, therefore, must be achieved either through the use of sheet piling or reinforced concrete walls on top of the existing earth embankments (see figure 10.7a) or by the complete replacement of the embankment with a piling, masonry or concrete floodwall.

Coastal floodwalls or sea walls are normally much more exposed than walls and embankments protecting estuaries and may be subjected to waves developed over fetches of several hundreds or even thousands of kilometres. In fact, sea walls are conventionally divided into two categories, those from which waves are reflected and those on which waves break. In turn, the ones on which waves break can be subdivided into two main groups (Thorn, 1960): first those where the depth of water in front of the wall is such that waves break on the structure (see figure 10.7c); and second those where the bigger waves break on the foreshore in front of the wall (see figure 10.7b). Apart from the danger of overtopping, the main problem with sea walls concerns their durability under wave attack. As waves break on and then fall back from the wall, the enormous variations of pressure may lift off the facing material, whether it is stone pitching, granite blockwork or interlocking or asphalt-jointed concrete blocks. Sheet piling of timber or steel is used mainly for toe-walls to protect the main wall from scour at the toe when the foreshore has been eroded by storm waves.

Permeable sea walls, more closely resembling natural defences, have many advantages. These may be constructed of large natural boulders, as on the eastern coast of the United States, or of multi-pronged concrete blocks which have the advantage of interlocking and so remaining stable even when built up with very steep slopes. The roughness of the surface reduces both swash height and the scouring effect of backwash on the foreshore, which is often such an undesirable effect of impermeable walls.

Despite the possible adverse effects on natural coastal processes of artificial flood protection structures and even of artificial attempts to consolidate natural defences, such structures have a proven and substantial effectiveness and are extensively used. An indication of the approximate extent of coastal flood protection is given by two coastlines which previously served as comparative examples, the eastern coasts of England and the United States. Craig-Smith (1974) estimated that 67 per cent of the East Anglian coastline was protected, although there are marked local variations. Similarly, Burton, Kates and Snead (1969) estimated that of the 1800 km of outer coastline from Maine to South Carolina, roughly 23 per cent was protected, with inter-state variations ranging from one per cent in Maryland to 50 per cent in Connecticut.

In both eastern England and the eastern United States the authors found that attitudes to coastal flood protection structures differed markedly from the normal response to similar structures along rivers. For example, Craig-Smith referred to pressure exerted by conservation groups preventing complete protection in Suffolk, while Burton, Kates and Snead found a prevalence of agitation against protective works on amenity grounds and quoted the extreme case where a sea wall proposal was rejected on the basis of opposition by local residents who suggested that if the wall must be built it should be a 'small' one! Not surpris-

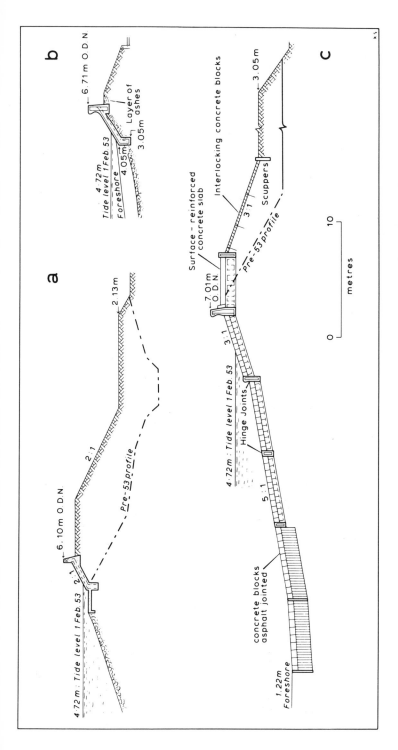

Figure 10.7 Coastal floodwalls: *a*, A concrete crest wall on an earth embankment, Isle of Sheppey; *b*, Cross-section of Seasalter wall, north coast of Kent; *c*, Cross-section of the Northern sea wall, which runs from Reculver to Birchington in Kent, and is one of the most massive sea walls in the United Kingdom
Source: Thorn (1960).

ingly, the land-use-intensifying effect of protective measures, almost invariably found on river floodplains, is less apparent and may even be reversed in some coastal areas. Burton and Kates (1964), for example, suggested that if the removal of a sand dune belt increases the amenity of a coastal site by giving more houses a view of the ocean, further development may be encouraged with a resultant increase in flood damages; while conversely, obliteration of an ocean view by construction of an artificial dune or a high sea wall may reduce amenity value and decelerate development.

Coastal barrages

On severely indented coastlines and on major estuaries the total length and therefore the construction and maintainance cost of adequate embankments and floodwalls is considerable. Thus attention has sometimes turned to the possibility of substantially shortening the exposed coastline by the construction of barrages across bays and estuaries. Such expensive schemes could seldom, if ever, be justified on the grounds of flood protection alone but since the barrage itself can serve as a basis for more direct road and rail links, at the same time creating a freshwater body on the landward side, there is clearly considerable potential for multiple resource development.

Proposals have been made for coastal barrages in many parts of the world, including several around the British coast, for example Morecambe Bay, the Dee estuary, Solway Firth and The Wash (Smith, 1972). However, concern about the possible economic and ecological consequences, through restrictions on navigation and fish migration, and the possible effects on coastal geomorphological processes has resulted in a very cautious approach, culminating so far as the proposals for Britain are concerned in only a number of feasibility studies. Of necessity, the Dutch have been more bold. For more than seven hundred years, in a continual battle with the sea, they have improved their system of sea dikes (embankments) and greatly reduced the length of the coastline. In the north, for example, the Barrier Dam, 30 km in length, pushed back the North Sea some 80 km and shortened the coastline by nearly 320 km. The former Zuyder Zee was dammed off to form the freshwater Ijselmeer, part of which has already been reclaimed as new polder land, and other shorter sea-arms have also been closed off by embankments (Volker, 1964). The largest scheme, however, was a direct consequence of the disastrous flooding which resulted from the storm surge of 1953 (see pp. 46–49).

The Delta Project (see figure 10.8) involved the construction of massive dams to close off four large sea inlets (the Haringvliet, the Brouwershavensche Gat, the Eastern Scheldt and the Veersche Gat), together with secondary dams in the Zandkreek, the Grevelingen and the Volkerak and a flood barrier above Rotterdam, thereby reducing the length of the coastline by 700 km and substantially improving the protection of the South-west Netherlands from flooding by the sea. Much of the work has now been completed and was described by Volker (1964). The approaches to Rotterdam and Antwerp via the Niewe Westerweg and the Western Scheldt will be left open but the embankments have been raised and strengthened. Excess floodwater and blocks of ice coming down the Meuse,

Waal and Lek are discharged through a series of sluices, nearly one kilometre in length, in the Haringvliet dam. Apart from its flood protection role, the Delta Project has created a large reserve of freshwater to combat the increasing threat of salination, improved road communications, linked hitherto isolated islands

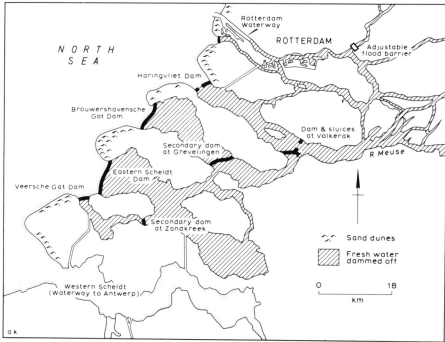

Figure 10.8   The Netherlands delta project
Source: Volker (1964).

to the mainland and greatly improved recreational facilities for water sports and sailing.

Flood barriers

Urbanised and industrialised estuaries that have major ports present one of the greatest flood protection problems, especially when they are in an area where subsidence and changing tidal conditions are reflected in a continually intensifying flood risk. On the one hand, traditional protection in the form of embankments and floodwalls is susceptible to only limited modification in urban areas without large-scale, expensive compulsory purchase of adjacent land. On the other hand, a permanent estuarine barrage with navigation locks would severely impede a busy shipping route. In such areas attention has therefore concentrated on the possibility of installing movable flood barriers which can be emplaced across the channel on the few days each year when a dangerously high tide threatens, but which are removed from the channel for most of the time. Several such schemes are currently at the planning or construction stage although undoubtedly the most spectacular is the Thames flood barrier, due for completion before 1980.

The gravity of the flood risk to central London was emphasised once again by the storm-surge of 1953. Continuing land subsidence and increasing tidal range mean that the high water level at Southend is increasing by 0.35 m per century while that at London Bridge is increasing by more than 0.6 m per century (Dock and Harbour Authority, 1974). The areas presently at risk at normal high tide and at the high tide level of 1 February 1953 are shown in figure 10.9a and amount to 62 and 116 km² respectively. Given a continuing intensification of the flood risk, the flood barrier currently under construction in the Woolwich reach at Silvertown is expected to give flood protection for about 60 years. By the end of that period the barrier will probably have to be raised about ten times a year, while when first in use, in 1979, it will be raised only twice a year (Dock and Harbour Authority, 1974).

The choice of both site and barrier design were difficult. The further upriver the barrier was located the smaller the inconvenience to shipping, but the greater were the complexity and cost of raising flood embankments downstream, and vice versa. The final choice is one of twelve original proposals and was determined in no small measure by the presence, at a shallow depth, of suitable chalk foundations. As far as the design of the barrier itself was concerned, the main requirements were unlimited headroom, maximum feasible span and pleasing appearance, and the solution was found in what has come to be known, incorrectly, as a rising sector gate (Hall, 1972). The basic principle of this is illustrated in figure 10.9b. This shows that the gate, which is in fact a *segment* of a circle, is normally housed in the bed of the river in a recessed concrete sill and can be swung upwards hydraulically into the defensive position in only 15 minutes.

Although the maximum span is limited to 61 m by both constructional materials and the differential head of water, there will be four main gates of this size, each more than 20 m high and weighing about 3300 tonnes, and six subsidiary gates, giving a total barrier width from bank to bank of about 520 m (GLC, 1974). Downstream of the flood barrier, embankments and floodwalls have been raised to give the same level of protection as the barrier itself and minor barriers have been built across the more important tributary channels, such as the Bow, Barking and Dartford Creeks.

A smaller tidal surge barrier is being constructed to protect low-lying areas of the city of Hull, in North Humberside, from the comparatively minor flooding which results whenever high spring-tides coincide with large freshwater discharges in the River Hull and the Humber estuary, and also from the major flooding which would inevitably accompany a high spring tide and tidal surge combination. More than 90 per cent of the city of Hull lies approximately two metres below the level of the highest recorded tide in the Humber estuary and River Hull, which occurred with the tidal surge of 29 September 1969. Because of land subsidence and increasing high-tide levels, it is expected that the number of times each year that the barrier is closed will gradually increase from the initial estimate of six at the outset (MacDonald and Shankland/Cox, 1974). The Hull flood barrier, which is due for completion before 1980, will consist of a gateway stretching nearly 100 m across the River Hull, some 200 m upstream of

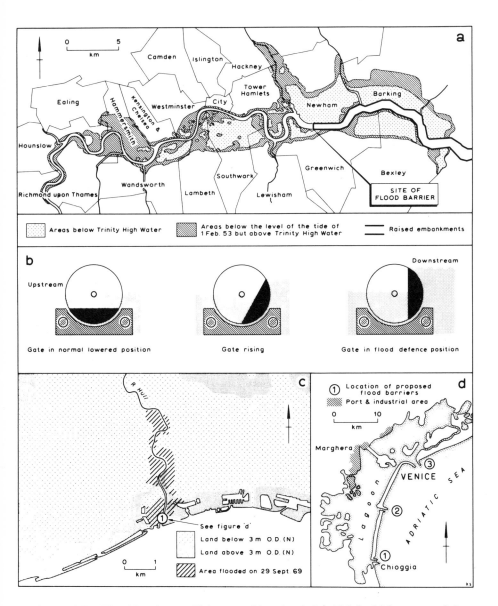

Figure 10.9   Flood barriers: *a*, The areas of London below Trinity high water and the high water attained on 1 February 1953; *b*, The basic principle of the so-called rising sector gate; *c*, Location of proposed flood barrier and areas most subject to flooding, Hull; *d*, Proposed location of flood barriers to protect Venice

Source: *a* and *b*, GLC (1974); *c*, Yorkshire Water Authority maps; *d*, Fay and Knightley (1975).

its confluence with the Humber (see figure 10.9c). A steel curtain 10.5 m in height and slung between concrete towers will be lowered into the river in less than half an hour. To reach the normal, fully open position, the curtain will be raised like an up-and-over garage door and stored in a horizontal position with its underside some 30 m above water level, allowing clearance for the largest vessels which use the Humber.

Like London and Hull, Venice is a major port in an area undergoing long-term subsidence which is subjected to occasional flooding from tidal surges. In addition to the port and industrial functions of its Marghera suburb, however, Venice itself is a tourist centre of international renown. It is perhaps surprising, therefore, that proposals for flood protection utilising movable flood barriers at the entrances to the lagoon (see figure 10.9d) are still at a comparatively early planning stage, although a number of systems have been suggested for temporarily closing off the lagoon, including floodable caissons and inflatable bags, both of which would lie unobtrusively on the sea bed when not in use (Fay and Knightley, 1975).

THE PRACTICAL RANGE OF CHOICE

A wide range of possible responses to the flood hazard has been discussed in some detail in the last three chapters. In a given situation, however, the effective, practical range of choice is likely to be quite limited, some indication of which was made at the end of chapter 8. In terms of coastal flooding, for example, not only are the possibilities for flood protection quite restricted in comparison with the possible response to river floods, but also the entire field of flood abatement, which can be applied so effectively to certain river flood situations, is completely inapplicable. The practical range of choice is narrowed down, therefore, to some form of adjustment and to a limited selection of structural measures.

Even within river basins there may be stringent physical limitations as, for example, when the non-availability of suitable reservoir sites limits the range of flood protection choices, or when the physical characteristics of the basin make flood abatement impossible. In other cases range of choice may be distorted by political considerations. Thus White (1964) observed that in the United States if the Federal flood control policy is to pay the total cost of reservoir projects but make no contribution, or only a limited one, towards floodproofing and land-use regulation, local agencies may consider floodproofing impracticable even though it is a less costly measure. In still other cases certain responses may prove to be technically impracticable or technical or other considerations may dictate a combined approach, involving not only several types of protection or abatement or adjustment but also a broader combination of aspects of all three main responses to the flood hazard.

But perhaps the greatest restraint on choice of response is imposed by economic considerations. Although this has not always been so (indeed many hundreds of superficially uneconomic 'make-work' projects were authorised by the U.S. Government during the depression of the early 1930s), virtually all schemes of flood-damage mitigation are now subjected to cost–benefit analysis. This topic is explored in the next chapter.

11 Economic Aspects of Response to the Flood Hazard

INTRODUCTION: TYPES OF FLOOD DAMAGE

The main characteristics of the flood hazard have been outlined (see p. 114), and it is on the economic implications of response to that hazard that the present chapter will concentrate. Floods, like most other natural hazards, cause considerable damage but do have some beneficial effects, such as silt deposition on agricultural land and the recharge of soil moisture, and they also have consequences which defy precise evaluation (Mitchell, 1974). The damage and financial loss caused by flooding and the extent to which these losses may be reduced by the various responses to the hazard have been subjected to increasingly rigorous appraisal during the past two or three decades, primarily in the United States and more recently in other countries. In all this work, data inadequacy has been a persistent problem which is still by no means entirely resolved.

Matthai (1969) referring to the June 1965 flooding of Denver, Colorado by the South Platte River, reported that, 'The flood peak passed through Denver during the night, and the immediate crisis was over by morning; but those in the inundated areas were faced with a Herculean task. . . . The colossal cleanup job, which would take months, began'. In this quotation, various types of damage are implied; there is, for example, the immediate damage which results when inundation occurs – cars are swept away and people knocked down by the swirling floodwaters. Other losses are involved in the cleanup and rehabilitation phase. Finally, there is a third type of damage such as the physical and mental ill-health which is so often the aftermath of a traumatic experience. More conventionally, flood damages are classified as in figure 11.1a, which is simply a visual precis of a most useful summary by Parker and Penning-Rowsell (1972) of some of the more important work in this field.

In the first place, it is usual to differentiate tangible and intangible damages according to whether or not they can be expressed in monetary terms. *Intangible damages* include fear, anxiety, annoyance, distress, insecurity, ill-health and ultimately loss of life (Parker and Penning-Rowsell, 1972). It will be emphasised later that a number of the major problems in flood damage estimation concern the quantification of intangibles, some of which are extremely suspect. An even more basic problem is the failure to agree on which intangibles it is possible or even desirable to attempt to quantify. (One approach to the evaluation of the personal annoyance caused by flooding was reported by Sterland (1973).)

Floods

Tangible damages can be further subdivided into direct and indirect categories. *Direct damages* result from the direct physical contact of damage-able property with floodwater and the extent of the damage is assumed to be the cost of restoration of that property to its preflood condition, or to its current market value if restoration impracticable. Direct damages thus include physical damage to buildings and their contents, bridges, roads and railways, physical damage to agricultural land, particularly in the case of coastal flooding by salt water which can result in long-term deterioration of soil structure and fertility, and finally the loss of agricultural crops. Direct damages are controlled by the physical characteristics of the floodplain or coastal land-use system and by its susceptibility to flooding (Middlesex Polytechnic, 1974). *Indirect damages* are

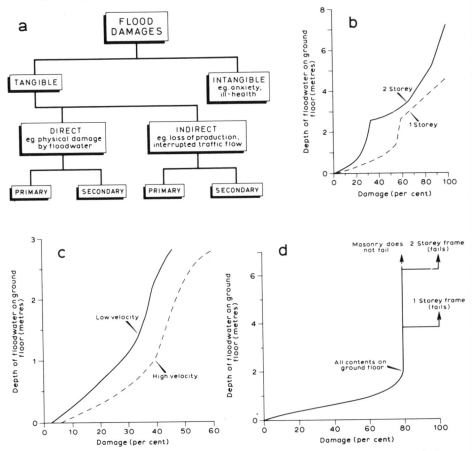

Figure 11.1   Flood damage and depth–damage curves: *a*, Types of flood damage; *b*, Average depth–damage curves for houses without basements, with 2.4 m ceilings and wooden sub-flooring and floor joists; *c*, Depth–damage curves for low value, two-storey houses at Pensford, Somerset for two classes of floodwater velocity; *d*, Average depth–damage curves for the contents of small business premises
Source: *b*, Kunreuther and Sheaffer (1970) pp. 659–67; *c*, TVA (1969); *d*, Porter (1971).

losses resulting from the breakdown of certain physical or economic linkages in the economy. Examples include loss of production, loss of income and business, and delays in transportation of goods and people involving the valuation of time. Steers (1953) reported that during the east coast flooding of 1953 some 350 km of railway track and 80 stations were temporarily out of service.

Some workers have further subdivided direct and indirect damages into primary and secondary categories. Thus *secondary direct damages* would include damage due to gas leakage and explosion caused by flooding and *secondary indirect damages* would include loss of retail business because of reduced local earnings consequent upon direct flood damage to industrial and commercial buildings. Parker and Penning-Rowsell (1972) suggested that additional complications were introduced in respect of indirect damages by the fact that a flood affects not only the area inundated but also, to a lesser extent, the adjacent areas so that a sort of shock wave having a multiplier effect spreads out from the flooded area.

Alternatively, flood damages can be classified according to the categories of land-use affected, in each of which flooding causes markedly different types of damage, for example agricultural, residential, retail/commercial/offices, public utilities, public buildings, industrial, transportational, recreational. Again, Kuiper (1965) referred to a simple fourfold classification as follows: (1) Physical damage to buildings and their contents, bridges, roads, railways, etc. (2) Agricultural crop losses, (3) Loss of income due to interruption of business, and (4) Cost of flood fighting, and the evacuation, care and rehabilitation of flood victims. Care must be taken to avoid double counting between items (3) and (4). Kuiper illustrated the relative importance of these four categories in the 1950 Red River flooding of Greater Winnipeg in which the total flood damage was $126 million, 82.5 per cent of which was accounted for by category (1), 2.4 per cent by category (2), 11.1 per cent by category (3) and the remaining 4.0 per cent by category (4).

The classification of damage illustrated in figure 11.1a is the most comprehensive and the most generally applicable and will be used where appropriate in the remainder of this chapter. It must, however, be emphasised that flood damages are highly variable and often extremely difficult to estimate, particularly the indirect and secondary damages.

FACTORS AFFECTING FLOOD DAMAGES

The variability of flood damage in both space and time reflects a large number of influencing factors. According to Parker and Penning-Rowsell (1972) the most important are the type of land use, characteristics of the floodwater (including depth, velocity, wave action, duration and solids load) and damage-reducing action taken by the occupants of flooded areas.

The effects of some of these factors are self-evident and need little further emphasis. Thus it is obvious that some types of land-use are more susceptible to the effects of flooding than others, although the relationships between land-use type and flood damage are not yet established precisely enough to enable useful generalisations to be made.

Another obvious effect is exerted by the depth of floodwater, each additional increment of depth increasing the damage in places already inundated and at the same time adding to the area of inundation. Although the relationship between floodwater depth and flood damage is seldom simple and linear in practice, it has proved possible to establish generalised depth–damage relationships for some land-use types in the form of *depth–damage curves* (see figure 11.1b, c, d), in which floodwater depth is plotted against damage expressed as a percentage of the total property value. Generally speaking such curves are established more easily for residential properties than for commercial and industrial establishments which are more variable in character. Damages may also be related to floods with certain occurrence frequencies in order to establish *damage–frequency curves*. Average depth–damage curves, based on the analysis of several hundreds of homes in Baltimore, Maryland, are shown in figure 11.1b. Major damage increments are associated with the inundation of the contents of each floor so that in the two-storey house the total inundation of the ground floor accounts for damage representing only 33 per cent of the property value, compared with 60 per cent in a one-storey dwelling. In many business properties, however, most of the contents are on the ground floor where flooding can account for a very high proportion of the damages. This is illustrated in figure 11.1d which also emphasises that the depth–damage relationship will vary considerably depending on the type of constructional materials. For example, timber-frame buildings commonly fail completely when critical water depths and pressures are attained, at which point the damage value escalates instantaneously to 100 per cent, whereas brick, stone and concrete buildings seldom fail even when completely inundated. The major difference in constructional materials between, say, North America where timber-frame construction is very common, and Britain where brick and stone are the norm, makes it difficult to transpose the results of flood damage studies and experience from one country to another. Depth–damage curves are clearly an appropriate way of quantifying flood damages for certain types of land-use but are probably less appropriate for others, such as an agricultural crop or a stretch of road or railway line, where the duration and velocity of floodwaters may be more important.

Since the *duration* of flooding often correlates positively with the depth of floodwaters and the area of inundation, it can be assumed that this factor is in part included in generalised depth–damage curves. However, this is not true of floodwater *velocity* which can produce widely different damages to the same land-use type, and whose effect may vary considerably from one land-use type to another. As Parker and Penning-Rowsell (1972) observed, many previous flood damage studies have assumed that floodwater velocities are low, which is frequently true, and that no additional damage could be caused by this factor. Some workers, for example White (1964), TVA (1969) and Porter (1971), have recognised the importance of the velocity component, however, and produced modified depth–damage curves to take this variable into account, albeit in a comparatively subjective way (see figure 11.1c).

The damage resulting from a given duration of flooding and from a given depth and velocity of floodwater may be further affected by the *solids load* carried by the water. Fine deposits not only cause damage to machinery and vehicle engines but also affect the time and cost of cleaning-up operations, as does the presence of sewage and other pollutants in the water, while heavier debris, such as rocks and boulders, may cause major direct damage. Only in the case of agricultural land use are floodwater deposits likely to prove beneficial, except in the event of salt-water flooding in coastal areas. Numerous other characteristics of floods such as *rate of rise* of floodwater, *turbulence, seasonality* and *timing* all affect the magnitude of flood damages (Parker and Penning-Rowsell, 1972) but are even more difficult to quantify and relate to damage estimates than those which have been discussed.

Finally, the damage resulting from a given floodwater duration, depth, velocity and quantity will depend on what *damage-reducing action* has been taken in the affected area. Adequate flood forecasting procedures, adjustments and protection measures (as discussed in chapters 7, 8 and 10) will do much to reduce the resulting damages and should be taken into account, although this is not always done, when generalised damage relationships, such as depth–damage curves, are being developed.

FLOOD DAMAGES: MAGNITUDES AND TRENDS

As will be demonstrated in more detail later in this chapter, flood damages are notoriously difficult both to measure and to estimate. This is due to the large number of influencing variables just discussed and, as Mitchell (1974) pointed out, to individual assessor's use of different loss evaluation criteria, some classes of damage being exaggerated or double-counted while others are omitted altogether, non-consideration of trends in adjustment to the flood hazard and, finally, the variability of damage estimates in relationship to economic assessments. Therefore, flood damage data, whether estimated or measured directly in the field, are subject to substantial errors and, in terms of regional or national totals, to major omissions as well. Thus in the United States, each of the three main data-collecting agencies, the Corps of Engineers, the Department of Agriculture and the Weather Bureau, pays attention to different aspects of flood damage. None of them, individually, gives a complete picture, nor unfortunately are their data mutually exclusive, otherwise simple summation might yield a useful composite result. The Weather Bureau data provide the longest continuous record, dating back to 1903, and it is mainly for this reason that they are used in the present chapter.

On a global scale the problem is even more intractable. Not all nations regularly collect or publish data on floods and other natural hazards nor is it easy to make comparisons of economic losses for those who do. Mitchell (1974) suggested that, in these circumstances, casualty reports may provide the best available guide to world patterns. Although estimates range widely, it is believed that natural hazards account for up to four per cent of the world's total annual deaths, of which 75 per cent result directly from riverine floods, tropical cyclones and associated sea surges. These casualties, however, are not evenly distributed throughout the world. Only 7 per cent occur in North America, Europe and Australia. Certainly in the United States absolute numbers reflect an apparent steady decline (see figure 11.2b) as forecasting and other responses to the flood hazard become gradually more efficient. It is, in fact, in the developing world that flooding and other natural hazards still take their greatest toll of human life, although in world monetary terms the economic losses in these areas are substantially smaller than those incurred in advanced industrial nations. On balance, then, world casualty rates do not appear to provide a particularly sensitive guide to flood damages on a global scale.

In the light of such problems one can only use, as examples to illustrate spatial and temporal variations in flood damages, those countries in which data have been systematically collected over long periods of time. Figure 11.2a illustrates annual flood damage data for the United States for the period 1903 through 1971, with damages expressed in 1971 dollar values thereby excluding early deflationary and subsequent, more marked, inflationary trends. There is clearly a wide variation in annual damages during this period with a range from low values of $7 million in 1906 and 1919 to high values of $1287 million in 1951 and $1292 million in 1955. Even so, nearly 70 per cent of the years had damages less than the $266 million average and in only three years did damages exceed $1000 million. Ten-year moving averages of these data are plotted in figure 11.2b and define an apparent upward trend throughout the data period representing an annual increase in damages of $6 million. Considering the large number of possible flood hazard responses, at least one of which is suited to virtually every floodplain and coastal situation, and particularly in view of the actual expenditure of over $7000 million on flood protection and prevention since adoption of a national flood control policy in 1936 (Task Force, 1966), it may seem strange that flood losses in the United States are not only as high as they are but also continue to increase. This is the great paradox of the flood problem, not only in America but in virtually every country of the world which has stimulated so much attention (White, 1964). The explanation is complex (but hinted at many times in our earlier discussions) and rests mainly on the fact that measures taken in response to the flood hazard, whether in the form of adjustments, abatement or protection, or simply reflected in a much improved forecasting procedure, create a sense of security which encourages further development of flood-prone areas. When, inevitably, the flood hazard response eventually proves inadequate, the resultant losses are infinitely greater than they would have been if that sense of security had not been engendered. Each renewed response to the flood hazard therefore adds an increment to subsequent flood damages. Even without this factor, the increasing pressure on land resources would result in some intensification of land use in flood-prone areas which, in itself, would result in considerable additional damages.

Deaths from flooding in the United States are shown only for the period 1925 through 1971. Again there is a wide variation from zero in 1931 to 423 in 1927,

Figure 11.2 Flood damage and deaths, United States: *a*, 1903–71 estimated annual totals (damage figures adjusted to 1971 values using the wholesale price index); *b*, Ten-year moving average graph, 1903–71 (damage figures adjusted to 1971 values using the wholesale price index); *c*, Distribution of estimated flood damages by major river systems, 1925–71
Source: U.S. Department of Commerce (1972).

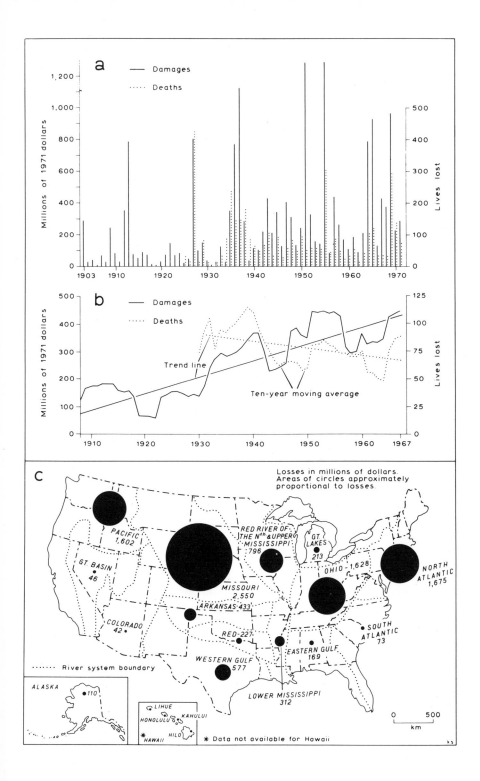

with an average of 82.5 deaths per year throughout the period. In this case, however, there is an apparent downward trend representing an annual decrease of 0.6 deaths per year. The direction, if not the magnitude, of this trend is confirmed by the estimate of Geraghty *et al.* (1973) that more than 20 000 deaths were caused by flooding between 1831 and 1940, an average of more than 185 per year. The marked improvement undoubtedly results largely from better flood and hurricane warning systems – it is significant that 60 per cent of the floods causing 100 or more deaths were associated with hurricanes (Geraghty *et al.*, 1973).

The geographical distribution of flood damages by major river basins is shown for the United States for the period 1925 through 1971 (figure 11.2c) and is largely self-explanatory. It will be seen that the greatest damages occurred in the basins of the Missouri and Ohio Rivers and on the Pacific and North Atlantic slopes.

COST–BENEFIT ANALYSIS

It must not be inferred from the foregoing comparison between the increasing response to and the increasing damages from flooding that large sums of money are spent inadvisedly on schemes of flood mitigation. Indeed, for many years in both Britain and the United States, as well as in many other countries, government-funded schemes (the major type in most countries) have had to produce preliminary cost–benefit analyses. In Britain, the Ministry of Agriculture, Fisheries and Food applied cost–benefit analysis relatively informally through 'worthwhileness tests' in connection with 'land drainage' (in effect flood alleviation) projects, although elsewhere a more formalised approach has usually been adopted. Whether applied formally or informally, however, the limitations of cost–benefit analysis are many. In view of the importance of its role in the decision-making process, consideration of the merits and drawbacks of cost–benefit analysis is appropriate at this stage and will be used as a framework for further discussion of economic aspects of response to the flood hazard.

Basis of the technique

As Johnson (1969) observed, any competent engineer could design schemes to avoid all flooding although ' . . . the cost would be fantastic, many of the schemes would be grossly uneconomic and the effect on amenities totally unacceptable. Real wisdom comes in knowing where and how money can be spent to the best advantage.' Clearly, what is needed are well defined, acceptable, general procedures whereby different schemes, based on one or more of the many possible responses to the flood hazard, may be evaluated and compared on a common basis. In this way, not only can the best of a number of possible schemes be identified, but also the viability of that particular scheme can be assessed in relationship to the total flood problem in the project area. A solution may be sought through the two related approaches of cost–benefit analysis and systems analysis, the latter being in some respects a more sophisticated and dynamic development of the former (O'Riordan and More, 1969).

Cost–benefit analysis, as the term suggests, is a technique for evaluating and comparing the benefits and costs of a scheme and is based on the assumption that the 'best' solution is represented either by the lowest-cost alternative or by that scheme which maximises the desired objective (O'Riordan and More, 1969). In terms of response to the flood hazard, *benefits* may be tangible and direct (reduction or prevention of direct physical damage, more intensive land use), indirect (reduction or prevention of indirect damages), or intangible (prevention of death, injury and sickness, and the maintenance of public morale). According to Kuiper (1965), it is considered conservative practice to judge the merits of a scheme on its tangible and direct benefits only.

Whatever the response to the flood hazard, there will be some degree of damage: for instance emergency evacuation is normally only successful for people and portable objects, fixed objects and property will be flooded irrespective of the warning time available; and an embankment provides protection only to a specified height, eventually it will be breached or overtopped. These damages which occur despite the adoption of a given response are called *residual damages* and may be used as the basis for defining benefits. Since benefits represent the damages prevented by a particular response they can be expressed simply as

Benefits = damages which would result from no response

$$- \text{residual damages} \qquad (11.1)$$

Costs are much easier to define and are simply the total expenditure involved in implementing a particular response to the flood hazard. Cost estimates should include all tangible costs, directly or indirectly indentifiable, incurred from the start of preliminary investigation of a scheme to its completion.

Difficulties in comparing the benefits and costs of a scheme result mainly from the fact that each is distributed differently in time – construction costs, usually a substantial proportion of the total, are incurred rapidly at the outset, while maintenance and administrative costs, together with benefits, are spread comparatively evenly over the very much longer post-construction period. Monetary value fluctuations during the economic life of a scheme add considerably to assessment problems. In order to overcome these, benefits and costs are based on price levels prevailing at the time of the analysis and are normally expressed as annual averages over the period of amortisation of the scheme. The excess of benefits over costs can be expressed as the ratio

$$\text{Benefit–Cost Ratio} = \frac{\text{benefits}}{\text{costs}}$$

$$(11.2)$$

The benefit–cost ratio can then be used to determine which particular response to the flood hazard should be adopted by using one of a number of criteria illustrated in figure 11.3a. In the United States, for example, Congress has long accepted the building of any project for which the benefit–cost ratio exceeds unity, that is when benefits exceed costs by even a small amount. All projects of a size between points *A* and *D* thus fulfil the basic Congressional requirement. In the case of projects smaller than A or larger than D, costs exceed benefits. The project which will produce the maximum benefit–cost ratio is at point B and yields the best return for a given amount of money invested. The project having the maximum net benefits (total benefits minus total costs) is shown at point C and represents the optimal development in that the last increment of cost invested just equals the value of benefit it produces. Theoretically, the construction of such a project makes the best use of resources and capital in the sense that no greater gain could be produced elsewhere in the economy (O'Riordan and More, 1969), and is the project size selected for most government-financed projects in the United States.

Cost–benefit analysis poses considerable problems particularly, as will be seen in subsequent discussion, in the calculation of residual damages and benefits. It does, however, have the advantage of simplicity and provides a means of establishing the relative feasibility of proposed schemes while, at the same time, demanding detailed identification and/or quantification of many variables which might otherwise be overlooked. Because of the comparative ease with which costs may be defined, little further consideration will be given to them in this chapter. Instead, attention will henceforth be concentrated on calculating damages, residual damages, damage reduction and total benefits.

Calculating damages

There are two main approaches to the calculation of flood damages. The first involves waiting for floods to occur and then calculating actual damage in the field through interview and observation; the second concerns the estimating of potential damages (the damages which would result from flooding of specified severity) mainly on the basis of generalised relationships between assumed water depths and assumed damages.

The calculation of *actual damages* is the approach which, so far, has been the most widely, if unsystematically, used in the British Isles. Its main advantage is that it deals with actual conditions of flooding and damage. The disadvantages, however, are considerable, not the least being that the work which is both complicated and time-consuming, requiring careful advance planning as well as valuation and survey expertise (Parker, 1973), must be carried out in the confused and unpropitious circumstances immediately following a flood event. Parker (1973) observed that in Britain it is left to the Water (formerly River) Authorities to collect the data with the result that a variety of data collection methods are used, some areas and floods being well documented, others not. Inevitably, the quality of data is highly variable. Another disadvantage is that the people affected tend to produce a substantial over-assessment of damage, particularly during the immediate post-flood period, so that calculated damages depend very much on the timing of questionnaire surveys. Finally, actual damage data are available only for the range of experienced floods whereas frequently one needs to estimate damages for the more serious design flood which has not yet occurred.

Clearly then there is need for a method of calculating *potential flood damages* which does not rely on the actual occurrence of flooding and which can be made for all areas, including those where flood experience is non-existent or not recent. If flooding should occur, comparison of potential and actual damage values and refinement of the method for calculating potential damages can be

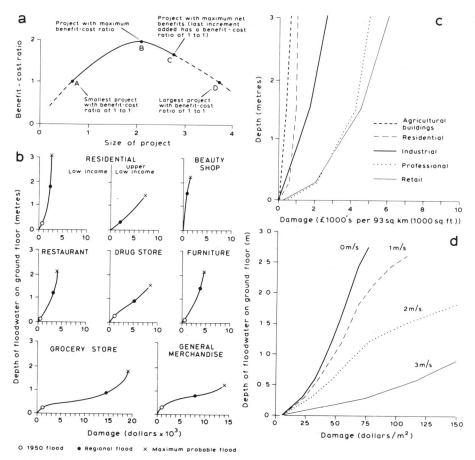

Figure 11.3   Damage calculation data: *a*, Selection of a flood mitigation project based on benefit–cost ratio; *b*, Depth–damage curves for representative establishments; *c*, Generalised depth–damage curves for five land-use categories, Lower Severn Valley; *d*, Depth–velocity–damage curves for one-storey frame houses in Nebraska
Source: *a*, Dixon (1964); *b*, White (1964); *c*, Middlesex Polytechnic (1974); *d*, U.S. Army Corps of Engineers (1970).

made (Middlesex Polytechnic, 1974). A number of approaches have been suggested (Kates, 1965; TVA, 1961; U.S. Army Corps of Engineers, 1970; White, 1964) and succinctly reviewed by Parker and Penning-Rowsell (1972). The main components of all such procedures are

(1) The identification of land-use categories, such as residential (sub-divided

according to value, constructional features), commercial, industrial and agricultural. Most work has concentrated on residential and commercial properties, although Kates (1965) extended the technique to industrial properties. Recent flood insurance legislation in the United States (see p. 130) has stimulated interest in estimating potential damages for a wide range of land-use categories.

(2) The determination of ground-floor elevations for each building.

(3) The determination of water depths for floods of varying severity: White (1964) used a recent, 1950, major flood, the Regional Flood and the Probable Maximum Flood (see p. 77).

(4) The determination of damages which would result from such flooding and the construction of depth–damage curves for each land-use type (see figure 11.3b).

This basic information can then be used in a number of ways, for example to develop composite, basin-wide damage estimates by the summation of generalised depth–damage curves for each land-use type, or the damages can be related to flood frequency thereby permitting the estimation of annual average potential damages and probable maximum damages for different periods of time.

Having discussed the merits and demerits of established methods, Parker and Penning-Rowsell (1972) proposed a modified and improved procedure for deriving generalised potential flood damage information relating mainly to direct flood damages to buildings and contents. Similar procedures are being developed for the substantially different cases of damage to agricultural, transportation and recreational land-use categories. The six main steps are

(1) Select land-use category for analysis, that is residential, industrial, etc.

(2) Identify the relative importance of the main flood characteristics (depth, velocity, duration, etc.) in causing flood damages to the selected land-use category. For example in the case of residential property floodwater depth may be the most important factor causing direct damage.

(3) Within each land-use category identify a limited number of sub-groups expected to be important in producing variations in flood damages. Obviously distinctions must be made between one and two storey dwellings or between the presence or absence of basements, or assessment could be based on rateable values.

(4) Establish a relationship between the main flood characteristic identified in (2) and damage, for example a depth–damage curve, using both actual flood damage data where available and estimates of potential damage based on detailed knowledge of sample properties. Figure 11.3c shows generalised depth–damage curves for five land-use categories in the Lower Severn valley.

(5) Use secondary flood characteristics such as velocity, that affect damage, to modify the depth–damage curve developed in (4). Thus curves relating depth to potential damage will vary depending on floodwater velocity just as did those for actual damages shown in figure 11.1c. Velocity induced variations of depth–damage curves for one-storey frame houses in Nebraska are illustrated in figure 11.3d. High velocities result in maximum damage, such as

building collapse, even with comparatively shallow depths of floodwater on the ground floor.

(6) Test the damage estimates so derived by comparing them with actual damage estimates as these become available and modify generalised potential estimates to conform more closely with actual damage experience.

Despite progress in estimating direct damages to certain land-use categories, many problems still must be solved before a satisfactory estimate of total, basin-wide potential flood damage is feasible. For example, damage estimates for transportation links and for agricultural crops are far from satisfactory although there are some advances in relating crop damage to varying water depths and flood duration on a seasonal basis, the heaviest losses usually occuring during the growing season. Again, the estimation of indirect damages is problematical, and some authorities feel that the time involved in attempting a detailed estimate is not justified. It may be necessary, therefore, to develop guidelines to define indirect damage as a fixed percentage of direct damage, as it is by the USDA Soil Conservation Service (Parker and Penning-Rowsell, 1972). The estimation of intangible damages represents another intractable problem for which as yet only tentative solutions have been advanced. Also there is a need for the establishment of more definitive relationships between damage and flood characteristics other than just depth. Finally, a much clearer understanding of flood frequency and of the causes and geomorphological repercussions of flooding (discussed in chapters 1–6) are necessary if depth–damage curves and other generalised damage relationships are to be satisfactorily developed into spatially integrated estimates of potential damage for specified periods of time.

Calculating benefits

The basic definition of benefits accruing from flood mitigation schemes was expressed as equation 11.1. This can be elaborated since benefits may, in fact, comprise three main elements: *damage reduction* (the difference between unmitigated and mitigated damages); the *enhancement of land values* in the protected area which is usually reflected in a more intensive use of land (for example residential or industrial use replacing agricultural use); and a variety of *miscellaneous benefits* (such as improved recreational and leisure facilities). Kuiper (1965) suggested that in most cases benefits will fall largely in the first category, with others playing only a secondary role, but that it is possible for benefits to be entirely in the first or second category. For example, prior to 1953 the Dutch utilised their low-lying land on the assumption that the sea defences were invulnerable, so the measures introduced after that year's disastrous flooding simply restored the pre-existing situation and did not induce more intensive land-use. On the other hand, the protection of some 400 000 ha of land in the Saskatchewan Delta by a new system of flood embankments creates a situation where the benefits are exclusively in the future use of the land, since the present use is nil. In exceptional circumstances benefits may fall largely in the third, miscellaneous category. For example, in the Metropolitan Toronto Plan, which was proposed in 1959 in the aftermath of a catastrophic flood associated with Hurricane

Hazel, only 22 per cent of the benefits were for flood damage reduction and over 40 per cent were for public recreation (Burton, 1969).

In view of the complex nature of flood mitigation benefits and the problems of calculating damages (and, by implication, damage reduction), it will clearly be extremely difficult to make more than an educated guess about the magnitude of total benefits. It is in this light that many of the published estimates must be regarded. Thus Hertzler (1961) suggested that in the United States the total benefits accruing from flood mitigation schemes since 1918 exceeded total costs by a ratio of 1.33 while TVA (1967) produced a benefit–cost ratio of 1.98. They estimated that by the end of the fiscal year 1967 total benefits from the TVA programme, since its inception in 1936, amounted to more than $517 million ($367 million in damage reduction and $150 million in enhanced value of 2.4 million ha of productive agricultural land along the lower Ohio and Mississippi rivers) compared with a total expenditure on flood mitigation of $261 million.

Disregarding the category of miscellaneous benefits, further consideration will now be given to the calculation of damage reduction and of the enhancement of land values resulting from flood mitigation schemes.

We have seen that average annual flood damages can be calculated from the combined use of depth–damage and depth–frequency relationships. Clearly, both relationships may be changed by flood mitigation schemes. Emergency evacuation or floodproofing, for example, will affect the shape of the depth–damage curve while the construction of reservoirs or flood embankments will materially affect the shape of the depth–frequency curve. In order, therefore, to evaluate the *damage reduction* likely to result from a proposed scheme it is necessary to determine the existing and to estimate the future modified form of the depth–damage, depth–frequency and damage–frequency relationships.

A hypothetical example, based on Kuiper (1965), is shown in figure 11.4a where the solid line in both parts of the diagram represents the existing damage–frequency curve. If an embankment system is constructed which is capable of withstanding the 30-year flood the modified damage–frequency curve will be as shown in figure 11.4a(i), reflecting the fact that benefits accrue only for floods smaller than the 30-year flood. After the failure or overtopping of the embankments damages will be as large as they would have been prior to their construction. Similarly, if a diversion channel is constructed, again to accommodate the 30-year flood, the modified damage–frequency curve will be as shown in figure 11.4a(ii), that is no damage will result from floods with return periods shorter than 30 years, while for larger floods the diversion will continue to function and will thus reduce damages below their unmitigated level. Depending on local discharge–stage–damage relationships, damage reduction may increase, decrease (as shown here) or remain constant as flood magnitude increases. Kuiper (1965) suggested that channel improvement schemes would have an effect similar to diversion schemes while the effect of reservoir construction on the damage–frequency curve would probably be intermediate between that of embankments and diversions.

Day and Lee (1975) used a detailed computer model to calculate the potential damage-reducing effects of three different types of adjustment at a number of flood-prone locations in the Connecticut River Basin in New England. Damage–frequency curves for one of these locations are shown in figure 11.4b. All three adjustments took the form of emergency evacuation following receipt of a flood warning. LWT is the partial evacuation of movable items to a higher

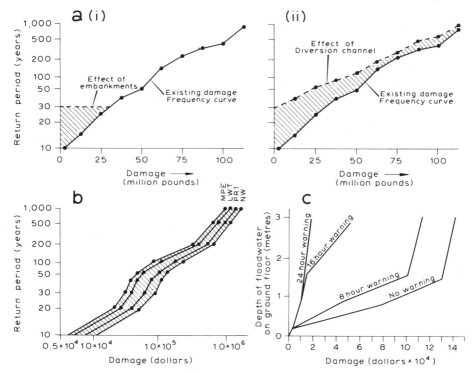

Figure 11.4   Damage reduction: *a*, Benefits (shaded area) accruing from two hypothetical flood mitigation schemes; (i) embankments and (ii) a diversion channel; *b*, Potential damage-reduction (benefits, shaded area) for residential property by three types of emergency evacuation, assuming 100 per cent response following floodwarning at Agawam, Massachusetts (see text for detailed explanation); *c*, Pennsylvania supermarket depth–damage curves related to length of floodwarning time, showing the damage reducing capability of emergency evacuation, assuming 100 per cent response
Source: *b*, Day and Lee (1975); *c*, Day *et al.* (1969) pp. 937–46.

elevation within a limited warning time of six to twelve hours; MPE the maximum practical evacuation of all movable items to a higher elevation within a warning time of twelve to twenty-four hours; and PRI the partial relocation of movable items to a storage area above the ground-floor ceiling. Their damage-reducing capability can be estimated by comparing the appropriate damage–frequency curve with the damage–frequency curve which would result with no warning (NW). Earlier work by Day *et al.* (1969) indicated the damage-reducing capability of emergency evacuation for supermarkets in relationship to the length of flood warning time received (see figure 11.4c).

One of the best known surveys of potential damage reduction was presented by White (1964) for six towns in the United States, the most intensively studied being LaFollette in Tennessee. White showed that at LaFollette floodproofing, engineering works and emergency action could reduce damages by as much as 85, 40 and 20 per cent respectively, although in fact no single response to the flood hazard would give larger net benefits than simply bearing the loss. In cost–benefit terms, emergency action was the most successful response, whereas the high costs of engineering works and of floodproofing greatly impaired their benefit cost ratios.

The *enhancement of land values* through more intensive use and greater pro-ductivity represents the second main component of benefits accruing from flood mitigation projects and is often referred to as project-induced economic growth (Whipple, 1969). However, the quantification of this type of benefit is difficult and the resulting errors may seriously impair the usefulness of cost–benefit analyses. Some of the problems of measuring the additional value of formerly flood-prone land, now protected from flooding, were highlighted by Struyk (1971) who calculated average differentials between flood-free and flood-prone areas along the Missouri River of about $62/ha, almost twice those prepared by the U.S. Army Corps of Engineers. It has already been pointed out (p. 168) that in some coastal areas flood protection measures may be accompanied by a reduction in the intensity of land use, reflecting the adverse aesthetic effect of the protection measure itself.

Two other problems, referred to by Chambers (1973), concern the ident-ification of true costs and the avoidance of double-counting. Thus where low-grade agricultural land is made suitable for residential development through flood protection, the value of the benefit cannot be taken directly as the differ-ence between the 'before and after' market value of the land. This is because, as Chambers pointed out, if a flood mitigation scheme is not introduced, resi-dential development will normally not be suppressed but will take place instead at some other site away from the flood-prone area. For the purposes of cost–benefit analyses, therefore, the likely effects of site works, loss of agricultural land, distances to employment and shopping centres, etc., at such other sites should also be considered. Double counting, which is the representation of a single benefit in two different ways and the subsequent inclusion of both values in the final analysis, may sometimes obfuscate the incorporation of land value enhancement in cost–benefit analyses. Thus for an individual house owner, the benefit accruing from a flood mitigation scheme may be taken as the amount of damage reduction or the expected appreciation in the market value of the house but not both. In other words, the increased market value is simply a reflection of the potential damage reduction and so is another way of ex-pressing the same benefit, not an additional benefit.

A further problem, illustrated by Theiler (1969), relates to the unpre-dictability of response by land-users to the actual and perceived change in flood hazard which results from a particular flood mitigation scheme. For example, it was expected that as a result of increased flood protection on the Coon Creek in south-western Wisconsin there would be an intensification of agricultural land-use and an expansion of agriculture into the newly protected areas. In fact, the local farmers did not respond as anticipated to the changed flood risk, largely because the flood protection scheme coincided with modifications to the local agricultural economy which lessened the demand for cropland. Also, an increased number of retired and semi-retired farmers did not fully use their land, and the opinion of some farmers was that they had no need for additional cropland.

SYSTEMS ANALYSIS

An alternative method of optimising response to the flood hazard is through systems analysis, a somewhat indefinite term which in this context implies a computerised analysis sufficiently complex to allow both for realistic changes of inputs and constraints, often containing a strong stochastic element, and also for greater flexibility in terms of changes of investment and target output levels during a number of time periods within the history of the project (Chorley and Kennedy, 1971). Systems analysis thus helps to overcome one of the main defects of conventional cost–benefit analysis, namely that the latter emphasises a static view of the project, whereas in fact objectives change both with the passage of time and as more data are collected, in effect there is often a dynamic interaction between policy making and project design (O'Riordan and More, 1969).

The systems analysis approach can be applied at widely differing levels of complexity. Thus in a consideration of non-structural methods of flood damage reduction, Day (1970) presented a recursive linear programming model for allocating specific land uses to specific parts of the floodplain according to a productivity index which took into account the hazard and the susceptibility of the use to damage. The model identified economically efficient combinations of spatial and temporal planning of urban land-use, site elevation through landfill and floodproofing of buildings. Day recognised that by not providing for structural measures the model was severely constrained in its ability to select fully optimal plans but felt that once the appropriate choice criteria and procedures for non-structural planning had been identified, the model could then be enlarged to incorporate the necessary structural alternatives.

Multi-reservoir flood control systems may be developed in a number of ways by means of different combinations of systems components. Selection of the best combination by conventional means normally involves a trial and error procedure based on the analysis of individual reservoirs in the system. Unfortunately, as Windsor (1975) pointed out, if the river basin system is at all complex, the number of possible design and operating policies can be extremely large, and there is no assurance that the best combination of structural measures will be found. Clearly the individual flood-control reservoirs can be planned and designed correctly only when they are considered as components of the larger system of projects within the river basin development. Windsor proposed a computer model, using mixed integer programming, in which it was assumed that the nonlinear cost functions for the reservoirs and damage centres within the basin were known and could be approximated by a set of linear segments. Flood variability was accounted for by using a representative range of recorded or synthetically derived flood hydrographs and the estimate of the probable maximum flood as input data to the model. Each potential flood combination was routed in turn through the proposed river basin development by using a decision policy that automatically minimised the expected total costs of the system and at the same time provided a reasonably high degree of assurance against hydraulic failure (Windsor, 1975).

Large-scale control of hydrological systems is rarely, if ever, attempted simply for the purposes of flood control. Even in a straightforward multi-reservoir scheme the reservoirs may be used not only to combat floods but also to maintain sufficient channel flow for navigation, irrigation, pollution control, etc. In more complex schemes not only reservoirs, but also channel improvements, embankments and other structural measures, flood abatement procedures, and various human adjustments to the flood hazard may be employed, together with the development of navigation and irrigation systems, public and industrial water supplies, the production of hydro-electric power and the development of water-based recreational and leisure facilities. In such situations economic and social variables interact with, and constrain, the purely hydrological ones, giving rise to the fusion of hydrological and socio-economic systems and the formation of a more complex hydro-economic system, so well exemplified in the Tennessee Valley (O'Riordan and More, 1969). Clearly, the prior evaluation of all the possible relationships and changing conditions through time would be impossible without a complex, systems-based computer model.

Hufschmidt and Fiering (1966) produced such a model for the Lehigh Valley in Pennsylvania which accommodated up to six reservoirs providing regulated flows of water for domestic and industrial water supply, recreation at the reservoir sites, storage for flood damage reduction, and storage and head for the generation of hydroelectric power. The model contained 42 major design variables related to the allocation of reservoir storage, the location of reservoirs and power generating sites, the presence or absence of a diversion channel, and the target outputs of water supply and energy. The model could accommodate up to 10 changes of capital investment and target output levels, making a grand total of 52 major design variables which, if accorded only three states – high, medium and low – would yield many millions of possible combinations. The model was designed to identify optimum combinations of variables consistent with four main constraints. In descending order of priority, these constraints were: first, the maintenance of streamflow and reservoir flood-storage capacity above specified minimum levels; second, the maintenance of reservoir water levels at an adequate elevation for recreational activity; third, the maintenance of water supply output; and finally, with the lowest priority, the maintenance of energy output. The total number of possible combinations was so great, even after preliminary sifting, that the model was eventually used to investigate likely combinations of variables which were randomly selected to give a wide range of capital investment and running costs and an equally wide range of benefits accruing from energy production, water supply, recreation and flood control (Chorley and Kennedy, 1971). Of these random combinations, only three showed net benefits over a 50-year period, the one finally selected yielding a benefit–cost ratio of 1.8 (Chorley and Kennedy, 1971).

AN APPRAISAL

Both simple cost–benefit analysis and the more complex systems analysis have their defects, not the least of which is that although such methods may work well where the problems are well defined in terms of risk probability and streams of costs and benefits, they are less appropriate in situations of uncertainty, or where rare and extreme events are involved (Penning-Rowsell and Underwood, 1972). In such situations it could be argued that common sense is the best guide; it has certainly stood the test of time for many centuries in Britain and elsewhere! A more important problem, though, is that however complex and accurate the benefit–cost procedure may be, the final choice of response to the flood hazard in many situations is based only partly on economic considerations. O'Riordan and More (1969), for example, noted that

> . . . multi-purpose resource-development projects can be implemented for a variety of objectives, such as redistribution of national income, regional economic growth, and increased aesthetic satisfaction, for which the overriding principles of economic efficiency do not rule. When one asks, 'Whose welfare is being maximized?' and 'Who is paying for this?' it is found that the biggest beneficiaries usually exert the greatest vested interest in the decision-making process, such that these pertinent questions cannot properly be answered in a rigorous economic framework. B–c analysis, therefore operates in the socio-political arena, where sub-optimum economic decisions must be partly based upon compromise and value judgements.
>
> (O'Riordan and More, 1969, p. 555)

Specific examples of the way the final choice of response to the flood hazard has been distorted by social, political or administrative considerations are manifold; a small selection of these will serve to illustrate this point.

Loughlin (1970; 1971) showed that the different and inconsistent cost-sharing arrangements existing in various U.S. government agencies for single and multiple purpose water resource programmes caused inefficiencies and inequities to arise. Beneficiaries might not choose the least cost alternative, the optimal scale might not be chosen and optimal use of existing capacity might not be realised. Equity problems included varying reimbursement requirements for similar or the same programmes, the 'tilting' of project costs towards non-reimbursable purposes and the arbitrariness of the existing cost-sharing provisions. In the particular case of flood protection, empirical evidence indicated that policy inconsistencies had resulted in distortions in the local decision-making process and discriminatory treatment of project beneficiaries. One source of discrimination was the differing reimbursement requirements within and among agency programmes for similar flood protection improvements. Loughlin then presented a cost-sharing formula which he claimed was consistent with the objectives of economic efficiency and social equity.

Johnson (1969) highlighted the role of government subsidies in distorting the flood hazard response in Britain when he observed that although for many areas it would be cheaper to rebuild elsewhere than to provide protection, there was unfortunately no way in which such removals could be aided from public funds. Indeed, there are many instances throughout the world where public relief funds and rehabilitation programmes have actually impeded attempts to rebuild in less hazardous locations (Mitchell, 1974).

Again, national interests may override simplistic cost–benefit procedures. For example in the case of the Great Ouse scheme (see p. 152), costs exceeded damage reduction benefits but, as Penning-Rowsell and Underwood (1972) pointed out, Britain cannot afford to allow such potentially rich, productive land to lie fallow. In other cases, national interests may severely impede the implementation of major flood mitigation programmes where flood-prone rivers cross international frontiers. Some of the problems arising on the lower Ganges–Brahmaputra system, which crosses both India and Pakistan, were discussed by Rogers (1969) and those of the Columbia River, flowing through the United States and Canada, were examined by Krutilla (1966).

Finally, a combination of factors may cause the distortion or rejection of an appropriate flood hazard solution. This was most clearly demonstrated in the lower Fraser valley in British Columbia. After catastrophic flooding in 1948, during which Vancouver was cut off from the rest of Canada except by air, the Fraser River Board proposed a comprehensive scheme in which revenue from the generation of hydroelectric power would cover the costs of developing both power facilities and a flood alleviation programme, including reconstruction of the flood embankment system (Sewell, 1965). The only costs of future flood mitigation, therefore, would be the costs of repairing the embankment system. According to Sewell (1969), three main factors have delayed the implementation of this scheme. First, it was uncertain at which level government lay responsibility for initiating action to deal with flood problems. Second, the power market was largely pre-empted by other projects in British Columbia, such as the major schemes on the Columbia and Peace rivers. And third, the scheme was delayed because of opposition by recreation interests and the salmon-fishing lobbyists, understandably perhaps since the river is one of the world's largest remaining sources of salmon.

Another factor which may greatly distort the choice of response to the flood hazard, in relationship to the solution 'selected' by cost–benefit analysis, is the reaction of the decision-makers to a 'probable' hazard. Figure 8.1 illustrates clearly that perception acts as a filter between the occurrence of the flood hazard and man's response to it. A growing body of work suggests that hazard perception is a function of four main variables (Mitchell, 1974): the decision-maker's interpretation of the physical characteristics of the hazard, the decision-maker's experience of the hazard, his personality traits and the situational characteristics of the decisions made.

In terms of the flood hazard the pertinent physical characteristics are the frequency and magnitude of flood events through time. Although the interpretation of the historical record, in terms of future expectations of flooding, is partly a function of experience (those with greater experience are more perceptive and respond more positively), this is not always the case. Burton, Kates and Snead (1969) observed that to assume that someone experienced a hazard simply because he lived at a site during a major hazard event is not valid; experience implies recognition of the hazard as such. Thus over 30 per cent of respondents who had experienced coastal flooding failed to assess the likelihood of future flood damage as significant (Mitchell, 1974). A further expression of distorted interpretation, which results in failure to adopt the optimum economic response to the flood hazard, is the self-satisfying rule adopted by many decision-makers (Kates, 1962). In other words, decision-makers who have experienced a flood and anticipate a repetition may well take action, but mainly to feel that they have done something to protect themselves; they will rarely anticipate a larger flood and may not even take sufficient action to protect against a flood equal to that already experienced. In general, though, there is a clear relationship between flood frequency and response to flooding. In areas with a high certainty of flooding there is a high level of response; where the occurrence of flooding is uncertain there is a correspondingly low level of perception and response (Kates, 1962).

Hazard perception is also affected by personality and situational characteristics, although investigations into the effects of the former are still at an early stage. For example, low educational attainment may dull perception of the dangers and problems of floodplain occupancy (Roder, 1961), while Burton (1961) found that the upper social classes were more concerned about the flood hazard, although not necessarily better informed than other sectors of society. More certainly, farmers have a keener awareness of flood hazard than city dwellers (Burton, 1962), and occupants of flood-prone coastal areas are found to perceive hazards more clearly than floodplain occupants (Burton and Kates, 1964).

It seems clear, whatever the factors involved, that lack of perception is a major cause of the increasing investment in and occupance of flood-prone areas along both rivers and coasts. However, as suggested in the preceding discussion of social and political influences on flood hazard response, the situation is far from simple and there are many instances where acute perception of flood risk is subordinated to other considerations. Residents of the coastal lowlands of Bangladesh, for example, are well aware of the cyclone hazard but do not migrate even when they know of opportunities elsewhere (Mitchell, 1974). The strong incentives to remain include the prospect of acquiring more land through government-sponsored flood embankment schemes, family ties and the existence of relief and rehabilitation programmes.

It would be wrong to conclude without remarking that the assumption of the 'rational man', on whom economic, social and political theories affecting response to the flood hazard are based, has been invalidated frequently in hazard situations. Kates (1962), supporting the concept of 'bounded rationality', observed that an approach based on the assumption that man is an absolutely rational being will not bring about any realistic solution until man has been educated to be totally rational in such situations. Irrationality emerges most strongly in situations where there is a high degree of uncertainty. Flooding is an essentially random phenomenon, with high magnitude events occurring relatively infrequently. Burton, Kates and Snead (1969) pointed out that while the scientist accepts this uncertainty within the framework of probability theory, the layman (educated or not) usually reacts to uncertainty in one of two fundamentally different ways. He may respond to the randomness of flooding either

> . . . by making the events knowable, finding order where none exists, ident-
> ifying cycles on the basis of the sketchiest of knowledge of folk insight, and in
> general, striving to reduce the uncertainty of the threat of hazard by making it
> certain.

or conversely, he may

> . . . deny all knowability, accept the uniqueness of natural phenomena, throw
> up [his] hands, and transfer [his] fate into the hands of a higher power.
>
> (Burton, Kates and Snead, 1969, p. 160)

12 Prospect

INTRODUCTION

Floods have been presented as a global phenomenon affecting both rich and poor, the prepared and unprepared. They are a complex, interdisciplinary problem – for some aspects satisfactory solutions have already been advanced, but for others no likely answers are as yet forthcoming. The essential characteristics of the flood problem have been expressed in terms, already unfashionable with the leftist fringe of geographers, of the interaction between man and his environment. Indeed, flooding and man's response to it is perhaps the most dramatic engagement of all, when the struggling inventiveness of myopic man is pitted against the majesty of Nature (and, if you will, the omnipotence of God) in an unceasing and unremittingly losing quest for 'control'. Sometimes succeeding in the short term, man is certain to be unsuccessful in the end.

Marie Morisawa (1968) succinctly summarised the progress of man's quest, 'Man's attempts to control rivers have often had little or no success. In fact, many times his efforts have aggravated the situation. The greatest natural disasters come as a result of ignorance or, even worse, half-knowledge.' The preceding chapters of this book have elaborated some of the successes, and have underlined the ignorance or half-knowledge which is responsible for so many of the failures.

Clearly one hopes for, and in the twentieth century has come to expect, an improvement in this situation as new understanding and improved techniques of accumulating and processing data reflect the current 'knowledge explosion'. In terms of the global flood problem, though, it seems unlikely that dramatic advances will develop in our understanding of the basic physical processes which cause flooding, or the emergence of new techniques of flood prediction or even the discovery of new responses to the flood hazard. In each of these fields substantial advances have been made during the past two or three decades and our present level of comprehension is high. In other areas, however, advances are long overdue which could do much to alleviate flood problems at the local, national and international scale.

It does not seem appropriate, at this late stage, to open detailed, technical discussion of prospective improvements, or even to compile an exhaustive catalogue of them. Rather, this brief concluding chapter will simply attempt to indicate, in largely qualitative terms, the potential scope of a limited number of prospective major developments – the collection and presentation of *data* on flooding, flood *forecasting*, the *perception* not only of the flood hazard but also of the choice of response to it, and finally the framework of *administration* through which response to the flood hazard is effected.

DATA

The basic data required to combat the flood problem were summarised by Snyder *et al.* (1971) as

(1) data identifying and characterising the area exposed to flood hazard
(2) flood stage and discharge data
(3) data describing the flood formation processes and enabling the determination of flood discharges by indirect methods
(4) data describing solids transport and the ice regime during flooding
(5) economic data relating to actual and potential flood damages

Although in some areas limited categories of flood data have been collected for very long periods, there are other areas in which programmes of data collection have only recently been initiated. Both long and short data runs tend to be characterised by the variable quality of the data and in many cases analysis and interpretation are impeded by the form in which the data have been collected.

Remedies for the inadequate quantity of data have been sought recently in the crash programmes of the International Hydrological Decade, which terminated in 1974. Much of this work was continued as part of the International Hydrological Programme; in IHD and UNESCO publications, such as the annual information summaries on natural disasters and catastrophic floods and the world catalogue of very large floods; and, finally, in the intensive data collection during the early stages of the recently completed Natural Environment Research Council's flood study in the United Kingdom. Unfortunately, except in some more enlightened countries such as the United States (where geographers have long been active in the formulation of flood mitigation policies, Gilbert White, for example, having chaired the Task Force on Federal Flood Control Policy which reported in 1966), there has been an inexcusable concentration on the collection of hydrometeorological data and a corresponding neglect of socio-economic data, even in recently initiated data collection programmes. For example, in the remarkably short-sighted document which set out the need for a government sponsored flood study in the United Kingdom, ICE (1967) relegated to the final paragraph a desultory mention of the collection of flood damage data. More significantly, at the present time, over a decade later, there is still no agreed procedure or responsible authority for the collection of damage data in the United Kingdom. Harding and Porter (1970) suggested that the two main agencies might be the River (now Water) Authorities and the Universities. Sheer practicalities, such as funding and the need for the instant availability of staff at the required times for periods of up to several weeks, would seem to obviate the Universities whose contribution must surely rest in the analysis and interpretation of the data rather than in their collection. This leaves the Water Authorities as the most appropriate agencies, for the task to which they were formally committed by Section 24 of the Water Act 1973.

The variable quality of both hydrometeorological and socio-economic data is likely to be a continuing problem, although some improvement will undoubtedly come with the introduction of better data collection techniques and instrumentation. There is, however, considerable scope for improving the form in which data are collected and presented. In Britain, for instance, most of the streamflow data collected by the River and Water Authorities in the past were intended to give information on minimum flow conditions, for example Minimum Acceptable Flow, in connection with the abstraction of water for public water supplies. Accordingly, maximum flows were often poorly recorded or not recorded at all. Until recently most major hydrometeorological programmes have concentrated on the volumes of floodwater discharged rather than its quality or, of even more importance, on the areal extent of the accompanying inundation.

As a result of attempts to rectify some of these deficiencies there have been considerable advances in mapping flood outlines and once again the best examples are provided by work done in the United States. There the earliest flood inundation maps were in the U.S. Geological Survey flood reports, which first appeared in 1903. Many subsequent flood reports, published as *Water-Supply Papers*, contained maps of the inundated areas, but not until 1959 did the U.S. Geological Survey start a new series of flood inundation maps, published as *Hydrologic Investigations Atlases*. The intention was to combine on a single sheet basic information on local flooding using a topographic map, history of past floods, flood frequency diagrams, flood profiles, aerial photographs when available and a brief explanatory text (Ellis, 1969). The greatest concentration of these atlases is in the Chicago region, where a co-operative programme between the U.S. Geological Survey and the Northeastern Illinois Planning Commission produced 53 atlases. These have been used to establish zoning regulations, and in county forest reserves and park districts to purchase land subject to flooding, thereby eliminating encroachment. They are also used to formulate new sewerage regulations and as the basis for assessing mortgage applications (Ellis, 1969; Sheaffer, 1964).

The U.S. Army Corps of Engineers, also involved in flood outline mapping, has concentrated largely on the depiction, on either topographic sheets or aerial photo-mosaics, of the outline of floods of selected frequencies, such as the Standard Project Flood with a return period of 100 years or more (see p. 69) and smaller floods (Intermediate Regional Floods) with return periods of 5, 10, 25 or 50 years. A minimum of two and sometimes three flood outlines are shown on the floodplain maps (see figure 12.1). These maps are an integral part of *Flood Plain Information Reports* prepared by the Corps of Engineers under the provisions of the amended Flood Control Act of 1960. According to Molinaroli (1965), the objectives of these reports are: the compilation of clear and useful information on floods and flood hazards; the encouragement of optimum use of valley-bottom lands; the dissemination of flood hazard information to the general public; and the reduction of future expenditure on flood alleviation resulting from improper use of floodplains.

More recently, an additional stimulus to floodplain mapping was given by the

Flood Disaster Protection Act of 1973 which made major changes in the National Flood Insurance Programme (see p. 130). This Act directed the U.S. De-

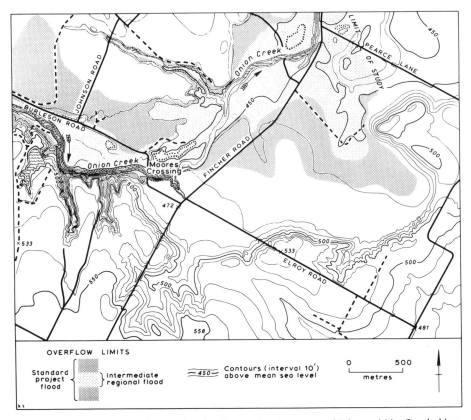

Figure 12.1 Onion Creek near Austin, Texas showing areas which would be flooded by the Intermediate Regional Flood and the Standard Project Flood
Source: U.S. Army Corps of Engineers (1973).

partment of Housing and Urban Development to accelerate the identification of flood hazard areas and the accumulation of data for the preparation of a flood insurance rate map. Largely through the assistance of the Geological Survey, this work is progressing rapidly. However, as Wolman (1971) and Dingman (1975) observed, despite this accelerating pace, the rate or urbanisation in the United States exceeds the rate of mapping of urbanised floodplains, so that alternative, quicker techniques of floodplain mapping should be adopted. One seemingly obvious way of delineating flood outlines more rapidly is to make use of aerial, and particularly satellite, photography. The feasibility of these techniques are discussed by Rango and Salomonson (1974) and by Rango *et al.* (1974). Hopefully similar ambitious programmes for mapping actual and probable floods will not only be developed in other countries, but will also be related to detailed studies of actual and potential damage data.

FORECASTING

There is undoubtedly scope for improving flood forecasts, largely along the lines suggested in chapter 7 (see p. 106). The main potential improvements seem likely to be brought about not by more rapid processing of data in larger and faster computers, but by reducing the time taken to input hydrometeorological data to the computers. In this respect improved precipitation or tidal-level forecasts based on satellite observations, together with improved techniques of areal precipitation assessment, for example through the use of radar, may play an important part. However, as has been frequently observed, in the case of river floods it is not only the precipitation input which matters but also the hydrological responsiveness of the catchment on which it falls. Clearly then, procedures which permit an accurate continuous accounting of catchment wetness, expressed perhaps in terms of soil moisture deficit (Grindley and Singleton, 1969) or by direct satellite observations of soil moisture status (Idso *et al.*, 1975), are likely to play a major role in improved forecasting. Flood forecasting will undoubtedly also benefit from direct satellite observations of the areal extent of upstream flooding and its change with time, particularly from satellites like those operated by the National Oceanic and Atmospheric Administration whose orbital configurations bring them over the same area of the earth's surface at intervals measured in hours rather than days or weeks.

PERCEPTION

One of the most pressing tasks in this field is to sharpen the perception of the flood hazard and the range of possible responses among those most at risk. From repeated experience it is obvious that more than the mere presentation of facts is required. For example, Roder (1961) showed the first *Hydrologic Investigations Atlas,* dealing with floods at Topeka, Kansas, to key decision makers in the locality, only one of whom showed any real interest or understanding. This and other individual experiences were later generalised by White (1973a), 'It was clear in the most elementary way that the definition of a flood hydrograph as developed by the meteorologists and hydrologists would be important in the decisions by individuals only to the extent that the described flood parameters were meaningful to the user'.

To a large extent, then, the task is to present the facts in a way in which they can be unambiguously understood by decision makers in floodprone areas. Since, as intimated in earlier discussions of perception in chapter 11, one of the areas of greatest misunderstanding concerns the concepts of probability and uncertainty, this is where attention must be concentrated. White told of conversing with a man rebuilding on the foundations of a house which had recently been swept away by floods.

'I asked if he thought there was any risk involved in building again on that place, and he said no, that, as a matter of fact, he had a very good friend in the U.S. Geological Survey who had assured him that there had been two floods that summer with a return interval of one hundred years. He didn't intend to build a house that would last two hundred years, he said. . .'

(White, 1973*b*, p. 14)

There are, of course, many other factors, including psychological ones, which determine the sharpness of hazard perception in ways not yet clearly understood. White (1973*a*) regarded as one of the truly difficult problems of social science 'the relationship, if any, between verbalized attitudes and actual behaviour'. Hopefully, continuing research in these fields will eventually improve our ability to communicate the realities of the flood hazard to the occupants of flood-prone areas.

ADMINISTRATION

One reasonable conclusion to be drawn from the various aspects of our discussion of floods is that the machinery for implementing responses to the flood hazard is often inexplicit and insufficiently co-ordinated. This weakness manifests itself in different ways and on many different levels, from the individual project report through local and national government to the magnitude of world co-operation. At each level there is scope for improvement which could lead to a more effective definition of and response to the flood hazard. A few examples may illustrate this point.

A type of tunnel vision appears to afflict many authors of technical reports on flooding and the flood hazard. Although each may see clearly the problems in his own field and equally clearly address his colleagues he rarely develops in detail the implications of his findings to workers in related fields, but assumes that his results will be interpreted and applied rationally by someone else. White (1973*b*) described a typical progression starting with A who prepares a flood probability estimate but expects B to make use of it in designing, say, a spillway. However, B then expects C to deal with the downstream engineering problems caused when that amount of water passes over the spillway and in turn, C expects D to cope with the socio-economic responses to these flows of water. White concluded.

I have yet to find in a comprehensive engineering document a precise charting of what it is assumed will have to be done all the way along the line in terms of both technical and social readjustments in order to attain the social aims that project is expected to serve. It can be done: the essential paths of analysis can be identified. But it is an extraordinarily rare practice. It needs to be done regularly and systematically.

(White, 1973*b*, p. 15)

This same lack of communication is witnessed so often in the machinery of local government. For example, one accepts that in areas already developed for residential, industrial, commercial, or even intensive agricultural use, costly programmes of flood mitigation must be devised and/or maintained. It is very difficult, however, to accept the frequent failure to subject future development programmes to adequate scrutiny. Too often, the existence of publicly funded flood mitigation schemes have tempted private land speculators to make a quick profit in flood-prone areas when the community would have been better served by locating new development away from the floodable areas, which could then remain unprotected either by embankments or insurance. A further anecdote from White drives the point home:

> I asked a man building a new apartment building on the Boulder flood plain if he thought there was any risk of flood. He replied he had no risk at all. I asked him if he knew about the flood of 1894. He said, of course, he knew about it, the flood of 1894 had come up chest-high where he was standing. How then, I said, could there be no risk. Well, he said there will be no risk, because he would sell the building within six months.
>
> (White, 1973*b*, p.14)

In more general terms White and his colleagues, at Chicago and elsewhere, have long pressed for a more rational and responsible attitude on the part of local government. His study of selected towns in the United States for example, led him to the belief that the concern of public policy must extend beyond the mere provision of flood protection works. He advocated the provision of public information and warning services, the education of public concern for floodproofing and land zoning, incentives for decision makers to adopt effective responses to the flood hazard and, above all, the adoption of an extensive educational programme (White, 1964). Similarly, Kates (1962) stressed the importance of education, publicity and community leadership, if only to counteract the often damaging attitude of many individuals that the flood problem and the proper response to it is a matter best left to the 'experts'.

Another point, made in chapter 8 but worth re-emphasising here, is that local governments themselves frequently fail to respond positively to the flood hazard or else fail to give the necessary leadership and encouragement to private decision makers because of the fear of damaging community interests in other fields, for example by discouraging the location of new industries. This problem can really only be solved through the extensive cooperation of local government authorities or by much stronger direction from central government.

Even at national government level, the administrative machinery for dealing with the flood problem can be cumbersome and unduly fragmented. Again using the United States as an example, if only because its activities are so excellently documented, the main federal agencies involved in response to the flood hazard are the Corps of Engineers, Department of Agriculture (Soil Conservation Service and Forest Service), Department of Housing and Urban Development, Geological Survey and the Tennessee Valley Authority, with the Water Resources Council acting as a coordinating body under the provisions of the Water Resources Planning Act. Task Force (1966) made recommendations which strengthened this role and explicitly stated that they expected the Council '. . . to exercise new leadership'. Despite the work of these agencies in adjustment, abatement and protection, floods naturally still occur, and when they do another group of federal agencies assumes the role of flood relief and reconstruction under the coordination of the Office of Emergency Planning (see table 12.1).

Similar fragmentation occurs in other countries, of course. In Britain the situ-

TABLE 12.1

PRINCIPAL U.S. FEDERAL AGENCIES PARTICIPATING
IN FLOOD RELIEF AND RECONSTRUCTION

Coordination:

OFFICE OF EMERGENCY PLANNING

Warning service	Weather Bureau
	Coast and Geodetic Survey
Flood fighting	Corps of Engineers
Emergency loans	Farmers Home Administration
	Small Business Administration
Income tax deductions	Internal Revenue Service
Rescue and direct relief	Army Navy Coastguard
	Public Health Service
	Food and Drug Administration
	Consumer Marketing Service
	Agricultural Stabilisation and Conservation Service
	American Red Cross (under national charter)
Grants or assistance in	Office of Emergency Planning
rebuilding public works	Corps of Engineers
	Bureau of Public Roads
	Community Facilities Administration

(From Task Force (1966). With acknowledgement)

ation has been exacerbated by the absence of an effective co-ordinating body (the present National Water Council seems little more than a 'paper sheep' disguised as a 'paper wolf' although this situation may be improved by legislation within a few years) and by a succession of half-baked legislation since 1965, when the old River Boards disappeared. This legislation has brought in useful innovations such as the Water Resources Board, only to scrap them again a few years later and has generally tinkered with, rather than restructured, the management of water resources in Britain, particularly in terms of an effective response to the flood hazard. Thus the ten regional Water Authorities have a general responsibility for flood protection and coastal protection within their areas, although schemes may be initiated by Internal Drainage Boards or local government authorities and funded from a variety of sources, including grants from the Ministry of Agriculture, Fisheries and Food and local government authorities. In addition to the regional Water Authorities are the Forestry Commission, responsible for programmes of forestry-based flood abatement; the

Meteorological Office and the Admiralty Hydrographic Office for river and coastal flood forecasting (and with the Water Authorities, for data collection); and, finally, conducting the main flood research effort are the Institute of Hydrology, the Water Research Centre and Departments of Civil Engineering and Geography in the Universities.

In other countries the absence of a centralised procedure for dealing with the flood hazard is quite deliberate. Thus in Canada, according to Burton (1969), the constitution as originally set out in the British North America Act and subsequently amended and interpreted in court rulings, regards natural resource development as a provincial, not a federal, responsibility, except when there is a flood disaster of such magnitude that it is beyond the capacity of a provincial government to handle. Finally, in many of the developing countries of the world a centralised administrative flood management machinery is either non-existent or else exists in only a rudimentary form.

In the light of such fundamental and diverse problems the United Nations Interregional Seminar on 'Flood Damage Prevention Measures and Management', held at Tbilisi in Russia in 1969, recommended that national governments consider the desirability of a number of measures, the first of which was the

> Formulation of a national flood management policy, taking into account present and perspective [sic?] flood hazards and possible damages. In implementation of such policy the appropriate institutional framework at central, state, and local levels of government safeguarding the necessary comprehensive approach to the problems of floods should be established.
>
> (Szesztay, 1970)

The Seminar further suggested that the effectiveness of national programmes would be greatly enhanced by global collaboration through the medium of the United Nations system of organisations such as UNESCO, WMO, WHO and FAO and that the United Nations itself should convene a series of regional and interregional seminars on problems related to flood management at intervals of two or three years. Finally, the Seminar recommended that

> In view of the intense suffering to which millions of human beings are subject as a result of floods in various parts of the world, and in view of the fact that the majority of the suffering people come from the poorer and weaker sections of the community, the participants feel it to be most desirable to follow the lead given in this Seminar and to establish under the auspices of the United Nations Economic and Social Council a permanent *Committee on the Management of Floods*.
>
> (Szesztay, 1970)

CONCLUSION

Fine sentiments and fine words may help to initiate effective action but it would be wrong to conclude this book without returning briefly to simple realities. One of the recurring themes in the preceding chapters has been that, while floods may be natural occurrences, the flood hazard is largely man-made and as long as man chooses to live in flood-prone areas disasters are inevitable. Certainly, much progress has been made already and further progress will undoubtedly come about as a wide range of skills is brought to bear on this complex and far-reaching problem – skills which include a knowledge of flood-forming processes, an understanding of probability theory, an acquaintance with economic analysis, an insight into the social behaviour of man and an awareness of the realities and constraints of the political process (Penning-Rowsell and Underwood, 1972).

But whatever man does, and however much he conquers ignorance and half-knowledge, floods will occur that overtop defences and decimate even the best-protected rural and urban areas. All this, of course, has been said before and it seems appropriate, therefore, to leave the final word with William Hoyt and Walter Langbein who, in the Prologue to their classic *Floods*, wrote a scenario for floodplains in about AD 2000 which is equally applicable to low–lying coastal areas

> Nature takes its inexorable toll. Thousand-year flood causes untold damage and staggering loss of life. Engineers and meteorologists believe that present storm and flood resulted from a combination of meteorologic and hydrologic conditions such as may occur only once a millenium. Reservoirs, levees, and other control works which have proved effective for a century, and are still effective up to their design capacity, are unable to cope with enormous volumes of water involved. This catastrophe brings home the lesson that protection from floods is only a relative matter, and that eventually nature demands its toll from those who occupy flood plains.
>
> (Hoyt and Langbein, 1955)

Bibliography of Works Cited

1 INTRODUCTION

American Water Resources Association (1972). Trends and commentary. *The Water Resources Newsletter,* 7, no. 4

Biswas, A. K. (1970). *History of Hydrology,* North-Holland, Amsterdam–London

Chow, V. T. (1956). Hydrologic studies of floods in the United States. *Int. Ass. Scient. Hydrol. Publ.* **42,** 134–70

Green, F. H. W. (1973). Aspects of the changing environment in recent years. *J. Environ. Management,* 1, 377–91

Lambert, W. G. and Millard, A. R. (1969). *Atra-ḫasīs – The Babylonian Story of the Flood,* Oxford University Press, London

Parsons, J. J., and Bowen, W. A. (1966). Ancient ridged fields of the San Jorge River floodplain, Colombia. *Geogrl. Rev.,* **61,** 317–43

Popov, I. V. and Gavrin, Y. S. (1970). Use of aerial photography in evaluating the flooding and emptying of river flood plains and the development of flood-plain currents. *Soviet Hydrol.* **5,** 413–25

Rostvedt, J. O., *et al.* (1968). Summary of floods in the United States during 1963. *U.S. geol. Surv., Wat.-Sup. Pap.,* 1830–B

Sheaffer, J. R. (1961). Flood-to-peak interval (ed. G. F. White) Papers on Flood Problems. *Univ. of Chicago, Dept. of Geog. Res. Pap.,* **70,** 95–113

Smith, K. (1972). *Water in Britain,* Macmillan, London

Strahler, A. N. (1964). Quantitative geomorphology of drainage basins and channel networks. *Handbook of Applied Hydrology* (ed. V. T. Chow), McGraw-Hill, New York, section 4-II

Walling, D. E. (1971). Streamflow from instrumented catchments in S.E. Devon. *Exeter Essays in Geography* (eds K. J. Gregory and W. L. D. Ravenhill) Exeter, p. 77

2 FLOODS CAUSED BY PRECIPITATION:
I RAINFALL

Barnes, H. H., and Bogart, D. B. (1961). Floods of September, 1960, in eastern Puerto Rico. *U.S. Geol. Surv. Circ.,* **451**

Biswas, A. K. (1970). *History of Hydrology*, North-Holland, Amsterdam

Bleasdale, A., and Douglas, C. K. M. (1952). Storm over Exmoor on August 15, 1952. *Met. Mag.*, **81**, 353–67

Carr, J. T. (1966). Hurricanes. *Texas Wat. Dev. Bd. Rept.*, **33**, 19–30

Colman, E. A. (1953). *Vegetation and Watershed Management*, Ronald, New York

De Wiest, R. J. M. (1965). *Geohydrology*, Wiley, New York

Dobbie, C. H., and Wolf, P. O. (1953). The Lynmouth flood of August, 1952. *Proc. Instn. Civ. Engrs*, **2**, 522–88

Harvey, A. M. (1971). Seasonal flood behaviour in a clay catchment. *J. Hydrol.*, **12**, 129–44

Hewlett, J. D. (1961a). Watershed management. *U.S.F.S., Southeast. For. exp. Sta. Rept.*, 61–6

Hewlett, J. D. (1961b). Soil moisture as a source of base flow from steep mountain watersheds. *U.S.D.A., Southeast For. exp. Sta. Pap.*, **132**

Hewlett, J. D., and Nutter, W. L. (1969). *An Outline of Forest Hydrology*, Univ. of Georgia, Athens

Horton, R. E. (1933). The role of infiltration in the hydrologic cycle. *Trans. Am. Geophys. Un.*, **14**, 446–60

Hudleston, F. (1933). The cloudbursts on Stainmore, Westmorland, June 18th, 1930. *British Rainfall*, 1930, 287–92

Hursh, C. R. (1944). Report of the subcommittee on subsurface flow. *Trans. Am. geophys. Un.*, **25**, 743–6

Hurst, H. E., and Phillips, P. (1931). *The Nile Basin*, Government Press, Cairo

IASH (1974). *Flash Floods,* Proceedings of the Paris Symposium, Sept. 1974, IASH/UNESCO/WMO

Institute of Hydrology (1972). *Research 1971–72*, Natural Environment Research Council

Jarvis, C. S. (1942). Floods. (ed. O. E. Meinzer), *Hydrology*, McGraw-Hill, New York

Jennings, A. H. (1950). Worlds greatest observed point rainfalls. *Mon. Weath. Rev.*, **78**, 4–5

Kidson, C. (1953). The Exmoor storm and the Lynmouth floods. *Geography*, **38**, 1–9

Kirkby, M. J., and Chorley, R. J. (1967). Throughflow, overland flow and erosion. *Bull. int. Ass. scient. Hydrol.*, **12**, 5–21

Lambor, J. (1956). Classification des types de crues de l'Europe Centrale et leur prévision. *Int. Ass. scient. Hydrol. Publ.*, **42**, 37–44

Manley, G. (1952). *Climate and the British Scene*, Collins, London

Marshall, W. A. L. (1952). The Lynmouth floods. *Weather,* **7**, 338–42

Morgan, C. W. (1966). Thunderstorms. *Texas Wat. Dev. Bd. Rept.,* **33**, 31–44

Orton, R. (1966). Easterly waves. *Texas Wat. Dev. Bd. Rept.*, **33**, 1–18

Rogers, P. (1969). A systems analysis of the lower Ganges–Brahmaputra basin. *Floods and their computation*, IASH/UNESCO/WMO, pp. 894–909

Schick, A. P. (1970). Desert floods. *Symposium on the results of research on representative and experimental basins*, IASH/UNESCO, 479–93

Schick, A. P. (1971). A desert flood. *Jerusalem Studies in Geography*, **2**, 91–155

Shell, J. D. (1962). Floods of December 1961 in Mississippi and adjoining States. *U.S. geol. Surv. Circ.*, **465**, 17

Texas Board of Water Engineers (1957). *Texas Floods of April, May and June 1957*, The Board in cooperation with U.S. Geol. Survey

Thorud, D. B., and Ffolliott, P. F. (1971). The 1970 Labor Day storm. *Arizona Watershed Symposium*, **15**, 46–55

Uppal, H. L., and Sehgal, S. R. (1956). *Int. Ass. scient. Hydrol. Publ.*, **42**, 14–21

Ward, R. C. (1975). *Principles of Hydrology*, 2nd edn, McGraw-Hill, London

Whipkey, R. Z. (1965). Subsurface stormflow from forested slopes. *Bull. Int. Ass. scient. Hydrol.*, **10**, 74–85

Whipkey, R. Z. (1967). Theory and mechanics of subsurface stormflow. *Forest Hydrology*, (eds W. E. Sopper and H. W. Lull), Pergamon, Oxford, pp. 255–60

Whipkey, R. Z. (1969). Storm runoff from forested catchments by subsurface routes. *Floods and their Computation*, IASH/UNESCO/WMO pp. 773–9

White, E. L., and Reich, B. M. (1970). *J. Hydrol.*, **10**, 193–8

Williams, G. E. (1970). The Central Australian stream floods of February–March 1967. *J. Hydrol.*, **11**, 185–200

Woolley, R. R. (1946). Cloudburst floods in Utah 1850–1938. *U.S. geol. Surv., Wat.-Sup. Pap.*, **994**

3 FLOODS CAUSED BY PRECIPITATION:
II SNOWMELT, RAIN-ON-SNOW AND ICEMELT

Beckinsale, R. P. (1969). River regimes. *Water, Earth and Man* (ed. R. J. Chorley), Methuen, London, pp. 455–71

Burton, I. (1969). Flood damage reduction in Canada. *Water* (eds J. G. Nelson and M. J. Chambers), Methuen, Toronto, pp. 77–108

Chebotarev, N. P. (1962). *Theory of Stream Runoff*, Israel Program for Scientific Translations, Jerusalem. Distributed by Oldbourne Press, London

Hoyt, W. G., and Langbein, W. B. (1955). *Floods*, Princeton University Press, Princeton

Khan, M. (1969). Influence of Upper Indus basin on the elements of the flood hydrograph at Tarbela-Attock. *Floods and their Computation*, IASH/UNESCO/WMO, pp. 918–25

Manley, G. (1952). *Climate and the British Scene*, Collins, London

Meier, M. F. (1964). Ice and glaciers. *Handbook of Applied Hydrology* (ed. V. T.

Chow), McGraw-Hill, New York, pp. 16-1–32

Nelson, J. G., and Byrne, A. R. (1966). Man as an instrument of landscape change. *Geogrl Rev.*, **56**, 226–38

Pardé, M. (1955). *Fleuves et Rivieres*, Armand Colin, Paris

Pardé, M. (1964). Floods, floods, floods! *UNESCO Courier*, **17**, July–August, 54–9

Sewell, W. R. D. (1969). Human response to floods. *Water, Earth and Man* (ed. R. J. Chorley), Methuen, London, pp. 431–51

Snyder, F., Sokolov, A., and Szesztay, K. (eds) (1971). *Flood Studies: an international guide for collection and processing of data*, UNESCO, Paris, p. 49

Thomas, C. A., and Lamke, R. D. (1962). Floods of February 1962 in southern Idaho and northeastern Nevada. *U.S. geol. Surv. Circ.*, **467**, 30

Thorarinsson, S. (1953). Some new aspects of the Grimsvötn problem. *J. Glaciol.*, **2**, 267–75

U.S. Corps of Engineers (1956). *Snow Hydrology*, Office of Tech. Serv., U.S. Dept. Commerce, Washington, D.C.

Wolf, P. O. (1952). Forecast and records of floods in Glen Cannich in 1947. *J. Instn Wat. Engrs*, **6**, 298–324

4 FLOODS NOT CAUSED BY PRECIPITATION

Admiralty Tide Tables (1970) vol. 1

Baird, A. W. (1884). Report on the tidal disturbances caused by the volcanic eruptions at Java, August 27th–28th, 1883. *Proc. R. Soc.*, **36**, 248–53

Balloffet, A., and Balloffet, A. F. (1974). Dam collapse wave in a river. *J. Hydraul. Div., ASCE*, **100**, no. HY5, 645–65

Bascom, W. (1959). Ocean waves. *Scient. Am.*, Aug., 2–12

Bernstein, J. (1954). Tsunamis. *Scient. Am.*, Aug., 3–6

Biswas, A. K. (1970). *History of Hydrology*, North-Holland, Amsterdam

Biswas, A. K., and Chatterjee, S. (1971). Dam disasters: an assessment. *Engng. J.*, **54**, 3–8

Bretschneider, C. L. (1967a). Storm surges. *Adv. Hydroscience*, **4**, 341–418

Bretschneider, C. L. (1967b). On wind tides and wind-driven longshore currents caused by winds blowing at an angle to the coastline. *11th Pacific Science Congress, Sympos. on Tsunami and Storm Surges*, 72

Brooks, C. E. P., and Glasspoole, J. (1928). *British Floods and Droughts*, Benn, London

Burton, I., Kates, R. W., and Snead, R. E. (1969). The human ecology of coastal flood hazard in megalopolis. *Univ. of Chicago, Dept. of Geog. Res. Paper, No. 115*, 196

Corkan, R. H. (1948). Storm surges. *Dock and Harbour Authority*, Feb., 3–19

Corkan, R. H. (1950). The levels in the North Sea associated with the storm disturbance of 8th January, 1949. *Phil. Trans. R. Soc. A*, **242**, 493–525

Davidson, D. D. and McCartney, B. L. (1975). Water waves generated by landslides in reservoirs, *J. Hydraul. Div., ASCE*, **101**, HY12, 1489–1501

Davies, W. E., Bailey, J. F., and Kelly, D. B. (1972). West Virginia's Buffalo Creek flood: a study of the hydrology and engineering geology. *U.S. geol. Surv. Circ.*, **667**, 32

Edwards, K. C. (1953). The Netherlands floods: some further aspects and consequences. *Geography*, **38**, 182–7

Fread, D. L., and Harbaugh, T. E. (1973). Transient simulation of breached earth dams. *J. Hydraul. Div., ASCE*, **99**, HY1, 139–54

Graftdijk, K. (1960). *Holland Rides the Sea*, World's Window Ltd., Baarn

Groen, P., and Groves, G. W. (1962). Surges. *The Sea* (ed. M. N. Hill), Interscience, New York, pp. 611–46

Harris, D. L. (1967). A critical survey of the storm surge protection problem. *11th Pacific Science Congress, Sympos. on Tusunami and Storm Surges*, 47–65

Heck, N. H. (1947). List of seismic sea waves. *Bull. seism. Soc. Am.*, **37**, 4

Khan, M. (1969). Influence of Upper Indus basin on the elements of the flood hydrograph at Tarbela-Attock. *Floods and their Computation*, IASH/UNESCO/WMO, pp. 918–25

Labzovskii, N. A. (1966). [Sea floods in the estuary of the Neva River]. Morskie navodneniia v ust'e r. Neva. *Moscow. Gosudarstvennyi Okeanograficheskii Institut, Trudy*, no. 79, 3–40

Miller, D. J. (1960). The Alaska earthquake of July 10, 1958: giant wave in Lituya Bay. *Bull. seism. Soc. Am.*, **50**, 253–66

Miyazaki, M. (1967). Storm surges along the Japanese coast and their prediction. *11th Pacific Science Congress, Sympos. on Tusunami and Storm Surges*, 74

Munk, W. H. (1962). Long ocean waves. *The Sea* (ed. M. N. Hill), Interscience, New York. pp. 647–63

Munk, W. H., Snodgrass, F., and Carrier, G. (1956). Edge waves on the continental shelf. *Science*, **123**, 127–32

Redfield, A. C., and Miller, A. R. (1957). Water levels accompanying Atlantic coast hurricanes. *Am. met. Soc., Met. Monog.*, **2**, 1–23

Riehl, H. (1965). *Introduction to the Atmosphere*, McGraw-Hill, New York

Robinson, A. H. W. (1953). The storm surge of 31st January–1st February, 1953. *Geography*, **38**, 134–41

Robinson, A. H. W. (1961). The Pacific tsunami of May 22nd, 1960. *Geography*, **46**, 18–24

Rossiter, J. R. (1954). The great tidal surge of 1953. *The Listener*, 8 July, 55–6

Scott, K. M., and Gravlee, G. C. (1968). Flood surge on the Rubicon River, California – hydrology, hydraulics and boulder transport. *U.S. geol. Surv. prof. Pap.*, **422–M**

Shepard, F. P. (1948). *Submarine Geology*, Harper, New York

Smith, K. (1975). *Principles of Applied Climatology*, McGraw-Hill, London

Steers, J. A. (1953). The east coast floods, January 31–February 1, 1953. *Georgl J.*, **119,** 280–98

Thornbury, W. D. (1969). *Principles of Geomorphology*, (2nd edn), Wiley, New York

Truitt, R. V. (1967). High winds . . . high tides, a chronicle of Maryland's coastal hurricanes. *Natural Resources Institute, Univ. of Maryland, Educational Series*, no. 77

Van Ufford, H. A. Q. (1953). The disastrous storm surge of 1st February. *Weather*, **8,** 116–21

Volker, M. (1953). La marée de tempête du 1er février 1953 et ses conséquences pour les Pays-Bas. *La Houille Blanche*, no. 2, 207–16

Walters, R. C. S. (1971). *Dam Geology*, Butterworths, London

5 FLOODS AS GEOMORPHOLOGICAL AGENTS

Barnes, F. A., and King, C. A. M. (1953). The Lincolnshire coastline and the 1953 storm flood. *Geography*, **38,** 141–60

Costa, J. E. (1974). Response and recovery of a piedmont watershed from tropical storm Agnes, June 1972. *Wat. Resour. Res.*, **10,** 106–12

Crisp, D. T., Rawes, M., and Welch, D. (1964). A Pennine peat slide. *Geogrl J.*, **130,** 519–24

Douglas, I. (1975). Private communication

Einstein, H. A. (1964). River sedimentation. *Handbook of Applied Hydrology*, (ed. V. T. Chow), McGraw-Hill, New York, pp. 17-35–67

Gagoshidze, M. S. (1969). Mud flows and floods and their control. *Soviet Hydrol.* **4,** 410–22

Gibbs, R. J. (1967). Amazon River: environmental factors that control its dissolved and suspended load. *Science*, **156,** 1734–7

Gifford, J. (1953). Landslides on Exmoor caused by the storm of 15th August, 1952. *Geography*, **38,** 9–17

Glover, B. J., and Johnson, P. (1974). Variations in the natural chemical concentration of river water during flood flows, and the lag effect. *J. Hydrol.*, **22,** 303–16

Grove, A. T. (1953). The sea flood on the coasts of Norfolk and Suffolk. *Geography*, **38,** 164–70

Gupta, A., and Fox, H. (1974). Effects of high-magnitude floods on channel form: a case study in Maryland piedmont. *Wat. Resour. Res.*, **10,** 499–509

Haggett, P., and Chorley, R. J. (1969). *Network Analysis in Geography*, Arnold, London

Heidel, S. G. (1956). The progressive lag of sediment concentration with flood waves. *Trans. Am. geophys. Un.* **37**, 56–66

Holeman, J. N. (1968). The sediment yield of major rivers of the world. *Wat. Resour. Res.*, **4**, 737–47

Howard, C. S. (1947). Suspended sediment in the Colorado River 1925–41. *U.S. Geol. Surv. Water-Supply Paper*, 998

Kherkheulidze, I. I. (1969). Estimation of basic characteristics of mudflows ('sel'). *Floods and their Computation*, IASH/UNESCO/WMO, pp. 940–8

Leopold, L. B., and Maddock, T. (1953). The hydraulic geometry of stream channels and some physiographic implications. *U.S. geol. Surv. prof. Pap.*, **252**

Leopold, L. B., Wolman, M. G., and Miller, J. P. (1964). *Fluvial Processes in Geomorphology*, Freeman, San Francisco

Lewin, J., and Manton, M. M. (1975). Welsh floodplain studies: the nature of the floodplain geometry. *J. Hydrol.*, **25**, 37–50

McPherson, H. J. (1971). Dissolved, suspended and bed load movement patterns in Two O'Clock Creek, Rocky Mountains, Canada, summer, 1969. *J. Hydrol.*, **12**, 221–33

McPherson, H. J., and Rannie, W. F. (1969). Geomorphic effects of the May 1967 flood in Graburn watershed, Cypress Hills, Alberta, Canada. *J. Hydrol.*, **9**, 307–21

Miller, A. A. (1951). Cause and effect in a Welsh cloudburst. *Weather*, **6**, 172–9

Pain, C. F., and Hosking, P. L. (1970). The movement of sediment in a channel in relation to magnitude and frequency concepts – a New Zealand example. *Earth Science J.*, **4**, 17–23

Popov, I. V., and Gavrin, Y. S. (1970). Use of aerial photography in evaluating the flooding and emptying of river flood plains and the development of floodplain currents. *Soviet Hydrol.*, **5**, 413–25

Schick, A. P. (1970). Desert floods. *Symposium on the results of research on representative and experimental basins*, IASH/UNESCO, pp. 479–93

Schumm, S. A., and Lichty, R. W. (1963). Channel widening and flood plain construction along Cimarron River in southwestern Kansas. *U.S. geol. Surv. prof. Pap.*, **352-D**

Steers, J. A. (1953). The east coast floods January 31–February 1 1953. *Geogrl J.*, **119**, 280–98

Williams, G. P., and Guy, H. P. (1973). Erosional and depositional aspects of Hurricane Camille in Virginia, 1969. *U.S. geol. Surv. prof. Pap.*, **804**

Wolman, M. G., and Leopold, L. B. (1957). River flood plains: some observations on their formation. *U.S. geol. Surv. prof. Pap.*, **282-C**, 87–109

6 FLOOD PREDICTION

ASCE (1972). Reevaluation of the adequacy of spillways of existing dams.

Report of the Task Committee of the Hydrometeorology Committee of the American Society of Civil Engineers

Alekhin, Y. M. (1964). *Short-range Forecasting of Lowland-river Runoff*, Israel Program for Scientific Translations, Jerusalem

Alexander, G. N. (1969). Application of probability to spillway design flood estimation. *Floods and their Computation,* IASH/UNESCO/WMO, pp. 536–43

Alexander, G. N., Karoly, A., and Susts, A. B. (1969*a*). Equivalent distributions with application to rainfall as an upper bound to flood distribution. *J. Hydrol.*, **9**, 322–44

Alexander, G. N., Karoly, A., and Susts, A. B. (1969*b*). Equivalent distributions with application to rainfall as an upper bound to flood distributions (contd). *J. Hydrol.*, **9**, 345–73

Benson, M. A. (1968). Uniform flood-frequency estimating methods for Federal Agencies, *Wat. Resour. Res.*, **4**, 891–908

Benson, M. A. (1969). Reply to comments by C. C. Kisiel on Uniform flood-frequency estimating methods for Federal Agencies. *Wat. Resour. Res.*, **5**, 911

Benson, M. A. (1973*a*). Discussion of precipitation and precipitation probability. *Floods and Droughts* (eds E. F. Schulz, V. A. Koelzer and K. Mahmood), Water Resources Publications, Ft. Collins, Colo., p. 101

Benson, M. A. (1973*b*). Thoughts on the design of floods. *Floods and Droughts* (eds E. F. Schulz, V. A. Koelzer and K. Mahmood), Water Resources Publications, Ft. Collins, Colo., pp. 27–33

Beran, M. A., and Sutcliffe, J. V. (1972). An index of flood-producing rainfall based on rainfall and soil moisture deficit. *J. Hydrol*, **17**, 229–36

Biswas, A. K. (1971). Some thoughts on estimating spillway design flood. *Bull. int. Ass. scient. Hydrol*, **16**, 63–71

Brater, E. F., Sangal, S., and Sherrill, J. D. (1974). Seasonal effects in flood synthesis. *Wat. Resour. Res.*, **10**, 441–5

Chebotarev, N. P. (1966). *Theory of Stream Runoff*, Israel Program for Scientific Translations, Jerusalem

Chow, V. T. (1951). A general formula for hydrologic frequency analysis. *Trans. Am. geophys. Un.*, **32**, 231–37

Chow, V. T. (1956). Hydrologic studies of floods in the United States. *Symposia Darcy, 3, Crues, IASH Publication*, No. 42, 134–70

Chow, V. T. (1957). Report of the Committee on Runoff, 1955–56. *Trans. Am. geophys. Un.*, **38**, 379

Chow, V. T. (1964). Runoff. *Handbook of Applied Hydrology* (ed. V. T. Chow), McGraw-Hill, New York, section 14

Cordery, I. (1971). Estimation of design hydrographs for small rural catchments. *J. Hydrol.*, **13**, 263–77

Crawford, N. H., and Linsley, R. K. (1966). Digital simulation in hydrology:

Stanford Watershed Model IV. *Stanford University, Civil Eng. Tech. Rept*, **39**, 210

Dalrymple, T. (1950). Regional flood frequency. *Surface Drainage, Highway Research Board, Rept.*, **11-B**, 4–20

Dalrymple, T. (1960). Flood frequency analysis. Manual of Hydrology, part 3, Flood flow techniques. *U.S. geol. Surv. Wat.-Sup. Pap.* **1543-A**,

Eagleson, P. S. (1970). *Dynamic Hydrology*, McGraw-Hill, New York

Eagleson, P. S. (1972). Dynamics of flood frequency. *Wat. Resour. Res.*, **8**, 878–98

Erickson, O. M., and McCorquodale, J. A. (1967). Applications of computers to the determination of snowmelt runoff. *Statistical Methods in Hydrology*, National Research Council of Canada, Ottawa, 361–78

Fiering, M. B. (1967). *Streamflow Synthesis*, Harvard U.P., Cambridge, Mass.

Foster, E. E. (1949). *Rainfall and Runoff*, Macmillan, New York

Francis, J. R. D. (1973). Rain, runoff and rivers. *Q. J. R. met. Soc.*, **99**, 556–68

Francou, J., and Rodier, J. A. (1969). Essai de classification des crues maximales. *Floods and their Computation*, IASH/UNESCO/WMO, pp. 518–27

Fuller, W. E. (1914). Flood flows. *Trans. Am. Soc. civ. Engrs*, **77**, 564–617

Garcia, L. E., Dawdy, D. R., and Mejia, J. M. (1972). Long memory monthly streamflow simulation by a broken line model. *Wat. Resour. Res.*, **8**, 1100–5

Gray, D. M. (1961). Interrelationships of watershed characteristics. *J. geophys. Res.*, **66**, 1215–23

Gray, D. M. (1970). *Handbook on the Principles of Hydrology*, National Research Council of Canada, Ottawa

Gray, D. M., and Wigham, J. M. (1970). Peak flow – rainfall events. *Handbook on the Principles of Hydrology* (ed. D. M. Gray), National Research Council of Canda, Ottawa, section VIII

Gumbel, E. J. (1941). The return period of flood flows. *Ann. math. Stats.*, **12**, 163–90

Gumbel, E. J. (1958). *Statistics of Extremes*, Columbia U.P., New York

Gumbel, E. J. (1967). Extreme value analysis of hydrologic data. *Statistical Methods in Hydrology*, National Research Council of Canada, Ottawa, pp. 147–81

Hardison, C. H. (1974). Generalized skew coefficients of annual floods in the United States and their application. *Wat. Resour. Res.*, **10**, 745–52

Henderson, F. M. (1963). Some properties of the unit hydrograph. *J. geophys. Res.*, **68**, 4785–93

Heras, R. (1969). Méthodes pratiques d'estimation des plus grandes crues. *Floods and their Computation*, IASH/UNESCO/WMO, pp. 492–504

Hershfield, D. M. (1961). Estimating the probable maximum precipitation. *J. Hydraul. Div. ASCE*, **87**, 5

Hershfield, D. M. (1965). Method for estimating probable maximum rainfall. *J. Am. Waterworks Ass.*, **57**, 965–72

Hershfield, D. M., and Kohler, M. A. (1960). An empirical appraisal of the Gumbel extreme-value procedure. *J. geophys. Res.*, **65**, 1737–46

Holtan, H. N., and Lopez, N. C. (1971). USDAHL-70 model of watershed hydrology. *U.S.D.A., agric. Res. Serv., Tech. Bull.*, **1435**, 84

Horton, R. E. (1933). The role of infiltration in the hydrologic cycle. *Trans. Am. geophys. Un.*, **14**, 446–60

Hoyt, W. G., and Langbein, W. B. (1955). *Floods*, Princeton U.P., New Jersey

IASH/UNESCO/WMO (1969). *Floods and their Computation*, 2 vols, Proceedings of the Leningrad Symposium, August 1967, IASH/UNESCO/WMO

Institute of Hydrology (1973). *Research 1972–73*, Natural Environment Research Council

Institute of Hydrology (1974). *Research 1973–74*, Natural Environment Research Council

Jarvis, C. S. (1926). Flood flow characteristics. *Trans. Am. Soc. civ. Engrs*, **89**, 985–1032

Jennings, M. E., and Benson, M. A. (1969). Frequency curves for annual flood series with some zero events or incomplete data. *Wat. Resour. Res.*, **5**, 276–80

Kerr, R. L., McGinnis, D. F., Reich, B. M., and Rachford, T. M. (1970). Analysis of rainfall-duration-frequency for Pennsylvania. *Pennsylvania State Univ., Inst. for Res. on Land and Water Resources, Res. Publ.*, **70**, 152

Kresge, R. F., and Nordenson, T. J. (1955). Flood frequencies derived from river forecasting procedures. *Proc. Am. Soc. civ. Engrs*, **81**, separate no. 630

Kuichling, E. (1889). The relation between the rainfall and the discharge of sewers in populous districts. *Trans. Am. Soc. civ. Engrs*, **20**, 1–56

Langbein, W. B. (1949). Annual floods and the partial-duration series. *Trans. Am. geophys. Un.*, **30**, 879–81

Langbein, W. B. *et al.* (1947). Topographic characteristics of drainage basins. *U.S. geol. Surv., Water-Supply Pap.*, **968-C**, 125–57

Levashov, A. A. (1966). Approximate determination of high flood frequency in rivers without hydrological observations. *Soviet Hydrol.*, **5**, 547–8

Linsley, R. K. (1967). The relation between rainfall and runoff. *J. Hydrol.*, **5**, 297–311

Lloyd-Davis, D. E. (1906). The elimination of storm water from sewerage systems. *Minut. Proc. Instn civ. Engrs*, **164**, 41–67

Mandeville, A. N., O'Connell, P. E., Sutcliffe, J. V., and Nash, J. E. (1970). River flow forecasting through conceptual models: Part III – the Ray catchment at Grendon Underwood. *J. Hydrol.*, **11**, 109–28

Mandlebrot, B. B., and Van Ness, J. W. (1968). Fractional Brownian motions, fractional noises, and their applications. *SIAM Rev.*, **10**, 422–37

Mandlebrot, B. B., and Wallis, J. R. (1968). Noah, Joseph, and operational hydrology. *Wat. Resour. Res.*, **4**, 909–18

Mandlebrot, B. B., and Wallis, J. R. (1969a). Computer experiments with fractional Gaussian noises, 1. Averages and variances. *Wat. Resour. Res.*, **5**, 228–41

Mandlebrot, B. B., and Wallis, J. R. (1969b). Computer experiments with fractional Gaussian noises, 2. Rescaled ranges and spectra. *Wat. Resour. Res.*, **5**, 242–59

Mandlebrot, B. B., and Wallis, J. R. (1969c). Computer experiments with fractional Gaussian noises, 3. Mathematical appendix. *Wat. Resour. Res.*, **5**, 260–7

Mandlebrot, B. B., and Wallis, J. R. (1969d). Some long-run properties of geophysical records. *Wat. Resour. Res.*, **5**, 321–40

Mandlebrot, B. B., and Wallis, J. R. (1969e). Robustness of the rescaled range R/S in the measurement of noncyclic long-run statistical dependence. *Wat. Resour. Res.*, **5**, 967–88

Mejia, J. M., Rodriguez-Iturbe, I., and Dawdy, D. R. (1972). Streamflow simulation, 2. The broken line process as a potential model for hydrologic simulation. *Wat. Resour. Res.*, **8**, 931–41

Melentijevich, M. (1969). Estimation of flood flows using mathematical statistics. *Floods and their Computation*, IASH/UNESCO/WMO, pp. 164–74

Miller, J. F. (1973). Probable maximum precipitation – the concept, current procedures and outlook. *Floods and Droughts*, (eds E. F. Schulz, V. A. Koelzer and K. Mahmood), Water Resources Publications, Ft. Collins, Colo., pp. 50–61

Mulvaney, T. J. (1851). On the use of self-registering rain and flood gauges in making observations of the relations of rainfall and of flood discharges in a given catchment. *Trans. Instn civ. Engrs Ir.* (Dublin), **4**, 18

Myers, V. A. (1969). The estimation of extreme precipitation as the basis for design floods; resume of practice in the United States. *Floods and their Computation*, IASH/UNESCO/WMO, pp. 84–104

Nash, J. E. (1960). A unit hydrograph study, with particular reference to British catchments. *Proc. Instn civ. Engrs*, **17**, 249–82

Nash, J. E., and Sutcliffe, J. V. (1970). River flow forecasting through conceptual models, Part I – a discussion of principles. *J. Hydrol.*, **10**, 282–90

NERC (1975). *Flood Studies Report*, 5 vols, Natural Environment Research Council

Newton, D. W. (1973). Discussion on Precipitation and precipitation probability. *Floods and Droughts* (eds E. F. Schulz, V. A. Koelzer and K. Mahmood), Water Resources Publications, Ft. Collins, Colo., p. 102

O'Connell, P. E., Nash, J. E., and Farrell, J. P. (1970). River flow forecasting through conceptual models, Part III – the Brosna catchment at Ferbane. *J. Hydrol.*, **10**, 317–29

Pilgrim, D. H. (1966). Storm loss rates for regions with limited data. *J. Hydraul. Div., ASCE*, **92**, 193–206

Potter, W. D. (1961). Peak rates of runoff from small watersheds. *U.S. Dept. Comm., Bur. Public Roads, Hydraul. Design Ser.*, no. 2

Reich, B. M. (1968). Predicting high flows from small watersheds. *Pennsylvania University, Inst. for Res. on Land and Water Resources, Inform. Rept.*, **55,** 24

Reich, B. M. (1969). Flood series for gaged Pennsylvania streams. *Penn. State Univ., Inst. for Research on Land and Water Resources, Res. Pub.*, 63

Reich, B. M. (1971). *Runoff Estimates for Small Rural Watersheds*, Contract FH-11-7429, Pennsylvania State Univ., Dept. Civ. Eng.

Robison, F. L. (1961). Floods in New York, magnitude and frequency. *U.S. geol. Survey, Circ.*, 454

Rodda, J. C. (1969). The significance of characteristics of basin rainfall and morphometry in a study of floods in the United Kingdom. *Floods and their Computation*, IASH/UNESCO/WMO, pp. 834–45

Rodriguez-Iturbe, I., Mejia, J. M., and Dawdy, D. R. (1972). Streamflow simulation, 1. A new look at Markovian models, fractional Gaussian noise, and crossing theory. *Wat. Resour. Res.*, **8,** 921–30

Rostomov, C. D. (1969). Method of estimating storm runoff from small drainage basins. *Floods and their Computation*, IASH/UNESCO/WMO, pp. 462–72

Schnackenberg, E. C. (1949). Extreme flood discharges. *Proc. N. Z. Soc. civ. Engrs*, **35,** 376

Sherman, L. K. (1932). Streamflow from rainfall by the unit-graph method. *Engng News-Record*, **108,** 501–5

Snyder, F. F. (1938). Synthetic unit-graphs. *Trans. Am. geophys. Un.*, **19,** 447–54

Sokolov, A. A. (1969a). Methods of snowmelt maximum discharge computation in cases of absence or insufficiency of hydrometric data. *Floods and their Computation*, IASH/UNESCO/WMO, pp. 671–80

Sokolov, A. A. (1969b). Closing address: the essence of the problem and the significance of the symposium. *Floods and their Computation*, IASH/UNESCO/WMO, pp. 971–80

Thomas, H. A., and Fiering, M. B. (1962). Mathematical synthesis of streamflow sequences for the analysis of river basins by simulation. *Design of Water Resource Systems* (eds A. Maass *et al.*), Harvard U.P., Cambridge, Mass., pp. 459–93

Todorovic, P., and Rousselle, J. (1971). Some problems of flood analysis. *Wat. Resour. Res.*, **7,** 1144–50

Todorovic, P. and Zelenhasic, E. (1970). A stochastic model for flood analysis, *Wat. Resour. Res.*, **6,** 1641–8

U.S. Corps of Engineers. (1956). *Snow Hydrology*, Office of Tech. Serv., U.S. Dept. Commerce, Washington, D.C.

U.S.D.A. (1957). Hydrology. *Engineering Handbook*, USDA, Soil Conservation Service, Washington, D.C., section 4

U.S.W.B. (1941). Maximum probable precipitation, Ohio River above

Pittsburgh. *USWB, Hydromet. Rept.*, **2**

U.S.W.B. (1960). Generalized estimates of probable maximum precipitation for the U.S. west of the 105th meridian. *USWB, Tech. Pap.*, **38**

U.S.W.B. (1961). Interim report probable maximum precipitation in California. *USWB, Hydromet. Rept*, **36**

Van der Made, J. W. (1969). Assessment of a design discharge of a river. *Floods and their Computation*, IASH/UNESCO/WMO, pp. 152–64

Ward, R. C. (1975). *Principles of Hydrology* (2nd edn), McGraw-Hill, London

Wiesner, C. J. (1970). *Hydrometeorology*, Chapman and Hall, London

Wilson, E. M. (1969). *Engineering Hydrology*, Macmillan, London

Wilson, W. T. (1968). Comment on 'Misconceptions in hydrology and their consequences' by V. Yevyevich. *Wat. Resour. Res.*, **4**, 1145–6

Wisler, C. O., and Brater, E. F. (1959). *Hydrology* (2nd edn), Wiley, New York

Wolf, P. O. (1966). Comparison of methods of flood estimation. *River Flood Hydrology*, Institution of Civil Engineers, London, pp. 1–23

Zelenhasic, E. (1970). Theoretical probability distributions for flood peaks. *Colorado State Univ., Hydrol. Papers*, **42**, 35

7 FLOOD FORECASTING

Alekhin, Y. M. (1964). *Short-range Forecasting of Lowland-River Runoff*, Israel Program for Scientific Translations, Jerusalem

Anon (1973). Hurricane prediction and control: impact of large computers. *Science*, **181**, 643–4

Barrett, E. C. (1973). Forecasting daily rainfall from satellite data. *Mon. Weath. Rev.*, **101**, 215–22

Battan, L. J. (1973). *Radar Observation of the Atmosphere*, University of Chicago Press, Chicago

Beard, L. R. (1969). Hypothetical flood compution (sic) for a stream system. *The Use of Analog and Digital Computers in Hydrology*, IASH/UNESCO, vol. 1, pp. 258–67

Beard, L. R. (1971). Closing the technology gap. *Computer Applications in Hydrology*, U.S. Army Corps of Engineers, Hydrologic Engineering Center, pp. 1–7

Bond, A. (1974). Early flood warning by computer will protect Bath area. *Process Engng*, 17 September

Church, J. E. (1942). Snow and snow surveying: ice. *Hydrology* (ed. O. E. Meinzer), McGraw-Hill, New York

Collins, E. H. (1934). Relationship of degree-days above freezing to runoff. *Trans. Am. geophys. Un.*, **15**, 624–9

Crawford, N. H., and Linsley, R. K. (1966). Digital simulation in hydrology: Stanford watershed model IV. *Stanford Univ., Dept. Civ. Engg., Tech. Rept.*, **39**, 210

Davar, K. S. (1970). Peak flow – snowmelt events. *Handbook on the Principles of Hydrology* (ed. D. M. Gray), National Research Council of Canada, Ottawa, section IX

Dooge, J. C. I. (1959). A general theory of the unit hydrograph. *J. geophys. Res.*, **64**, 241–56

Eagleson, P. S. (1970). *Dynamic Hydrology*, McGraw-Hill, New York

Eagleson, P. S. (1972). Dynamics of flood frequency. *Wat. Resour. Res.*, **8**, 878–98

Erickson, O. M., and McCorquodale, J. A. (1967). Applications of computers to the determination of snowmelt runoff. *Statistical Methods in Hydrology*, National Research Council of Canada, Ottawa, pp. 361–78

Fox, W. E. (1965). Methods of river forecasting. *Proc. conf. Hydrologic Activities in the South Carolina region,* Clenison Univ., Clenison

Garstka, W. U. (1964). Snow and snow survey. *Handbook of Applied Hydrology* (ed. V. T. Chow), McGraw-Hill, New York, pp. 10.1–57

Goodhew, R. C. (1970). Weather is my business. 1. The hydrologist. *Weather*, **25**, 33–9

Gray, D. M., and Wigham, J. M. (1970). Peak flow – rainfall events. *Handbook on the Principles of Hydrology* (ed. D. M. Gray), National Research Council of Canada, Ottawa, section VIII

Grieve, H. (1959). *The Great Tide*, County Council of Essex, Chelmsford

Grindley, J. (1967). The estimation of soil moisture deficits. *Met. Mag.*, **96**, 97–108

Grindley, J., and Singleton, F. (1969). The routine estimation of soil moisture deficits. *Floods and their Computation*, IASH/UNESCO/WMO, pp. 811–20

Hall, D. G., and White, K. E. (1976). Warning systems for river management. *Proc. Instn civ. Engrs*, **60**, 295–8

Harding, D. M., and Parker, D. J. (1972). A study of the flood hazard at Shrewsbury, United Kingdom. Paper presented at 22nd Internat. Geog. Cong., Calgary

Harrold, T. W., and Nicholass, C. A. (1972). The accuracy of some recent radar estimates of surface precipitation. *Met. Mag.*, **101**, 193–205

Horton, R. E. (1933). The role of infiltration in the hydrologic cycle. *Trans. Am. geophys. Un.*, **14**, 446–60

Hoyt, W. G., and Langbein, W. B. (1955). *Floods*, Princeton U.P., New Jersey

Hydrocomp (1970). *Water Resource Systems HSP/FLOODS*, Hydrocomp International, Palo Alto

Jensen, C. E. (1974). *The Federal Plan for Meteorological Services and Supporting Research*, U.S. Dept. Commerce, NOAA

Johnson, E. P. (1967). Example of radar as a tool in forecasting tidal flooding. *U.S. Weath. Bur., Eastern Region Tech. Mem.*, WBTM-ER-24

Labzovskii, N. A. (1966). (Sea floods in the estuary of the Neva River) Morskie navodneniia v ust'e r. Neva. *Moscow. Gosudarstvennyi Okeanograficheskii Institut, Trudy*, no. 79, 3–40

Lane, L. J., Diskin, M. H., and Renard, K. G. (1971). Input–output relationships for an ephemeral stream channel system. *J. Hydrol.*, **13**, 22–40

Lawler, E. A. (1964). Flood routing. *Handbook of Applied Hydrology* (ed. V. T. Chow), McGraw-Hill, New York, section 25–II

Linsley, R. K. (1967). The relation between rainfall and runoff. *J. Hydrol.*, **5**, 297–311

Linsley, R. K., and Crawford, N. H. (1974). Continuous simulation models in urban hydrology. *Geophys. Res. Lett.*, **1**, 59–62

Linsley, R. K., Kohler, M. A., and Paulhus, J. L. H. (1949). *Applied Hydrology*, McGraw-Hill, New York

McCarthy, G. T. (1938). The unit hydrograph and flood routing. Unpublished paper presented at Conference of North Atlantic Div., U.S. Army Corps of Engineers, New London, Conn., 24 June 1938

Mandeville, A. N., O'Connell, P. E., Sutcliffe, J. V., and Nash, J. E. (1970). River flow forecasting through conceptual models: Part III – The Ray catchment at Grendon Underwood. *J. Hydrol.*, **11**, 109–28

Miljukov, P. I. (1972). State and trends in hydrological forecasts. *Status and Trends of Research in Hydrology 1965–74*, UNESCO, Paris, pp. 85–100

Nash, J. E. (1958). The form of the instantaneous unit hydrograph. *IASH Publ.*, **45**, 114

Nash, J. E., and Sutcliffe, J. V. (1970). River flow forecasting through conceptual models: Part I – A discussion of principles. *J. Hydrol.*, **10**, 282–90

NERC (1972). *Natural Environment Research Council, Report of the Council*, House of Commons Paper 411, HMSO

NOAA (1973a). *The National Weather Service and Water Management*, U.S. Dept. Commerce, NOAA/PA 71004

NOAA (1973b). *Floods, Flash Floods and Warnings*, U.S. Dept. Commerce, NOAA/PA 71009 (Rev)

O'Connell, P. E., Nash, J. E., and Farrell, J. P. (1970). River flow forecasting through conceptual models: Part III – The Brosna catchment at Ferbane. *J. Hydrol.*, **10**, 317–29

Østrem, G. (1964). Glacio-hydrological investigations in Norway. *J. Hydrol.*, **2**, 101–15

Popov, E. G. (1964). River forecasts. *Methods of Hydrological Forecasting for the Utilization of Water Resources*, U.N. Water Resources Series, no. 27, pp. 38–54

Porath, A., and Schick, A. P. (1974). The use of remote sensing systems in monitoring desert floods. *Flash Floods*, IASH-UNESCO-WMO, pp. 133–9

Richards, M. M. (1964). Prediction of runoff volume from storm rainfall. *Methods of Hydrological Forecasting for the Utilization of Water Resources*, U.N. Water Resources Series, no. 27, pp. 15–37

Robinson, A. R., Tomasin, A., and Artegiani, A. (1973). Flooding of Venice: phenomenology and prediction of the Adriatic storm surge. *Q. J. R. met. Soc.*, **99**, 688–92

Rockwood, D. M. (1958). Columbia basin streamflow routing by computer. *J. Waterways Harbors Div., ASCE*, **84**, paper 1874

Rockwood, D. M. (1969). Application of streamflow synthesis and reservoir regulation – 'SSARR' – program to the Lower Mekong River. *The Use of Analog and Digital Computers in Hydrology*, IASH-UNESCO, vol. 1, pp. 329–44

Schermerhorn, V. P., and Kuehl, D. W. (1969). Operational streamflow forecasting with the ssarr model. *The Use of Analog and Digital Computers in Hydrology*, IASH-UNESCO, vol. 1, pp. 317–28

Sugawara, M. (1969). On a method of flood forecasting using a digital computer connected with a weather radar. *The Use of Analog and Digital Computers in Hydrology*, IASH-UNESCO, vol. 1, pp. 161–9

Thornthwaite, C. W., and Mather, J. R. (1955). The water balance. *Publs Climat.*, **8**, 1–86

Townsend, J. (1975). Storm Tide Warning Service – surge forecasting methods. Meteorological Office (cyclostyled)

U.S. Army Corps of Engineers (1956). *Snow Hydrology*, North Pacific Div., Portland, Oregon

U.S. Army Corps of Engineers (1960). *Runoff from Snowmelt*, EM 1110–2–1406, USGPO, Washington, D.C.

U.S. Coast and Geodetic Survey (1965). *Tsunami! The Story of the Seismic Sea-Wave Warning System*, USGPO, Washington, D.C.

Ward, R. C. (1975). *Principles of Hydrology* (Second edn), McGraw-Hill, London

Warnick, C. C., and Penton, V. E. (1971). New methods of measuring water equivalent of snow pack for automatic recording at remote mountain locations. *J. Hydrol.*, **13**, 201–15

Wilson, E. M. (1969). *Engineering Hydrology*, Macmillan, London

Woodley, W. L., and Sancho, B. (1971). A first step towards rainfall estimation from satellite cloud photographs. *Weather*, **26**, 279–89

Yevjevich, V. M. (1964). Bibliography and discussion of flood-routing methods and unsteady flow in open channels. *U.S. geol. Surv., Water-Sup. Pap.*, 1690

Yevjevich, V. M., and Barnes, A. H. (1970). Flood routing through storm drains. Part I – solution of problems of unsteady free surface flow in storm drains. *Colorado State Univ., Hydrol. Papers*, no. 43

8 HUMAN RESPONSE TO THE FLOOD HAZARD:
I INTRODUCTION AND POSSIBLE ADJUSTMENTS

Bue, C. D. (1967). Flood information for flood-plain planning. *U.S. Geol. Surv. Circ.*, no. 539

Burton, I. (1961). Some aspects of flood loss reduction in England and Wales. *Papers on Flood Problems* (ed. G. F. White), Univ. of Chicago, Dept. of Geog., Res. Pap. no. 70, pp. 203–21

Burton, I., Kates, R. W., and Snead, R. E. (1969). *The Human Ecology of Coastal Flood Hazard in Megalopolis*, Univ. of Chicago, Dept. of Geog., Res. Pap., no. 115

Douglas, I., and Hobbs, J. (1974). Deluge in Australia. *Geogrl Mag.*, **46**, 465–71

Gately, J. E. (1973). The idea of a flood. *Middlesex Polytechnic, Flood Hazard Research Project, Spec. Publ.*, no. 1

Gillett, P. (1974). National flood insurance program enlarged. *Water for Texas*, **4**, 9–11

Goddard, J. E. (1969). Man should manage the flood plains. *Flood Plain Management, Iowa's Experience* (ed. M. D. Dougal), Iowa State Univ. Press, Ames, pp. 11–22

Harding, D. M., and Parker, D. J. (1972). A study of the flood hazard at Shrewsbury. Paper presented at seminar on Natural Hazards, Institute of British Geographers, January 1973

Heap, D. (1969). *An Outline of Planning Law* (5th edn), Sweet and Maxwell, London

Hewitt, K., and Burton, I. (1971). The hazardousness of a place. A regional ecology of damaging events. *Univ. Toronto, Dept. of Geog., Res. Publ.*, **5**, 154

Hoyt, W. G., and Langbein, W. B. (1955). *Floods*, Princeton U.P., New Jersey

Kates, R. W. (1962). *Hazard and Choice Perception in Flood Plain Management*, Univ. of Chicago, Dept. of Geog., Res. Pap. no. 78

Kates, R. W. (1971). Natural hazard in human ecological perspective: hypotheses and models. *Econ. Geog.*, **47**, 438–51

Kates, R. W., and White, G. F. (1961). Flood hazard evaluation. *Papers on Flood Problems* (ed. G. F. White), Univ. of Chicago, Dept. of Geog., Res. Pap. no. 70, pp. 135–47

Krutilla, J. V. (1966). An economic approach to coping with flood damage. *Wat. Resour. Res.*, **2**, 183–90

Kunreuther, H., and Sheaffer, J. R. (1970). An economically meaningful and workable system for calculating flood insurance rates. *Wat. Resour. Res.*, **6**, 659–67

Linsley, R. K., and Franzini, J. B. (1972). *Water-Resources Engineering* (2nd edn), McGraw-Hill, New York

Loughlin, J. C. (1971). A flood insurance model for sharing the costs of flood protection. *Wat. Resour. Res.*, **7**, 236–44

Miller, D. H. (1966). Cultural hydrology: a review. *Econ. Geog.*, **42**, 85–9

Murphy, F. C. (1958). *Regulating Flood Plain Development*, Univ. of Chicago. Dept. of Geog., Res. Pap. no. 56

Newson, M. D. (1975). Private communication

Nixon, M. (1963). Flood regulation and river training in England and Wales. *Conservation of Water Resources in the United Kingdom*, Institution of Civil Engineers, London, pp. 137–50

Penning-Rowsell, E. (1972). Flood hazard research project: progress report. *Middlesex Polytechnic, Flood Hazard Research Project, Prog. Rept.*, no. 1

Penning-Rowsell, E., and Parker, D. J. (1973). The control of flood plain development: a preliminary analysis. *Middlesex Polytechnic, Flood Hazard Research Project, Prog. Rept.*, no. 4

Sewell, W. R. D. (1969). Human response to floods. *Water, Earth and Man* (ed. R. J. Chorley), Methuen, London, pp. 431–51

Sheaffer, J. R. (1960). *Flood Proofing: An Element in a Flood Damage Reduction Program*, Univ. of Chicago, Dept. of Geog., Res. Pap. no. 65

Task Force (1966). *A Unified National Program for Managing Flood Losses*, Rept. by Task Force on Federal Flood Control Policy, 89th Congress House Doc. no. 465, USGPO, Washington

U.S. Army Corps of Engineers (1959). *Flood Emergency Manual*, Chief of Engineers, Washington

U.S. Army Corps of Engineers (1973). *Special Flood Hazard Information: White Oak Creek, Diboll, Texas*, The Engineers, Fort Worth, Texas (cyclostyled)

White, G. F. (1939). Economic aspects of flood forecasting. *Trans. Am. geophys. Un.*, **20**, 218–33

White, G. F. (1964). Floodplain adjustments and regulations. *Handbook of Applied Hydrology* (ed. V. T. Chow), McGraw-Hill, New York, Section 25-V

White, G. F., Calef, W. C., Hudson, J. W., Mayer, H. M., Sheaffer, J. R., and Volk, D. J. (1958). *Changes in Urban Occupance of Flood Plains in the United States*, Univ. of Chicago, Dept. of Geog., Res. Pap. no. 57

9 HUMAN RESPONSE TO THE FLOOD HAZARD: II FLOOD ABATEMENT

Ackerman, W. C., *et al.* (1966). *Recommendations for Watershed Research Programs*, U.S. Dept. Interior, OWRR Panel on Watershed Research, Washington, D.C.

Anderson, D. G. (1968). *Effects of Urban Development on Floods in Northern*

Virginia, U.S. Geol. Surv., Water Resource Div., Open File Report, Richmond, Va.

AWRA (1972). Research and Technology. *The Water Resources Newsletter*, **7**, no. 4, American Water Resources Association.

Ayers, H. D. (1965). Effect of agricultural land management on winter runoff in the Guelph, Ontario region. *Research Watersheds: Proc. Hydrol. Sympos.*, no. 4, Univ. of Guelph, Ontario, 167–82

Bailey, R. W., and Copeland, O. L. (1960). Low flow discharges and plant cover relations in two mountain watersheds in Utah. *General Assembly of Helsinki, I.A.S.H. Publ.*, **51**, 267–78

Bedell, G. D., Kohnke, H., and Hickok, R. B. (1946). The effects of two farming systems on erosion from cropland. *Soil Sci. Soc. Amer. Proc.*, **11**, 522–6

Berndt, H. W. (1964). Inducing snow accumulation on mountain grassland watersheds. *J. Soil and Water Cons.*, **19**, 196–8

Black, P. E. (1968). Streamflow increases following farm abandonment on east- ·n New York watershed. *Wat. Resour. Res.*, **4**, 1171–8

Brown, J. A. H. (1972). Hydrological effects of a bushfire in a catchment in south-eastern New South Wales. *J. Hydrol.*, **15**, 77–96

Bunyan, J. E. (1975). The development of a flood storage area at Basildon. *J. Instn Wat. Engrs*, **29**, 174–82

Burdick, M. D. (1966). Public Law 566 Projects in Arizona. *Proc. A. Arizona Watershed Symp.*, **10**, 29–31

Ciriacy-Wantrup, S. V. (1964). Water policy. *Handbook of Applied Hydrology* (ed. V. T. Chow), McGraw-Hill, New York, section 28

Corbett, E. S., and Green, L. R. (1965). Emergency revegetation to rehabilitate burned watersheds in Southern California. *U.S. For. Serv. Res. Pap.* PSW-22

Costin, A. B. (1952). Hydrological studies in the Upper Snowy catchment area with special reference to the effects of land utilization. *J. Soil. Cons. N.S.W.*, **8**, 5–17

Costin, A. B., Gay, L. W., Wimbush, D. J., and Kerr, D. (1961). Studies in catchment hydrology in the Australian Alps: III – preliminary snow investigations. *CSIRO Div. Plant. Ind. Tech. Pap.*, **15**

Douglas, I. (1972). *The Environment Game*, Univ. of New England, Armidale, N.S.W.

Dragoun, F. J. (1969). Effects of cultivation and grass on surface runoff. *Wat. Resour. Res.*, **5**, 1078–83

Dunin, F. X., and Downes, R. G. (1962). The effect of subterranean clover and wimmera rye grass in controlling surface runoff in four-acre catchments near Bacchus Marsh, Victoria. *Aust. J. exp. Agric. Anim. Husbandry*, **2**, 148–52

Espey, W. H., Morgan, C. W., and Masch, F. D. (1966). A study of some effects of urbanization on storm runoff from a small watershed. *Texas Wat. Dev. Board Rept.*, no. 23

Felton, P. M., and Lull, H. W. (1963). Suburban hydrology can improve watershed conditions. *Public Works*, **94**, 93–4

Harrold, L. L. (1962). *Hydrology of Agricultural Watersheds*, USDA Agric. Res. Service and Ohio Soil Cons. Cttee. with Ohio Agric. Expt. Station

Harrold, L. L., Triplett, G. B., and Youker, R. E. (1967). Watershed tests of no-tillage corn. *J. Soil and Water Cons.*, **22**, 98–100

Harrold, L. L., Brakensiek, D. L., McGuinness, J. L., Amerman, C. R., and Driebelbis, F. R. (1962). Influence of land use and treatment on the hydrology of small watersheds at Coshocton, Ohio, 1938–1957. *USDA Tech. Bull.*, **1256**, 194

Hewlett, J. D., and Helvey, J. D. (1970). Effects of forest clear-felling on the storm hydrograph. *Wat. Resour. Res.*, **6**, 768–82

Hewlett, J. D., and Nutter, W. L. (1969). *An Outline of Forest Hydrology*, Univ. of Georgia Press, Athens, Ga.

Hibbert, A. R. (1967). Forest treatment effects on water yield. *Forest Hydrology*, (eds W. E. Sopper and H. W. Lull), Pergamon, Oxford, pp. 527–43

Hickok, R. B. (1963). Hydrology research needs for upstream flood prevention. *5th Cong. Internat. Irrig. and Drainage Comm., Tokyo, Japan*, **R6**, question 18, 75–88

Hopkins, W., Bentley, J., and Rice, R. (1961). Research and a land management model for Southern California watersheds. *U.S. For. Serv., Pacific Southwest For. Range exp. Sta. Misc. Pap.*, no. 56

Howe, G. M., Slaymaker, H. O., and Harding, D. M. (1967). Some aspects of the flood hydrology of the upper catchments of the Severn and Wye. *Trans. Inst. Br. Geog.*, **41**, 33–58

Keppel, R. V. (1961). Watershed research on semi-arid rangelands. *Proc. A. Arizona Watershed Symp.*, **5**, 33–5

Klein, R. M. (1969). The Florence floods were no act of God. *The Washington Post*, Sunday August 24, B3

Krammes, J. S., and Rice, R. M. (1963). Effect of fire on the San Dimas experimental forest. *Proc. A. Arizona Watershed Symp.*, **7**, 31–4

Law, F. (1956). The effect of afforestation upon the yield of water catchment areas. *J. Br. Waterworks Ass.*, **38**, 489–94

Leopold, W. B., and Maddock, T. (1954). *The Flood Control Controversy*, Ronald, New York

Linsley, R. K., Kohler, M. A., and Paulhus, J. L. H. (1949). *Applied Hydrology*, McGraw-Hill, New York

Lull, H. W., and Reinhart, K. G. (1967). Increasing water yield in the northwest by management of forested watersheds. *U.S. For. Serv. Res. Pap.*, NE-66

McCuen, R. H. (1974). A regional approach to urban storm water detention. *Geophys. Res. Lett.*, **1**, 321–2

McGuinness, J. L. Harrold, L. L., and Dreibelis, F. R. (1958). The effects of land use practices on runoff, erosion, and crop yields as evaluated by small single-crop watersheds. *USDA Research Rept.*, **310,** 23

Martinelli, M. (1964). Watershed management in the Rocky Mountain alpine and subalpine zones. *U.S. For. Serv. Res. Note*, RM-36

Minshall, N. E. (1961). Effect of cover and soils on surface runoff. *J. Soil Water Cons.*, **16,** 259–64

Nelson, J. G., and Byrne, A. R. (1966). Man as an instrument of landscape change. *Geogrl Rev.*, **56,** 226–38

Pase, C. P., and Ingebo, P. A. (1965). Burned chaparral to grass: early effects on water and sediment yields from two granitic soil watersheds in Arizona. *Proc. A. Arizona Watershed Symp.*, **9,** 8–11

Satterlund, D. R., and Eschner, A. R. (1965). Land use, snow and streamflow regimen in central New York. *Wat. Resour. Res.*, **1,** 397–405

Schneider, W. J. (1969). Reforestation effects on winter and spring flood peaks in central New York State. *Floods and their Computation*, IASH/UNESCO/WMO, pp. 780–7

Sharp, A. L., Bond, J. J., Neuberger, J. W., Kuhlman, A. R., and Lewis, J. K. (1964). Runoff as affected by intensity of grazing on rangeland. *J. Soil and Water Cons.*, **19,** 103–6

Smith, R. M., and Henderson, R. C. (1961). Some interpretations of runoff and erosion from terraces on blackland soil. *U.S.D.A. agric. Res. Serv.*, **41–42,** 15

Sodemann, P. C., and Tysinger, J. E. (1967). Effects of forest cover upon hydrologic characteristics of a small watershed in the limestone region of east Tennessee. *Hydrology of Fractured Rocks.*, IASH Publ. 73, pp. 139–51

Ursic, S. J. (1968). Reforestation and water resources of the Yazoo-Little Tallahatchi watershed. *Miss. Water Resources Conf. Proc.*, 9–13

Ward, R. C. (1971). *Small Watershed Experiments.*, Univ. of Hull Occ. Papers in Geography, no. 18

Ward, R. C. (1975). *Principles of Hydrology* (2nd ed), McGraw-Hill, London

10 HUMAN RESPONSE TO THE FLOOD HAZARD: III FLOOD PROTECTION

Aagaard, K., and Coachman, L. K. (1975). Toward an ice-free Arctic Ocean. *EOS, Trans. Am. Geophys. Un.*, **56,** 484–6

Barnes, F. A., and King, C. A. M. (1953). The Lincolnshire coastline and the 1953 storm flood. *Geography*, **38,** 141–60

Beckinsale, R. P. (1969). Human responses to river regimes. *Water, Earth and Man* (ed. R. J. Chorley), Methuen, London, pp. 487–509

Burton, I. (1969). Flood-damage reduction in Canada. *Water* (eds J. G. Nelson and M. J. Chambers), Methuen, Toronto, pp. 77–108

Burton, I., and Kates, R. W. (1964). The floodplain and the seashore: a comparative analysis of hazard-zone occupance. *Geogrl Rev.*, **54**, 366–85

Burton, I., Kates, R. W., and Snead, R. E. (1969). *The Human Ecology of Coastal Flood Hazard in Megalopolis*, Univ. of Chicago, Dept. of Geog., Res. Pap. no. 115

Craig-Smith, S. J. (1974). The East Anglian coastal research programme, 1973–1976. Paper presented to a Conference of River Engineers, Norwich, 1974 (cyclostyled)

Dock and Harbour Authority (1974). Thames flood protection: plans and progress on the barrier and associated defences up to Autumn 1974. *Dock and Harbour Authority Magazine*, September 1974

Dorozynski, A. (1975). After the dam the depression? *Nature*, **255**, 570

Fay, S., and Knightley, P. (1975). Will inflation sink Venice rescue party? *The Sunday Times*, 13 April 1975, p. 5

GLC (1974). *Thames Flood Defences*, Information brochure about the Thames Barrier, obtainable from the Greater London Council, Director of Public Health Engineering (R), 10 Great George Street, London SW1P 3AB

Hall, A. (1972). *The Thames Barrier*, The Greater London Council

Hewlett, J. D., and Nutter, W. L. (1969). *An Outline of Forest Hydrology*, Univ. of Georgia Press, Athens, Ga.

Hoyt, W. G., and Langbein, W. B. (1955). *Floods*, Princeton U.P., New Jersey

Kuiper, E. (1965). *Water Resources Development*, Butterworths, London

Linsley, R. K., and Franzini, J. B. (1972). *Water-Resources Engineering* (2nd edn), McGraw-Hill, New York

Linsley, R. K., Kohler, M. A., and Paulhus, J. L. H. (1949). *Applied Hydrology*, McGraw-Hill, New York

MacDonald, Sir M., and Partners, and Shankland/Cox Partnership (1974). *River Hull Tidal Surge Barrier*, Yorkshire Water Authority, Planning Report

Medrington, N. (1969). Twenty years of land drainage progress in the area of the Lee Conservancy Catchment Board. *Association of River Authorities Yearbook* (eds N. Whincup *et al.*), The Association, London, pp. 304–20

Mrowka, J. P. (1974). Man's impact on stream regimen and quality. *Perspectives on Environment* (eds I. R. Manners and M. W. Mikesell), Association of American Geographers, Washington, D.C., pp. 79–104

Newson, M. D. (1975). *Flooding and Flood Hazard in the United Kingdom*, Oxford Univ. Press

Nixon, M. (1963). Flood regulation and river training in England and Wales. *Conservation of Water Resources in the United Kingdom*, The Institution of Civil Engineers, London, pp. 137–50

Ogrosky, H. O., and Mockus, V. (1964). Hydrology of agricultural lands. *Handbook of Applied Hydrology* (ed. V. T. Chow), McGraw-Hill, New York, section 21

Pardé, M. (1964). Floods, floods, floods! *UNESCO Courier*, **17**, July–August, pp. 54–9

Radley, J., and Simms, C. (1971). *Yorkshire Flooding – Some Effects on Man and Nature*, Sessions Book Trust, York

Rutter, E. J., and Engstrom, L. R. (1964). Hydrology of flow control: Part III – reservoir regulation. *Handbook of Applied Hydrology* (ed. V. T. Chow), McGraw-Hill, New York, section 25–III

Smith, K. (1972). *Water in Britain*, Macmillan, London

Steers, J. A. (1953). The East coast floods, January 31–February 1, 1953. *Geogrl J.*, **119**, 280–98

Thorn, R. B. (1960). *The Design of Sea Defence Works*, Butterworths, London

TVA (1967). *TVA 1967 – The Principal Text of the Tennessee Valley Authority's Annual Report*, Tennessee Valley Authority, Knoxville

United Nations (1951). *Methods and Problems of Flood Control in Asia and the Far East*, Flood Control Series no. 2, United Nations, Bangkok

United Nations (1966). *Compendium of Major International Rivers in the ESCAPE Region*, Water Resources Series 29

Volker, A. (1964). The high wall of the Low Countries. *UNESCO Courier*, **17**, July–August, 48–51

White, G. F. (1964). Floodplain adjustments and regulations. *Handbook of Applied Hydrology* (ed. V. T. Chow), McGraw-Hill, New York, section 25-V

11 ECONOMIC ASPECTS OF RESPONSE TO THE FLOOD HAZARD

Burton, I. (1961). Invasion and escape on the Little Calumet. *Papers on Flood Problems* (ed. G. F. White), Univ. of Chicago, Dept. of Geography, Res. Paper 70, pp. 84–92

Burton, I. (1962). *Types of Agricultural Occupance of Flood Plains in the United States*, Univ. of Chicago, Dept. of Geography, Res. Paper 75

Burton, I. (1969). Flood-damage reduction in Canada. *Water* (eds J. G. Nelson and M. J. Chambers), Methuen, Toronto, pp. 77–108

Burton, I., and Kates, R. W. (1964). The floodplain and the seashore: a comparative analysis of hazard-zone occupance. *Geogrl Rev.*, **54**, 366–85

Burton, I., Kates, R. W., and Snead, R. E. (1969). *The Human Ecology of Coastal Flood Hazard in Megalopolis*, Univ. of Chicago, Dept. of Geography, Res. Paper 115

Chambers, D. N. (1973). Economic aspects of flood alleviation. *Economic Aspects of Floods* (eds E. C. Penning-Rowsell and D. J. Parker), Middlesex Polytechnic Flood Hazard Research Project, pp. 33–5

Chorley, R. J., and Kennedy, B. A. (1971). *Physical Geography: A Systems Approach*, Prentice-Hall, London

Day, H. J., Bugliarello, G., Ho, P. H. P., and Houghton, V. T. (1969). Evaluation of benefits of a flood warning system. *Wat. Resour. Res.*, **5**, 937–46

Day, H. J., and Lee, K. K. (1975). Flood damage reduction potential of river forecast (cyclostyled)

Day, J. C. (1970). A recursive programing model for nonstructural flood damage control. *Wat. Resour. Res.*, **6**, 1262–71

Dixon, J. W. (1964). Water Resources, Part I. Planning and development. *Handbook of Applied Hydrology* (ed. V. T. Chow), McGraw-Hill, New York

Geraghty, J. J., Miller, D. W., Van der Leeden, F., and Troise, F. L. (1973). *Water Atlas of the United States*, Water Information Center, Port Washington, New York

Hertzler, R. A. (1961). Corps of Engineers' experience relating to flood plain regulation. *Papers on Flood Problems* (ed. G. F. White), Univ. of Chicago, Dept. of Geography, Res. Paper 70, pp. 181–202

Hufschmidt, M. M., and Fiering, M. B. (1966). *Simulation Techniques for Design of Water-Resource Systems*, Harvard University Press

Johnson, E. A. G. (1969). Land drainage. *Association of River Authorities Yearbook 1969*, The Association, London, pp. 231–42

Kates, R. W. (1962). *Hazard and Choice Perception in Flood Plain Management*, Univ. of Chicago, Dept. of Geography, Res. Paper 78

Kates, R. W. (1965). *Industrial Flood Losses: Damage Estimation in the Lehigh Valley*, Univ. of Chicago, Dept. of Geography, Res. Paper 98

Krutilla, J. V. (1966). International Columbia River treaty. *Water Research* (eds A. V. Kneese and S. C. Smith), Johns Hopkins, Baltimore

Kuiper, E. (1965). *Water Resources Development*, Butterworths, London

Loughlin, J. C. (1970). Cost-sharing for Federal water resource programs with emphasis on flood protection. *Wat. Resour. Res.*, **6**, 366–82

Loughlin, J. C. (1971). A flood insurance model for sharing the costs of flood protection. *Wat. Resour. Res.*, **7**, 236–44

Matthai, H. F. (1969). Floods of June 1965 in South Platte River Basin, Colorado. *U.S. geol. Surv., Water-Supply Pap.*, **1850-B**

Middlesex Polytechnic (1974). Flood damage assessment: A preliminary analysis. Paper presented at the conference of University Specialists in Hydrology, Sheffield University, 19 September, 1974, by members of the Middlesex Polytechnic Flood Hazard Research Project (cyclostyled)

Mitchell, J. K. (1974). Natural hazards research. *Perspectives on Environment* (eds I. R. Manners and M. W. Mikesell), Association of American Geographers, Washington, D.C., pp. 311–41

O'Riordan, T., and More, R. J. (1969). Choice in water use. *Water, Earth and Man* (ed. R. J. Chorley), Methuen, London, pp. 547–73

Parker, D. J. (1973). The assessment of flood damages. *Economic Aspects of Floods* (eds E. C. Penning-Rowsell and D. J. Parker), Middlesex Polytechnic Flood Hazard Research Project, pp. 9–20

Parker, D. J., and Penning-Rowsell, E. C. (1972). *Problems and Methods of Flood Damage Assessment*, Middlesex Polytechnic Flood Hazard Research Project, Prog. Rept 3

Penning-Rowsell, E. C., and Underwood, L. (1972). *Flood Hazard and Flood Plain Management: Survey of Existing Studies*, Middlesex Polytechnic Flood Hazard Research Project, Progress Report Z

Porter, E. (1971). Assessing flood damage. *Spectrum, British Science News*, **84**, 2–5 (Central Office of Information)

Roder, W. (1961). Attitudes and knowledge on the Topeka flood plain. *Papers on Flood Problems* (ed. G. F. White), Univ. of Chicago, Dept. of Geography, Res. Paper 70, pp. 62–83

Rogers, P. (1969). A systems analysis of the lower Ganges-Brahmaputra basin. *Floods and their Computation*, IASH/UNESCO/WMO, pp. 894–909

Sewell, W. R. D. (1965). *Water Management and Floods in the Fraser River Basin*, Univ. of Chicago, Dept. of Geography Res. Paper 100

Sewell, W. R. D. (1969). Human response to floods. *Water, Earth and Man* (ed. R. J. Chorley), Methuen, London, pp. 431–51

Steers, J. A. (1953). The east coast floods January 31–February 1, 1953. *Geogrl J.*, **119**, 280–98

Sterland, F. K. (1973). An evaluation of personal annoyance caused by flooding. *Economic Aspects of Floods* (eds E. C. Penning-Rowsell and D. J. Parker), Middlesex Polytechnic Flood Hazard Research Project, pp. 21–31

Struyk, R. J. (1971). Flood risk and agricultural land values: a test. *Wat. Resour Res.*, **7**, 789–97

Task Force (1966). *A Unified National Program for Managing Flood Losses*, Report by the Task Force on Federal Flood Control Policy, USGPO, Washington, D.C.

Theiler, D. F. (1969). Effects of flood protection on land use in the Coon Creek, Wisconsin, watershed. *Wat. Resour Res.*, **5**, 1216–22

T.V.A. (1961). *Potential Damage Appraisal – Residences*, Unpublished report of the Tennessee Valley Authority, Knoxville, Tenn.

T.V.A. (1967). *TVA–1967*, USGPO, Washington, D.C.

T.V.A. (1969). *Potential Damage Appraisal – Small Businesses Report*, Unpublished report of the Tennessee Valley Authority, Knoxville, Tenn.

U.S. Army Corps of Engineers (1970). *Lincoln, Nebraska Flood Insurance Study*, Report prepared for Federal Insurance Administration by Corps of Engineers, Omaha

Whipple, W. (1969). Optimizing investment in flood control and floodplain zoning. *Wat. Resour Res.*, **5**, 761–6

White, G. F. (1964). *Choice of Adjustment to Floods*, Univ. of Chicago, Dept. of Geography, Research Paper 93

Windsor, J. S. (1975). A programing model for the design of multireservoir flood control systems. *Wat. Resour Res.*, **11,** 30–6

12 PROSPECT

Burton, I. (1969). Flood-damage reduction in Canada. *Water* (eds J. G. Nelson and M. J. Chambers), Methuen, Toronto, pp. 77–108

Dingman, S. L. (1975). An expedient approach to community-wide flood-plain delineation and regulation. *EOS, Trans. Am. geophys. Un.*, **56,** 360 (abstract only)

Ellis, D. W. (1969). Flood plain mapping by the U.S. Geological Survey. *Flood Plain Management* (ed. M. D. Dougal), Iowa State Univ. Press, Ames, pp. 197–206

Grindley, J., and Singleton, F. (1969). The routine estimation of soil moisture deficits. *Floods and their Computation*, IASH/UNESCO/WMO, pp. 811–20

Harding, D. M., and Porter, E. A. (1970). Flood loss information and economic aspects of flood plain occupance. *Proc. Instn civ. Engrs*, **46,** 403–9

Hoyt, W. G., and Langbein, W. B. (1955). *Floods*, Princeton Univ. Press, Princeton

ICE (1967). *Floods Studies for the United Kingdom*, Report of the Committee on Floods, The Institution of Civil Engineers, London

Idso, S. B., Schmugge, T. J., Jackson, R. D., and Reginato, R. J. (1975). The utility of surface temperature measurements for the remote sensing of surface soil water status. *EOS, Trans. Am. geophys. Un.*, **56,** 295 (abstract only)

Kates, R. W. (1962). *Hazard and Choice Perception in Flood Plain Management*, Univ. of Chicago, Dept. of Geography, Research Paper 78

Molinaroli, R. (1965). Flood plain studies. *Proc. Conf. Hydrologic Activities in the South Carolina Region*, Clemson Univ., Clemson, pp. 1–6

Morisawa, M. (1968). *Streams: Their dynamics and morphology*, McGraw-Hill, New York

Penning-Rowsell, E. C., and Underwood, L. (1972). *Flood Hazard and Flood Plain Management: Survey of existing studies*, Middlesex Polytechnic, Flood Hazard Research Project, Progress Rept 2

Rango, A., and Salomonson, V. V. (1974). Regional flood mapping from space. *Wat. Resour. Res.*, **10,** 473–84

Rango, A., McGinnis, D. F., Salomonson, V. V., and Wiesnet, D. R. (1974). New dimensions in satellite hydrology. *EOS, Trans. Am. geophys. Un.*, **55,** 703–11

Roder, W. (1961). Attitudes and knowledge on the Topeka flood plain. *Papers on Flood Problems* (ed. G. F. White), Univ. of Chicago, Dept. of Geography, Research Paper 70, pp. 62–83

Sheaffer, J. R. (1964). The use of flood maps in northeastern Illinois. *Highway Res. Board*, **58,** 44–6, Natn. Acad. Sci., Washington, D.C.

Snyder, F., Sokolov, A., and Szesztay, K. (1971). *Flood Studies: An International Guide for Collection and Processing of Data*, UNESCO, Paris

Szesztay, K. (1970). Flood damage prevention measures and management. *Bull. int. Ass. scient. Hydrol.*, **15,** 170–6

Task Force (1966). *A Unified National Program for Managing Flood Losses*, Report by Task Force on Federal Flood Control Policy, 89th Congress House Doc. no. 465, USGPO, Washington, D.C.

U.S. Army Corps of Engineers (1973). *Flood Plain Information: Onion Creek, Austin, Texas*, U.S. Army Corps of Engineers, Galveston, Texas

White, G. F. (1964). *Choice of Adjustment to Floods*, Univ. of Chicago, Dept. of Geography, Research Paper 93

White, G. F. (1973*a*). Natural hazards research. *Directions in Geography* (ed. R. J. Chorley), Methuen, London, pp. 191–216

White, G. F. (1973*b*). Prospering with uncertainty. *Floods and Droughts* (eds E. F. Schulz, V. A. Koelzer and K. Mahmood), Water Resources Publications, Ft. Collins, Colo., pp. 9–15

Wolman, M. G. (1971). Evaluating alternative techniques of floodplain mapping. *Wat. Resour. Res.*, **7,** 1383–92

Addendum to Bibliography

During the final stages of production of this book an important new publication on flood benefit/damage assessment, based on the results of the Flood Hazard Research Project at Middlesex Polytechnic, appeared as:

Penning-Rowsell, E. C., and Chatterton, J. B. (1977). *The Benefits of Flood Alleviation: A Manual of Assessment Techniques,* Saxon House, Farnborough, Hants.

SIMPLIFIED METRIC CONVERSION TABLES

In the Distance, Area and Volume tables the figures in the central columns may be read as either the metric or the imperial unit, for example, 1 inch = 25.4 millimetres; or 1 millimetre = 0.039 inches.

Distance

inches		(mm) millimetres	feet		(m) metres
0.039	1	25.4	3.281	1	0.305
0.079	2	50.8	6.562	2	0.610
0.118	3	76.2	9.843	3	0.914
0.158	4	101.6	13.123	4	1.219
0.197	5	127.0	16.404	5	1.524
0.236	6	152.4	19.685	6	1.829
0.276	7	177.8	22.966	7	2.134
0.315	8	203.2	26.247	8	2.438
0.354	9	228.6	29.528	9	2.743

yards		(m) metres	miles		(km) kilometres
1.094	1	0.914	0.621	1	1.609
2.187	2	1.829	1.243	2	3.219
3.281	3	2.743	1.864	3	4.828
4.375	4	3.658	2.486	4	6.437
5.468	5	4.572	3.107	5	8.047
6.562	6	5.486	3.728	6	9.656
7.656	7	6.401	4.350	7	11.265
8.750	8	7.316	4.971	8	12.875
9.843	9	8.230	5.592	9	14.484

Area

sq. feet		(m²) sq. metres	sq. yards		(m²) sq. metres
10.764	1	0.093	1.196	1	0.836
21.528	2	0.186	2.392	2	1.672
32.292	3	0.279	3.588	3	2.508
43.056	4	0.372	4.784	4	3.345
53.819	5	0.465	5.980	5	4.181
64.583	6	0.557	7.176	6	5.016
75.347	7	0.650	8.372	7	5.853
86.111	8	0.743	9.568	8	6.690
96.875	9	0.836	10.764	9	7.526

acres		(ha) hectares	sq. miles		(km²) sq. kilometres
2.469	1	0.405	0.386	1	2.588
4.938	2	0.810	0.772	2	5.176
7.407	3	1.215	1.158	3	7.764
9.876	4	1.620	1.544	4	10.352
12.345	5	2.025	1.930	5	12.940
14.814	6	2.430	2.316	6	15.528
17.283	7	2.845	2.702	7	18.116
19.752	8	3.240	3.088	8	20.704
22.221	9	3.645	3.474	9	23.292

Volume

cu. feet		(m³) cu. metres	gallons (imp)		(l) litres
35.315	1	0.028	0.220	1	4.544
70.629	2	0.057	0.440	2	9.087
105.943	3	0.085	0.660	3	13.631
141.258	4	0.113	0.880	4	18.174
176.572	5	0.142	1.101	5	22.718
211.887	6	0.170	1.321	6	27.262
247.201	7	0.198	1.541	7	31.805
282.516	8	0.227	1.761	8	36.349
317.830	9	0.255	1.981	9	40.892

Temperature
(Centigrade to Fahrenheit)

°C	0	1	2	3	4	5	6	7	8	9
+40	104.0	105.8	107.6	109.4	111.2	113.0	114.8	116.6	118.4	120.2
+30	86.0	87.8	89.6	91.4	93.2	95.0	96.8	98.6	100.4	102.2
+20	68.0	69.8	71.6	73.4	75.2	77.0	78.8	80.6	82.4	84.2
+10	50.0	51.8	53.6	55.4	57.2	59.0	60.8	62.6	64.4	66.2
+ 0	32.0	33.8	35.6	37.4	39.2	41.0	42.8	44.6	46.4	48.2
− 0	32.0	30.2	28.4	26.6	24.8	23.0	21.2	19.4	17.6	15.8
−10	14.0	12.2	10.4	8.6	6.8	5.0	3.2	1.4	−0.4	−2.2
−20	−4.0	−5.8	−7.6	−9.4	−11.2	−13.0	−14.8	−16.6	−18.4	−20.2
−30	−22.0	−23.8	−25.6	−27.4	−29.2	−31.0	−32.8	−34.6	−36.4	−38.2
−40	−40.0	−41.8	−43.6	−45.4	−47.2	−49.0	−50.8	−52.6	−54.4	−56.2

Index